Peach Girl

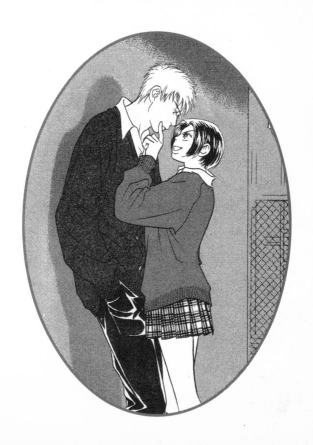

Peach Girl

by Miwa Ueda

8

TOKYOPOP®

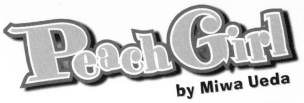

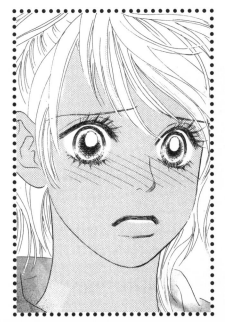

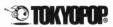

A  MANGA

TOKYOPOP® Presents
Peach Girl 8 by Miwa Ueda
TOKYOPOP is a registered trademark
of Mixx Entertainment, Inc.
ISBN: 1-931514-18-6
First Printing December 2002

10 9 8 7 6 5 4 3 2 1

Translator - Dan Papia.
Retouch and Lettering - Max Porter.
English Adaptation - Jodi Bryson.
Graphic Designer - Anna Kernbaum.
Senior Editor - Julie Taylor.
Production Managers - Jennifer Wagner and Jennifer Miller.
Art Director - Matt Alford.
VP of Production - Ron Klamert.
President & C.O.O. - John Parker. Publisher - Stuart Levy.

Email: editor@TOKYOPOP.com
Come visit us at www.TOKYOPOP.com

TOKYOPOP®

Los Angeles - Tokyo

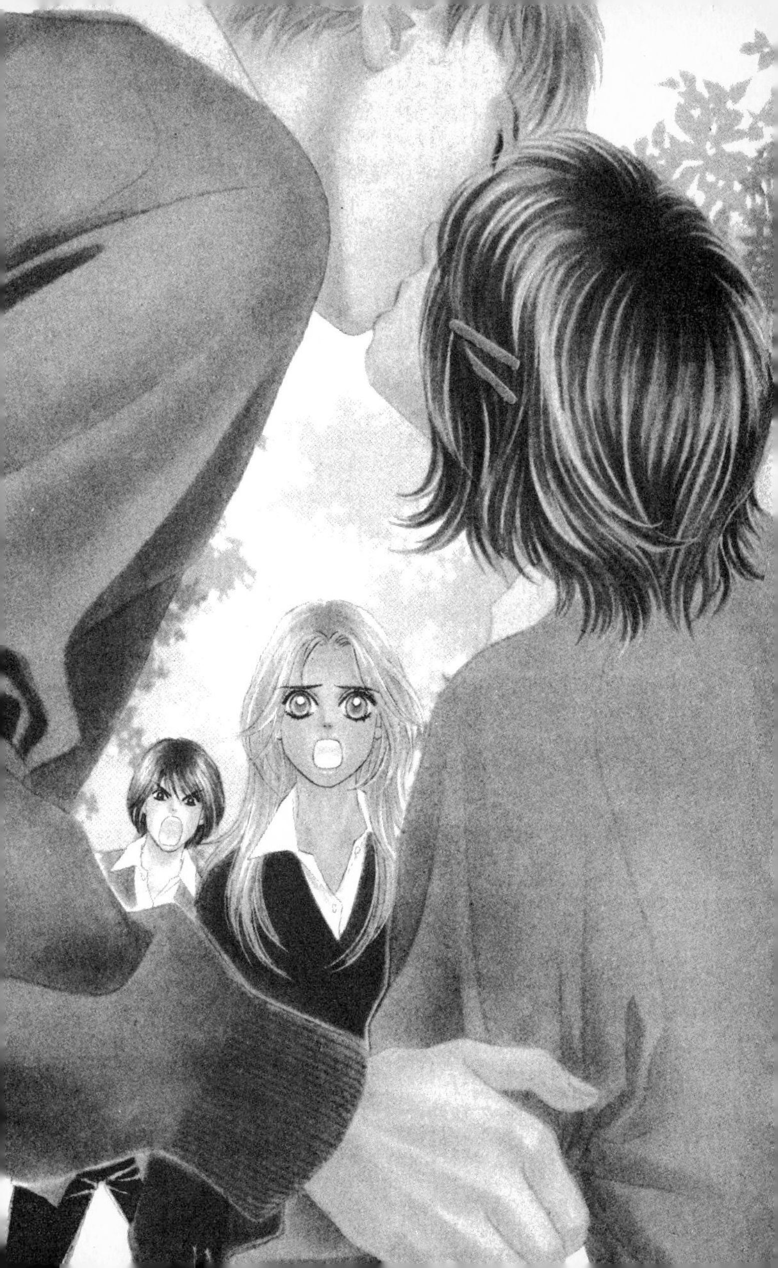

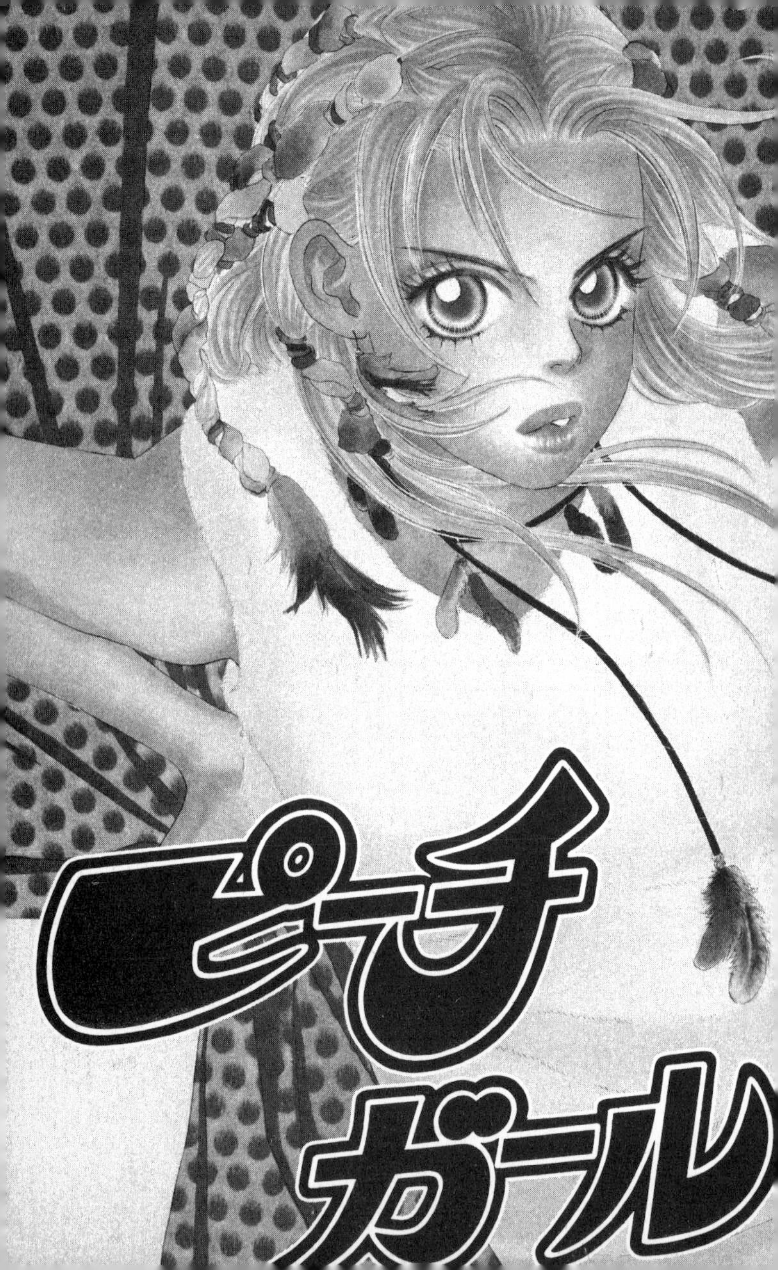
ピーチ
ガール

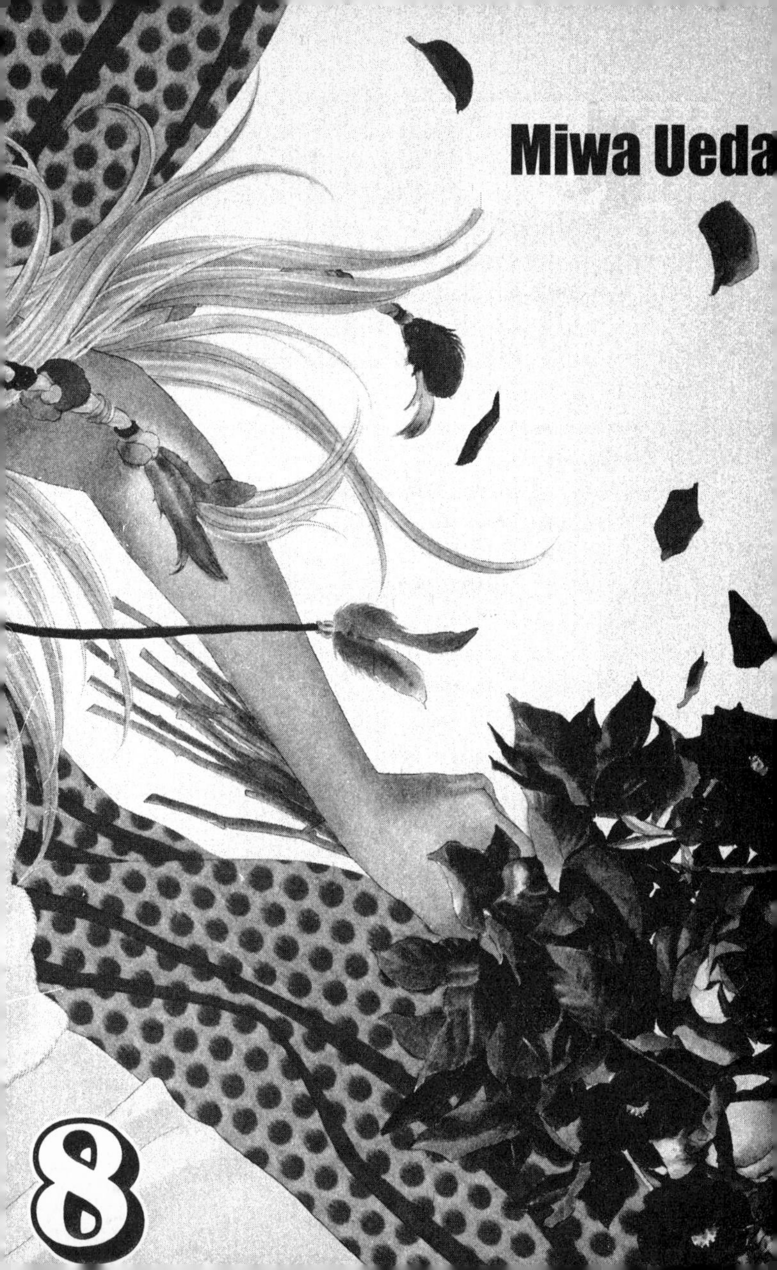
Miwa Ueda
8

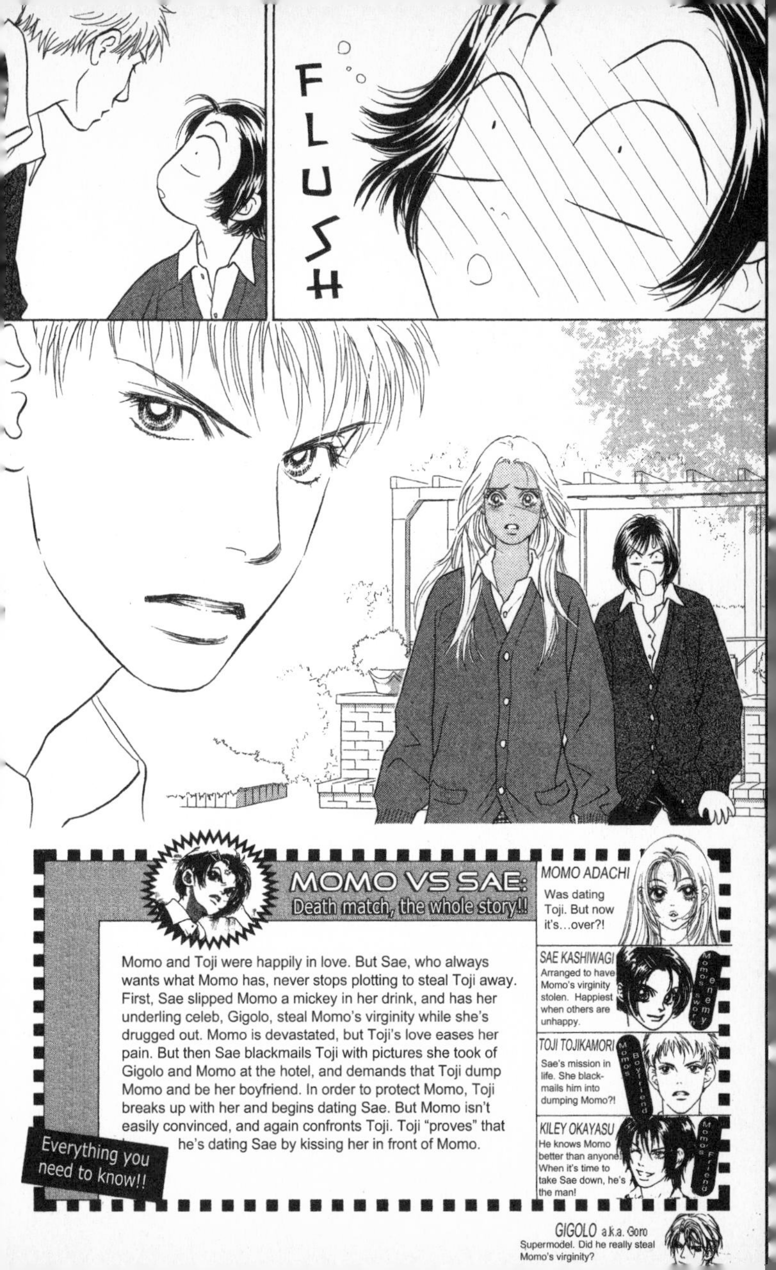
FLUSH

MOMO VS SAE:
Death match, the whole story!!

Momo and Toji were happily in love. But Sae, who always wants what Momo has, never stops plotting to steal Toji away. First, Sae slipped Momo a mickey in her drink, and has her underling celeb, Gigolo, steal Momo's virginity while she's drugged out. Momo is devastated, but Toji's love eases her pain. But then Sae blackmails Toji with pictures she took of Gigolo and Momo at the hotel, and demands that Toji dump Momo and be her boyfriend. In order to protect Momo, Toji breaks up with her and begins dating Sae. But Momo isn't easily convinced, and again confronts Toji. Toji "proves" that he's dating Sae by kissing her in front of Momo.

Everything you need to know!!

MOMO ADACHI
Was dating Toji. But now it's…over?!

SAE KASHIWAGI — Momo's sworn enemy
Arranged to have Momo's virginity stolen. Happiest when others are unhappy.

TOJI TOJIKAMORI — Momo's Boyfriend
Sae's mission in life. She blackmails him into dumping Momo?!

KILEY OKAYASU — Momo's Friend
He knows Momo better than anyone. When it's time to take Sae down, he's the man!

GIGOLO a.k.a. Goro
Supermodel. Did he really steal Momo's virginity?

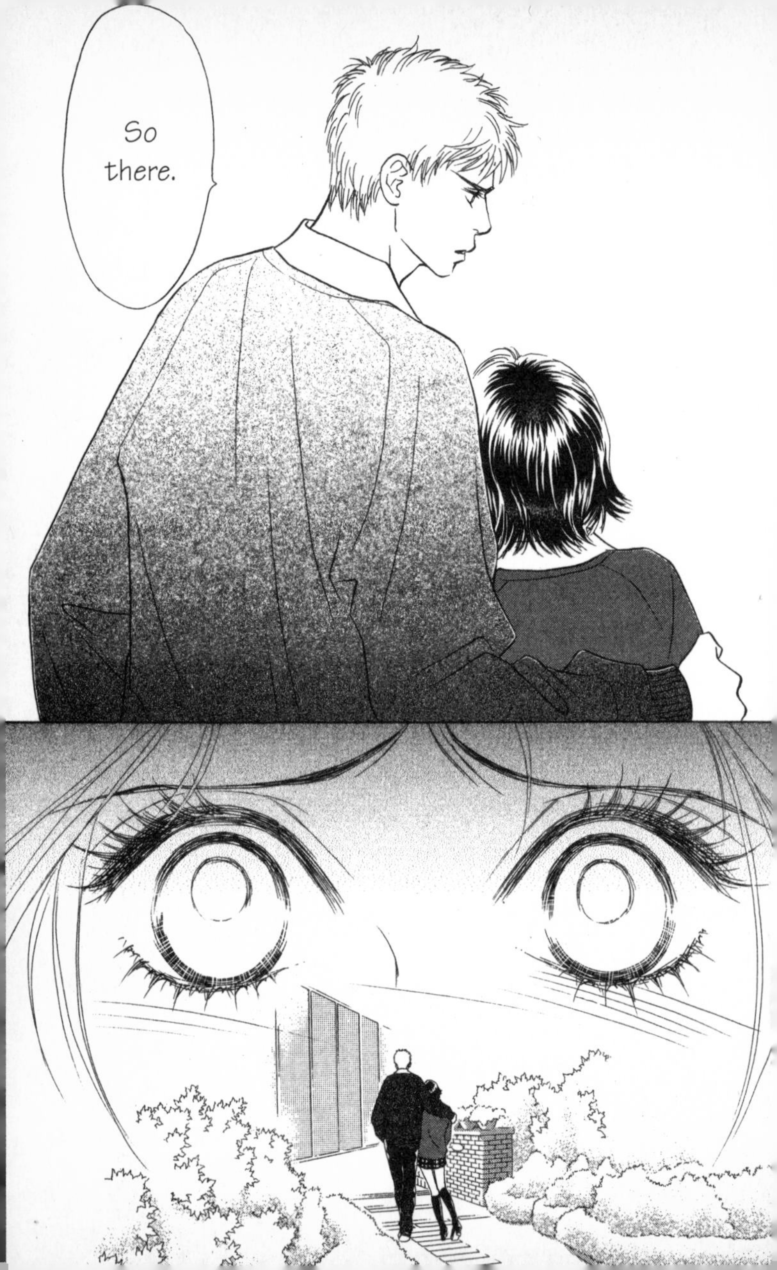
So there.

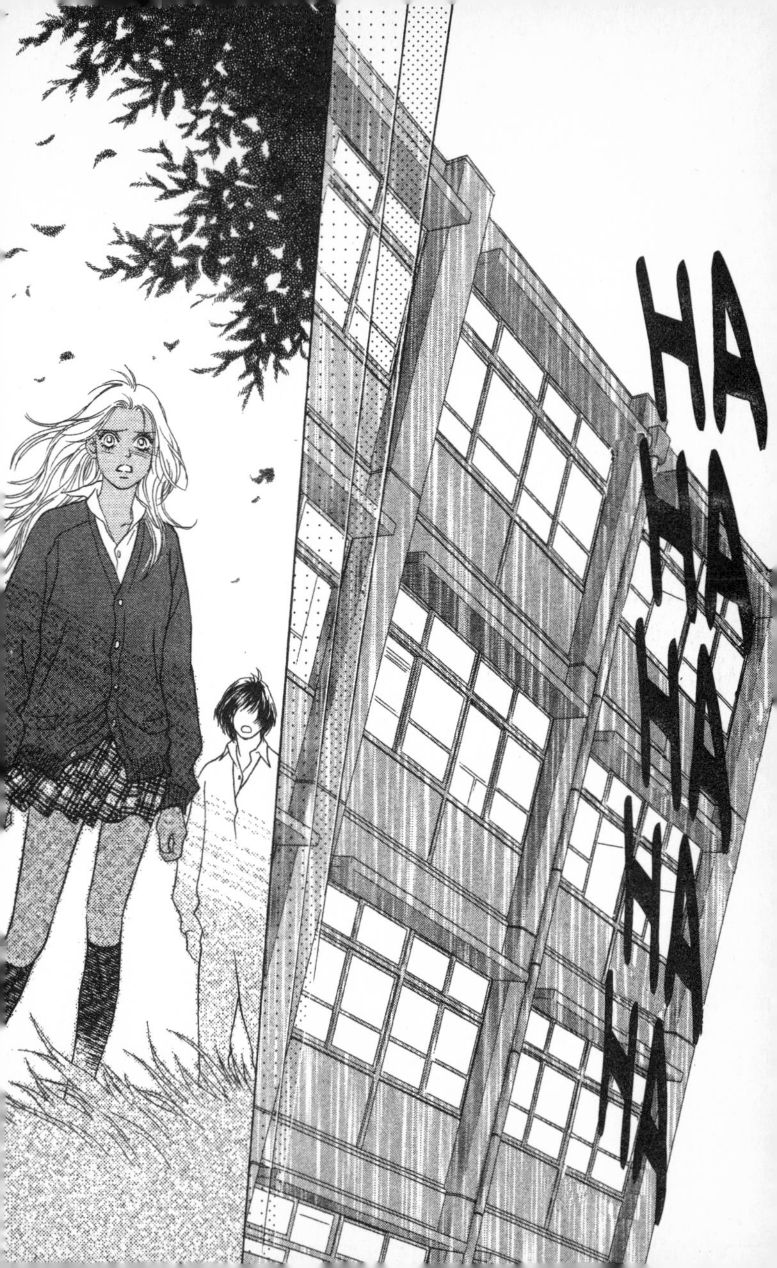
HA
HA
HA
HA
HA

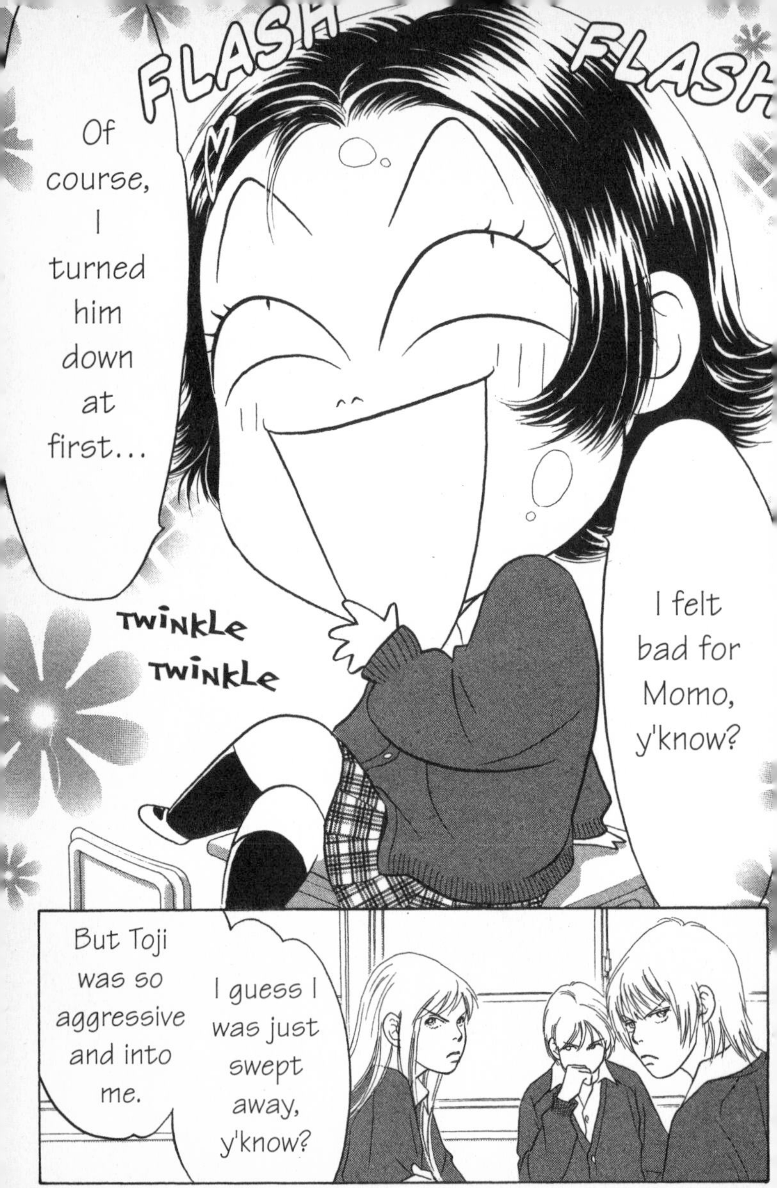
FLASH
FLASH
Of course, I turned him down at first...
I felt bad for Momo, y'know?
TWINKLE
TWINKLE
But Toji was so aggressive and into me.
I guess I was just swept away, y'know?

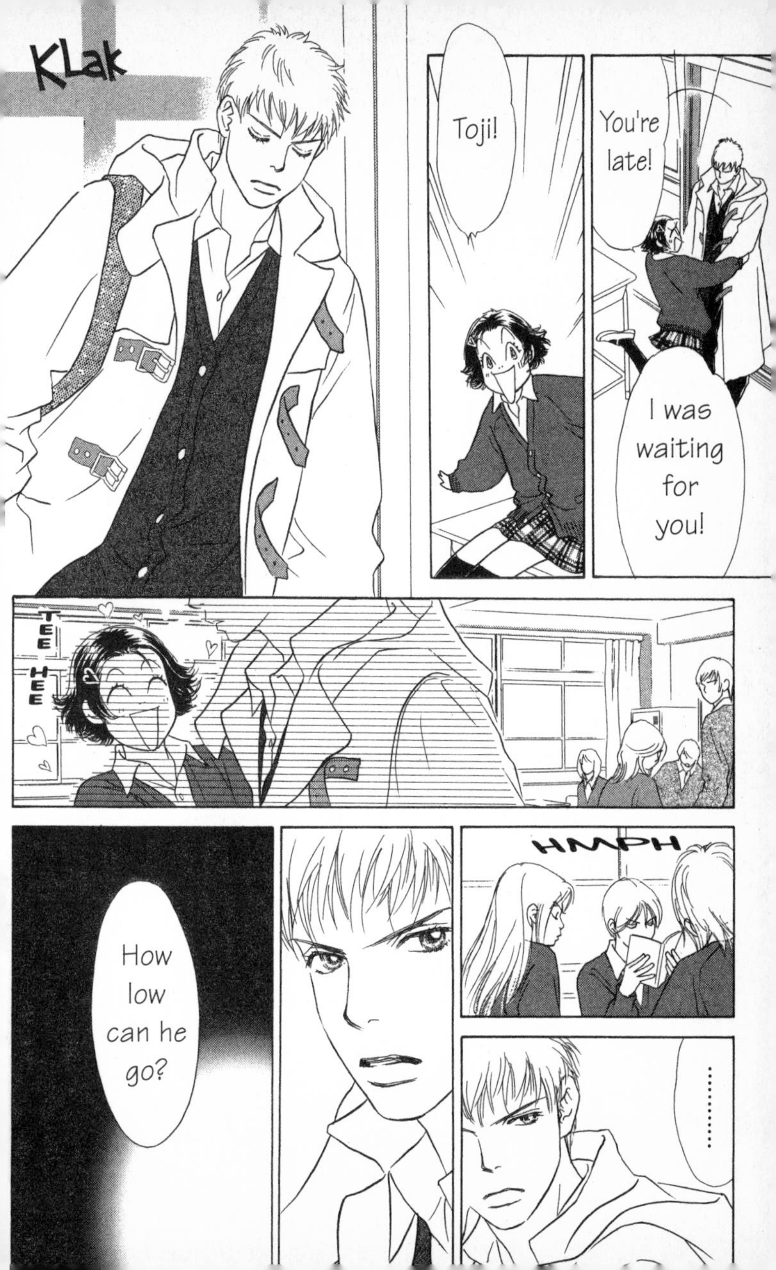
KLAK
Toji!
You're late!
I was waiting for you!
TEE HEE
How low can he go?
HMPH
....

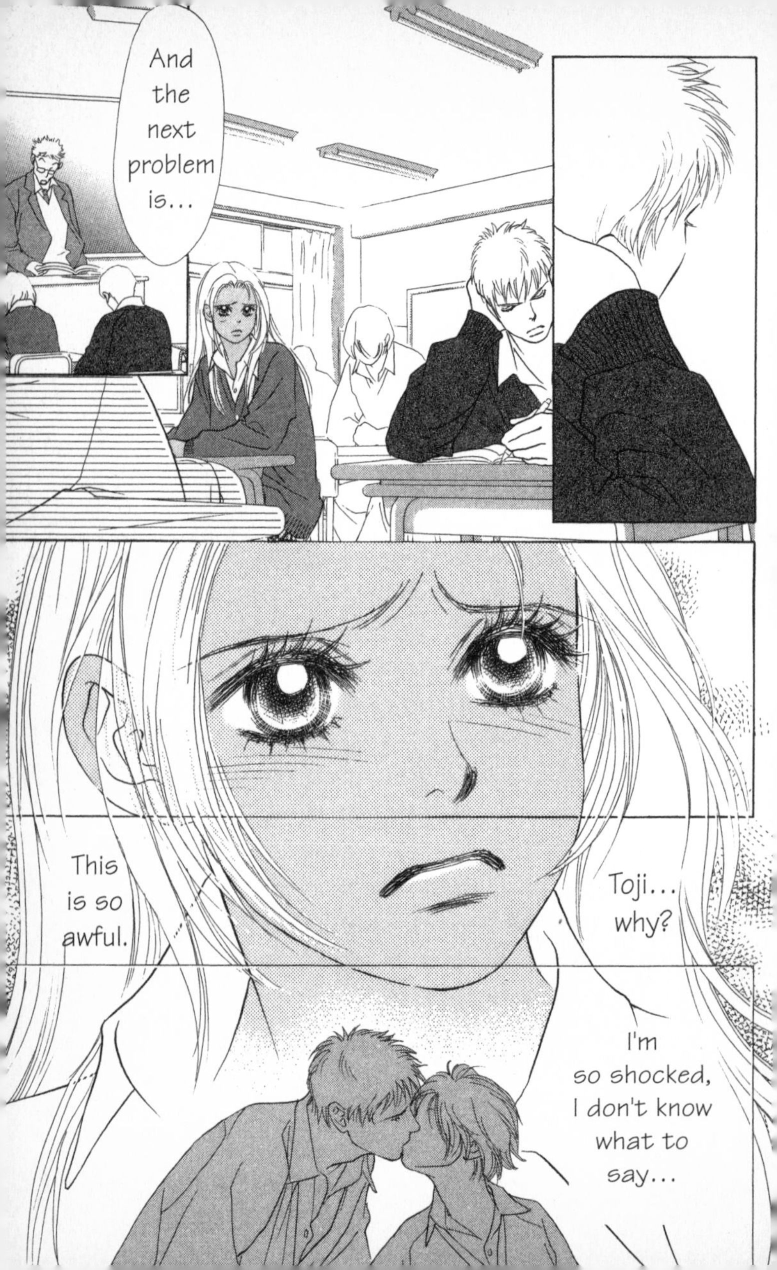
And the next problem is...
Toji... why?
This is so awful.
I'm so shocked, I don't know what to say...

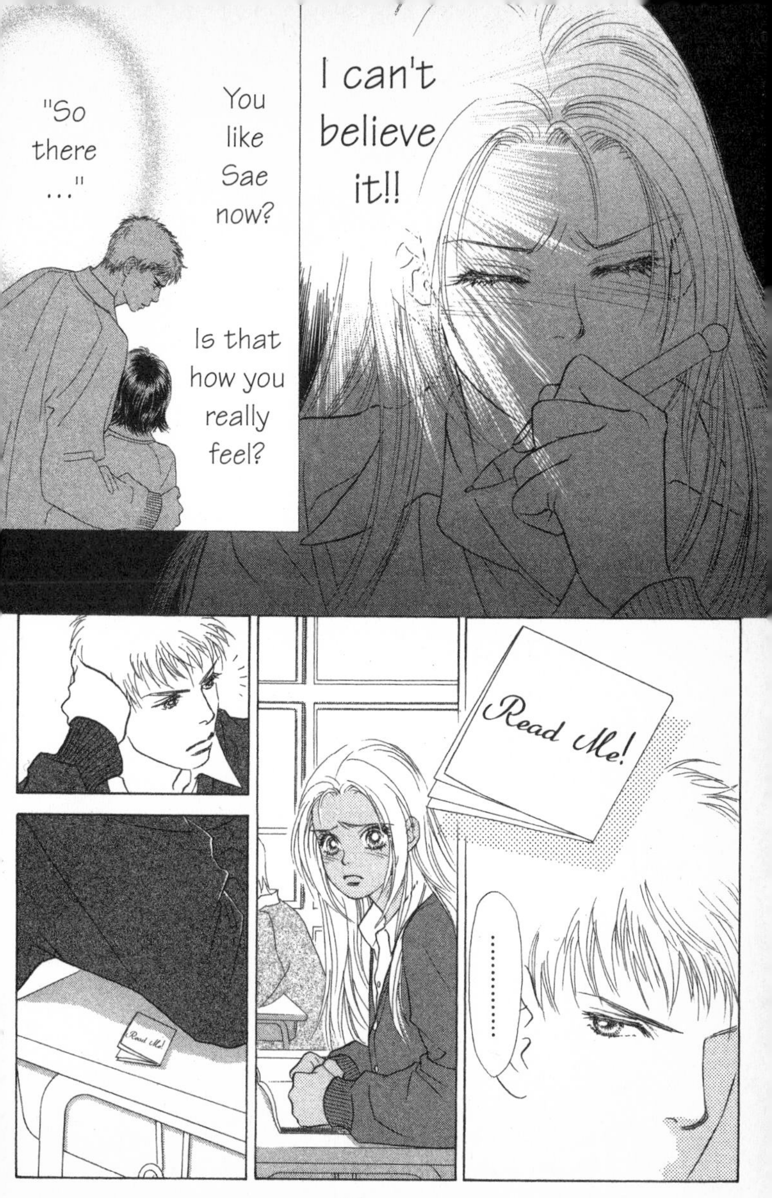
I can't believe it!!
You like Sae now?
"So there ..."
Is that how you really feel?
Read Me!
......
Read Me!

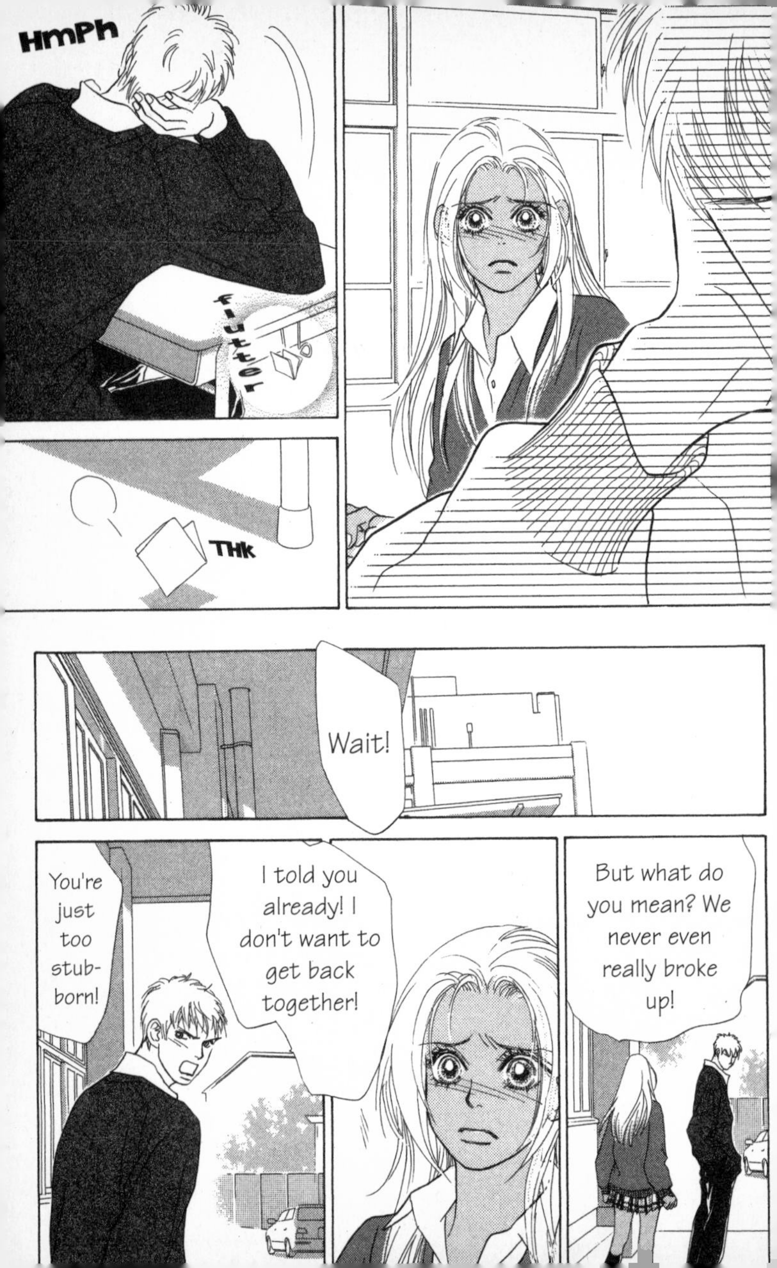
HmPh
flutter
THK
Wait!
But what do you mean? We never even really broke up!
I told you already! I don't want to get back together!
You're just too stubborn!

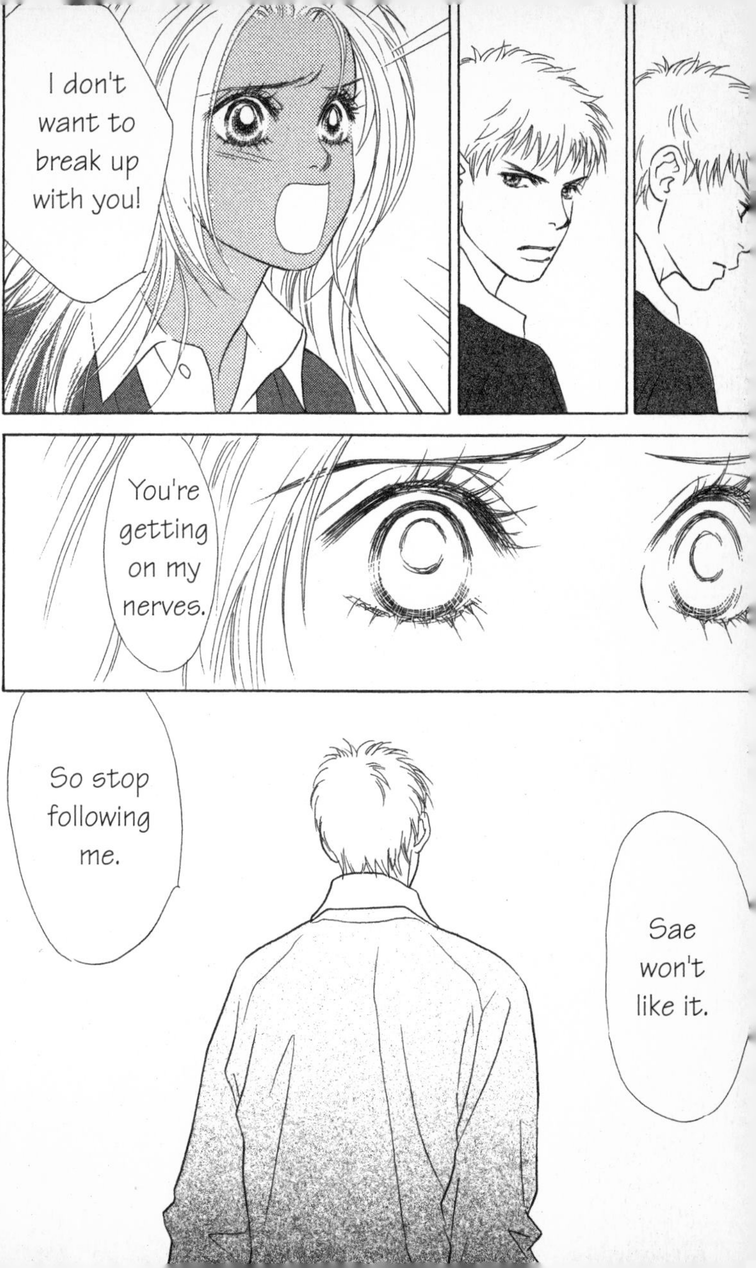
I don't want to break up with you!
You're getting on my nerves.
Sae won't like it.
So stop following me.

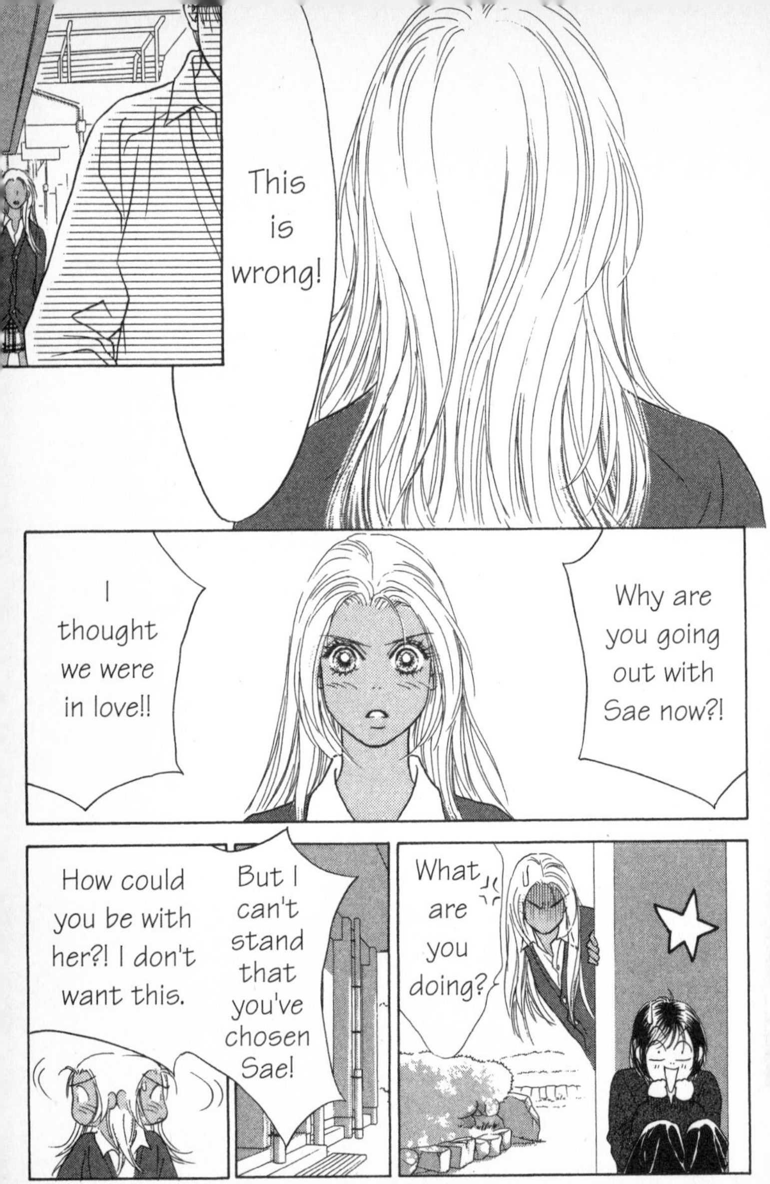
This is wrong!
Why are you going out with Sae now?!
I thought we were in love!!
What are you doing?
But I can't stand that you've chosen Sae!
How could you be with her?! I don't want this.

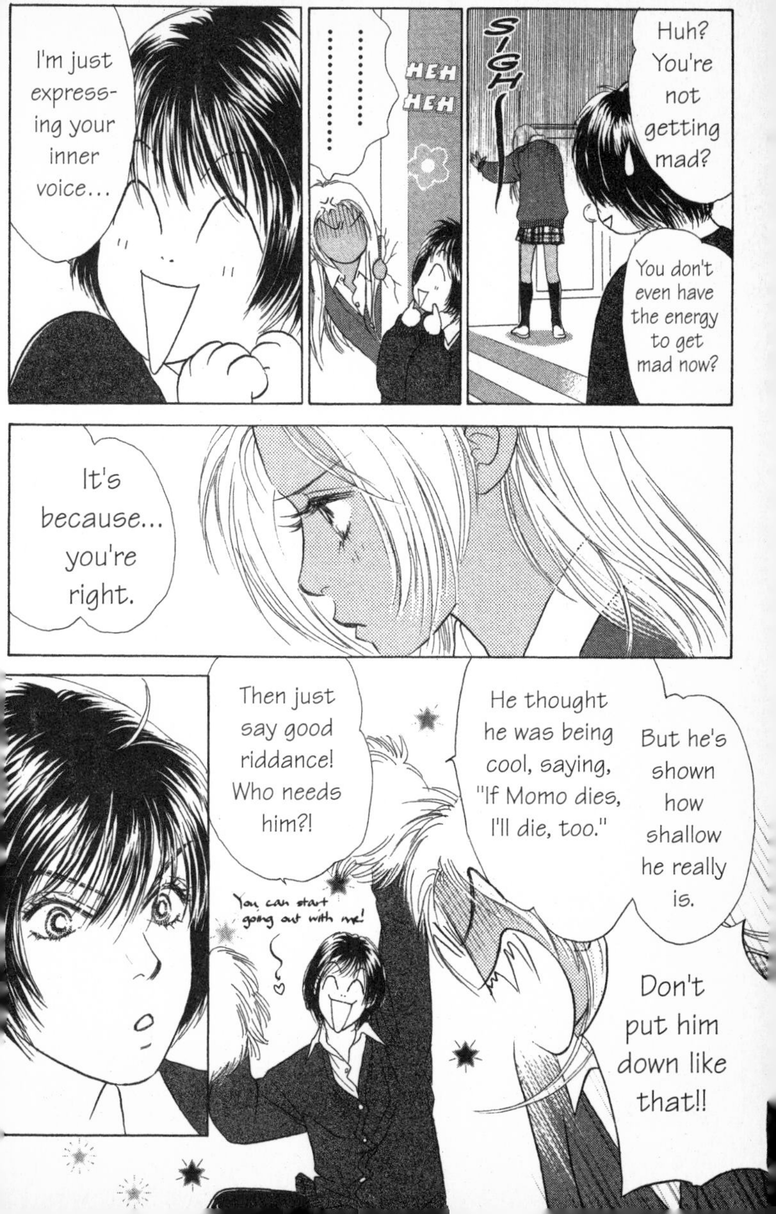
I'm just express-ing your inner voice...
......
HEH HEH
SIGH
Huh? You're not getting mad?
You don't even have the energy to get mad now?
It's because... you're right.
Then just say good riddance! Who needs him?!
You can start going out with me!
He thought he was being cool, saying, "If Momo dies, I'll die, too."
But he's shown how shallow he really is.
Don't put him down like that!!

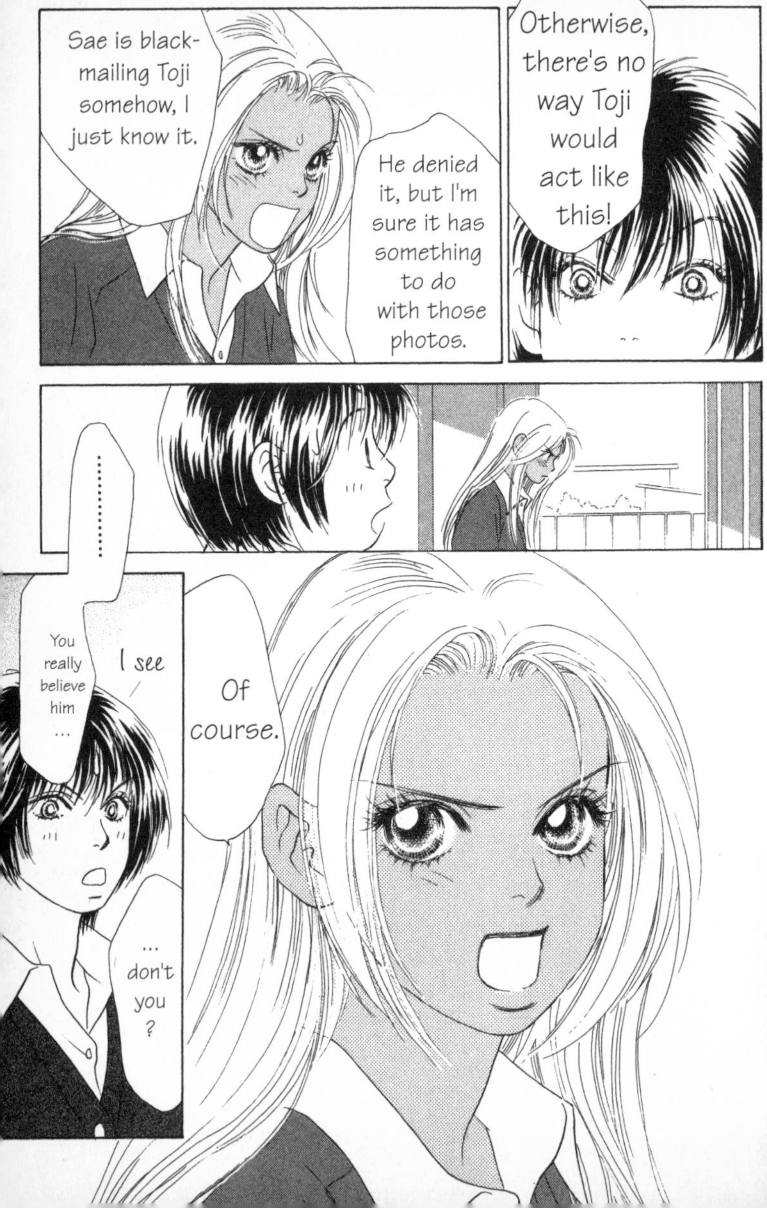
Sae is black-mailing Toji somehow, I just know it.
He denied it, but I'm sure it has something to do with those photos.
Otherwise, there's no way Toji would act like this!
....
You really believe him ...
I see
... don't you ?
Of course.

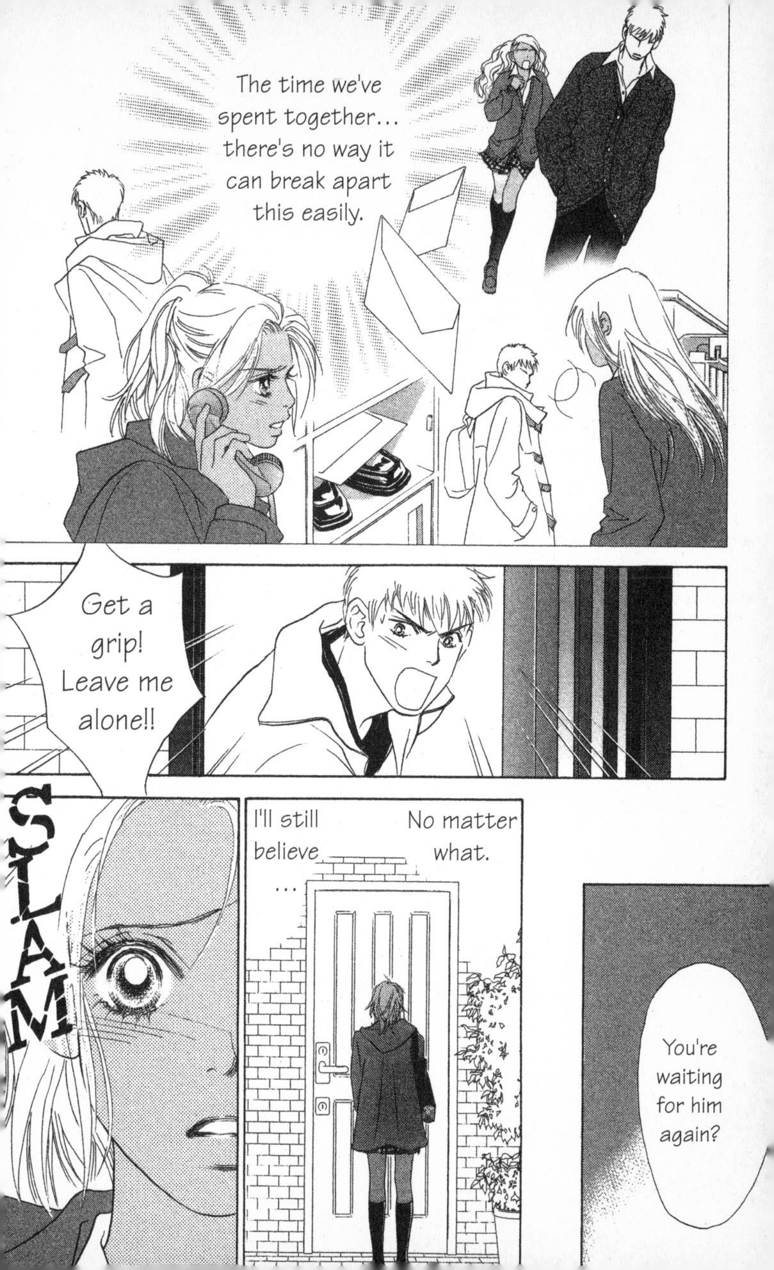
The time we've spent together... there's no way it can break apart this easily.
Get a grip! Leave me alone!!
You're waiting for him again?
No matter what.
I'll still believe...
SLAM

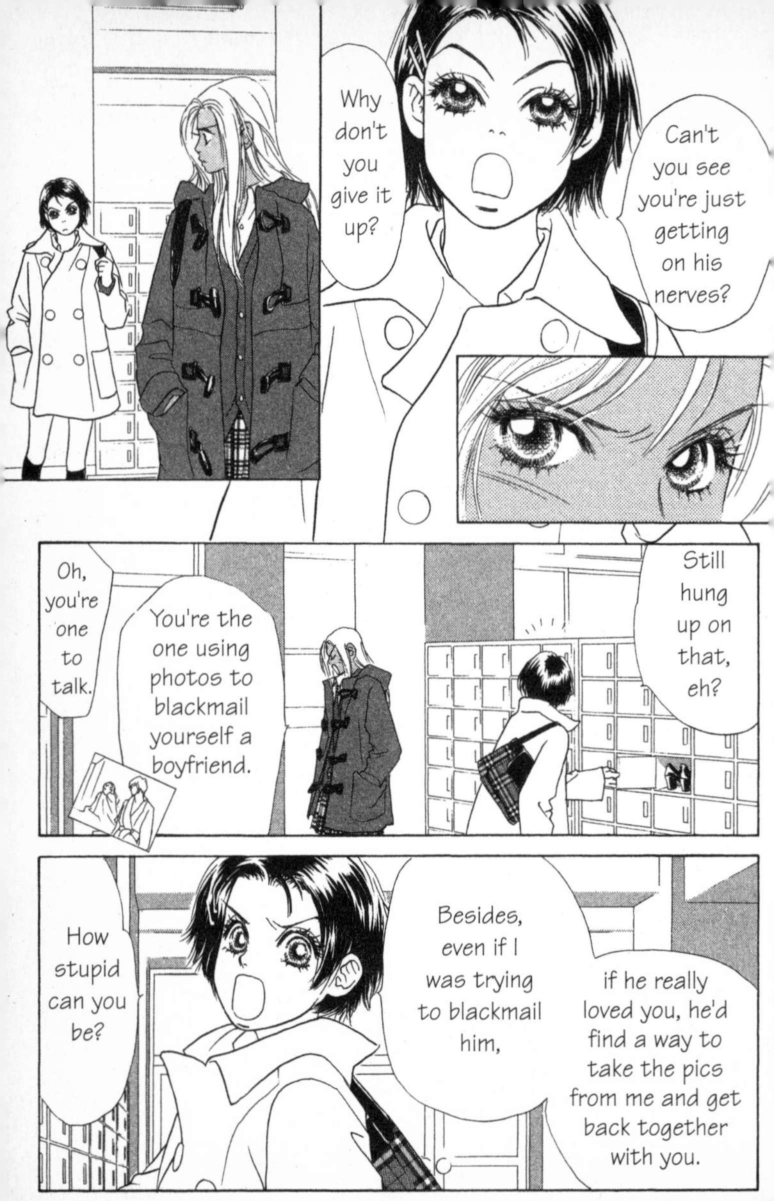
Why don't you give it up?
Can't you see you're just getting on his nerves?
Still hung up on that, eh?
Oh, you're one to talk.
You're the one using photos to blackmail yourself a boyfriend.
How stupid can you be?
Besides, even if I was trying to blackmail him,
if he really loved you, he'd find a way to take the pics from me and get back together with you.

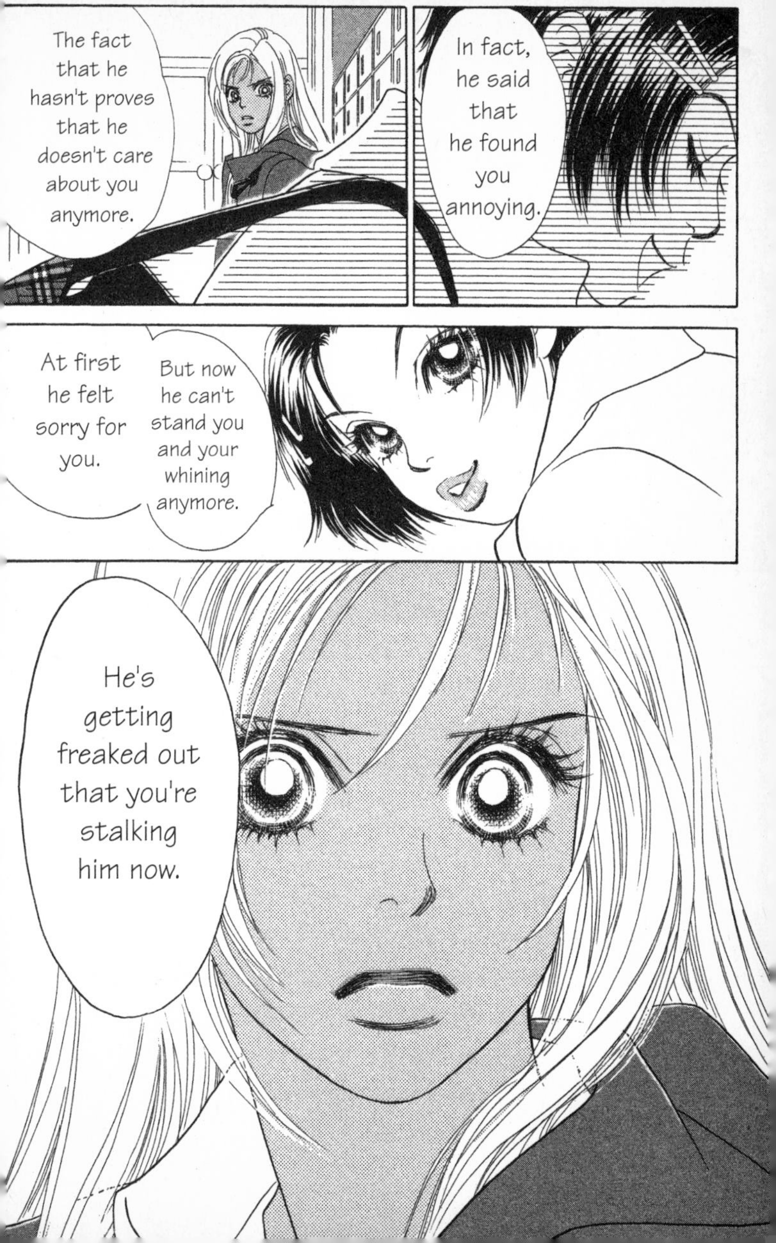
The fact that he hasn't proves that he doesn't care about you anymore.
In fact, he said that he found you annoying.
At first he felt sorry for you.
But now he can't stand you and your whining anymore.
He's getting freaked out that you're stalking him now.

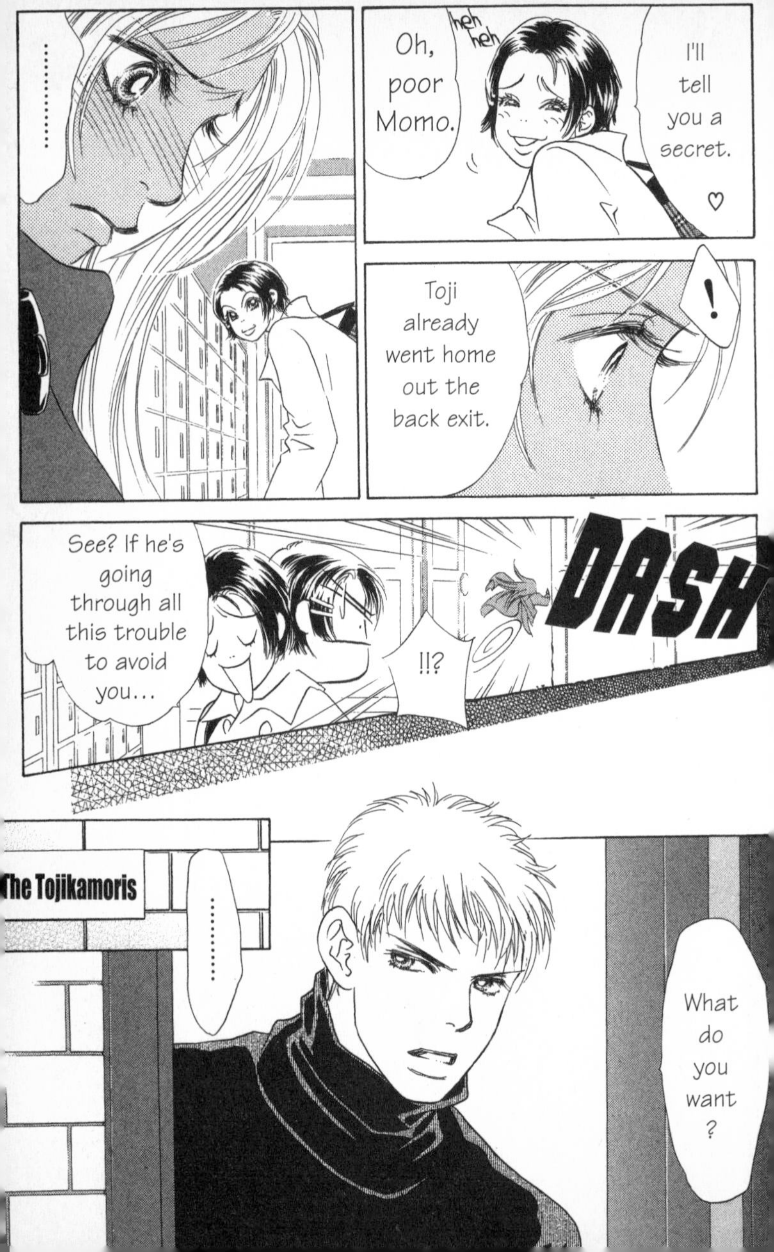
heh heh
Oh, poor Momo.
I'll tell you a secret. ♡
!
Toji already went home out the back exit.
......
DASH
!!?
See? If he's going through all this trouble to avoid you...
What do you want?
......
The Tojikamoris

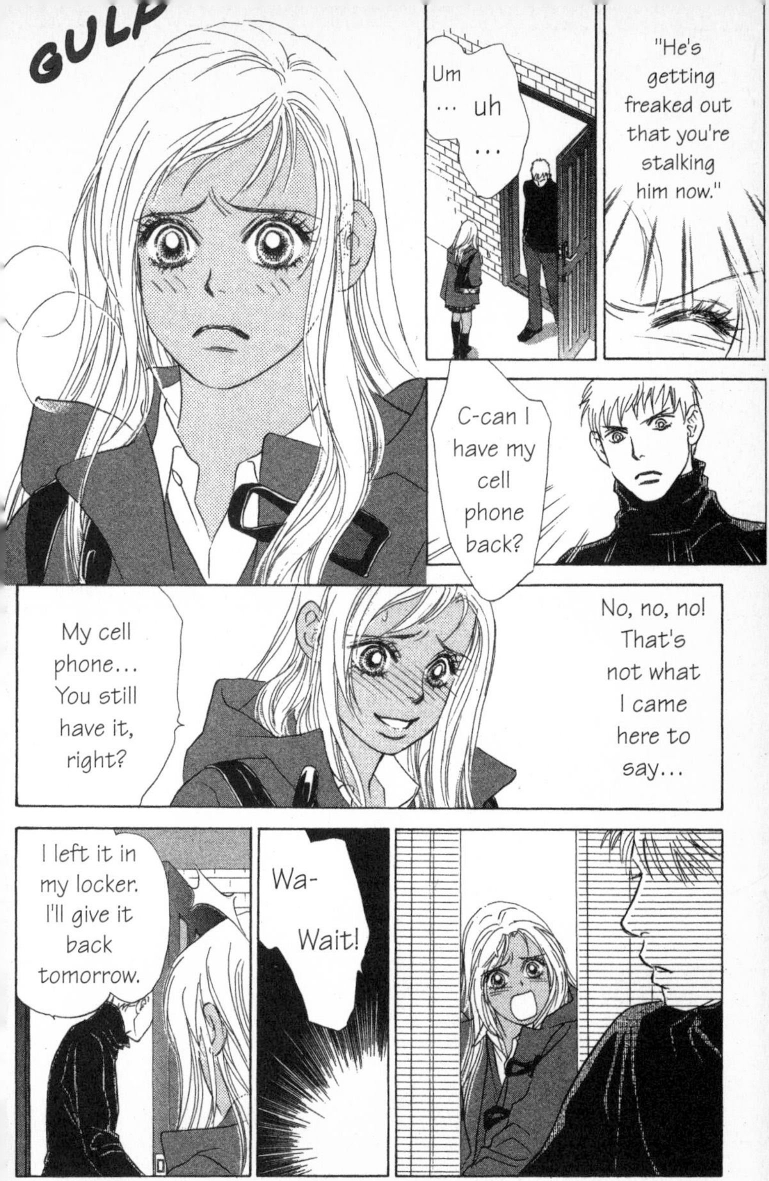
"He's getting freaked out that you're stalking him now."
Um … uh …
C-can I have my cell phone back?
GULP
No, no, no! That's not what I came here to say…
My cell phone… You still have it, right?
Wa- Wait!
I left it in my locker. I'll give it back tomorrow.

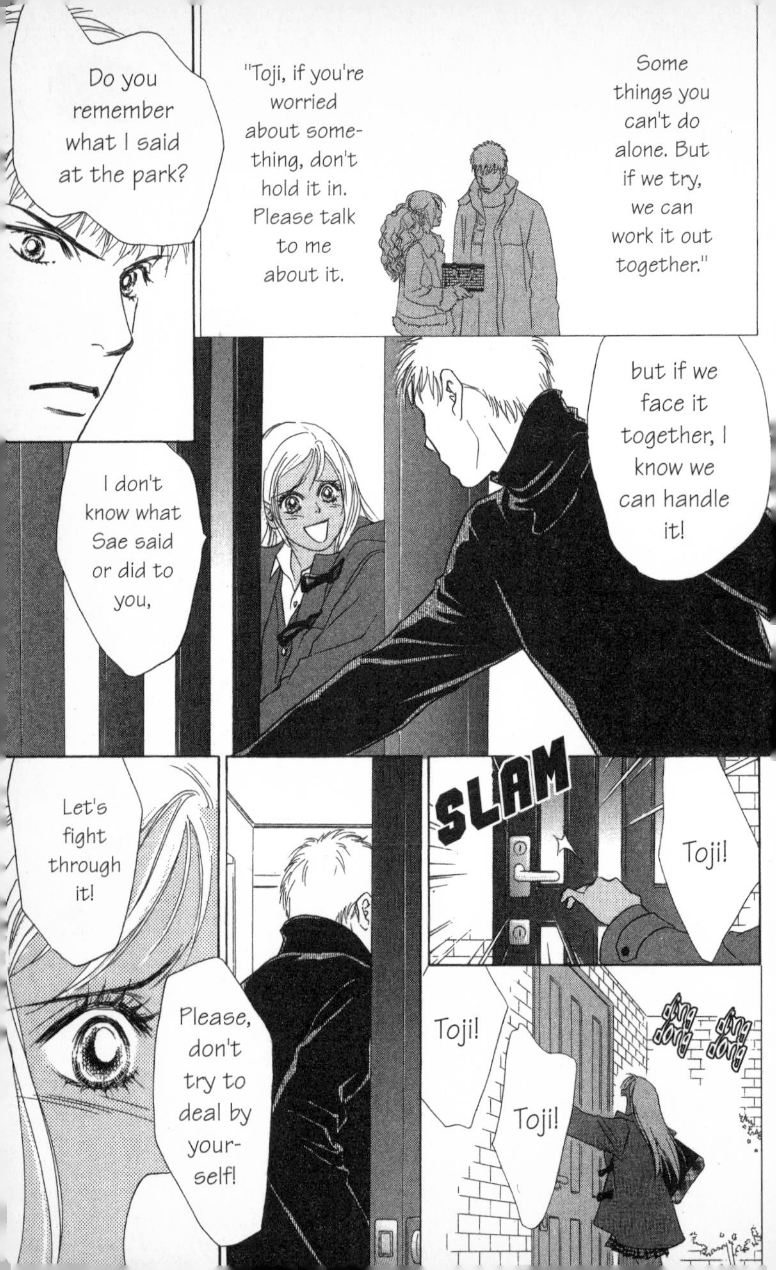

Do you remember what I said at the park?
"Toji, if you're worried about some-thing, don't hold it in. Please talk to me about it.
Some things you can't do alone. But if we try, we can work it out together."
I don't know what Sae said or did to you,
but if we face it together, I know we can handle it!
Let's fight through it!
Please, don't try to deal by your-self!
SLAM
Toji!
Toji!
Toji!
ding dong
ding dong

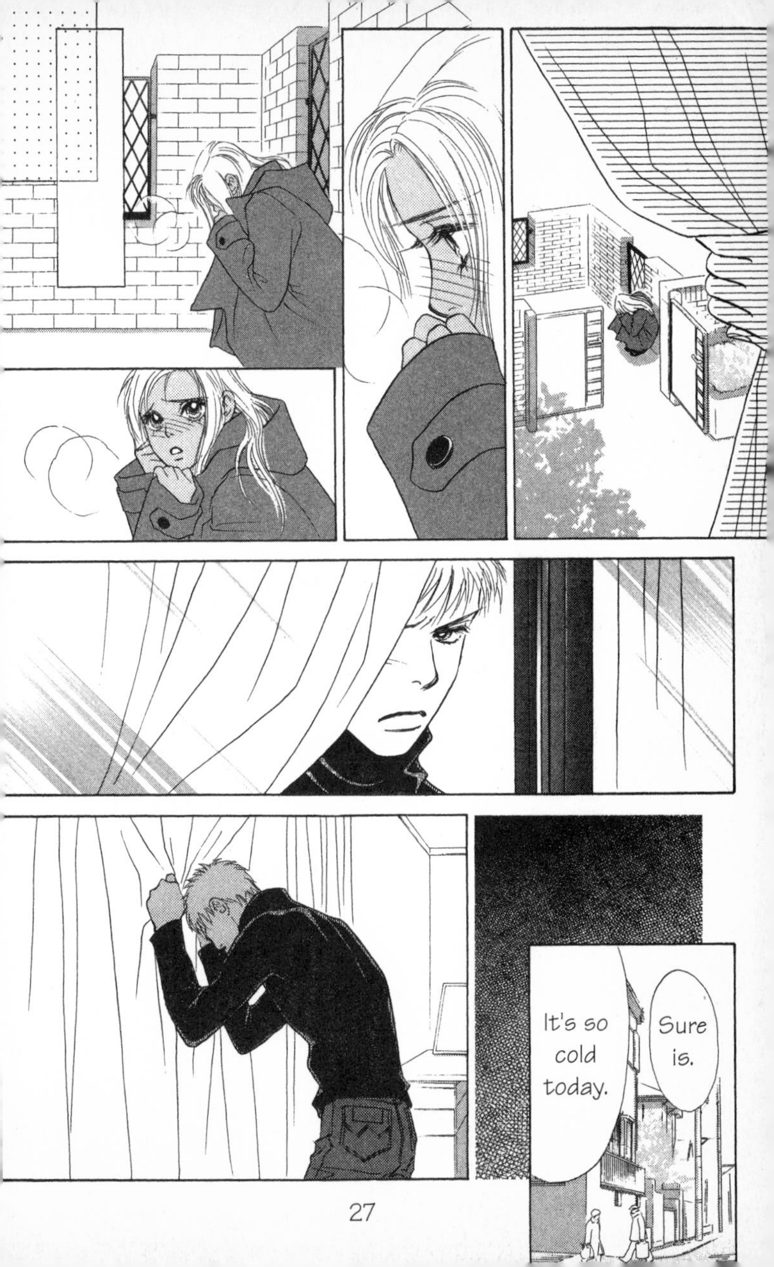
It's so cold today.
Sure is.

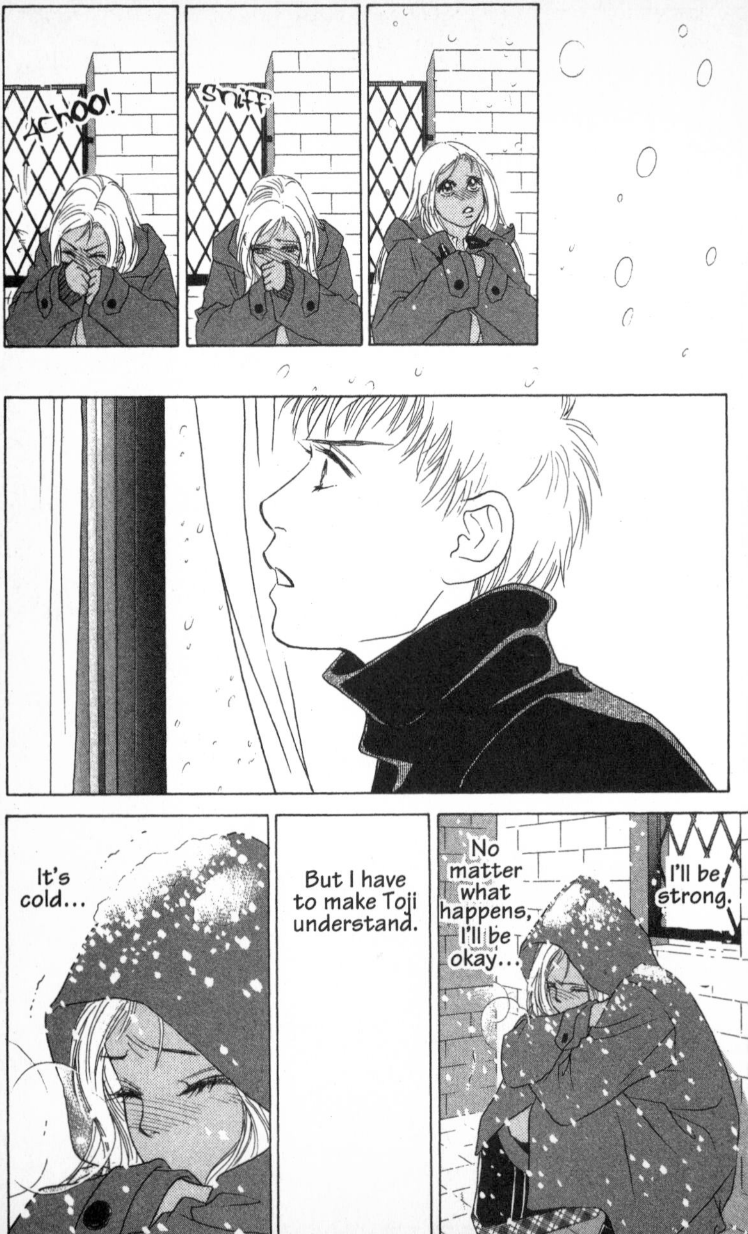
ACHOO!
SNIFF
It's cold...
But I have to make Toji understand.
No matter what happens, I'll be okay...
I'll be strong.

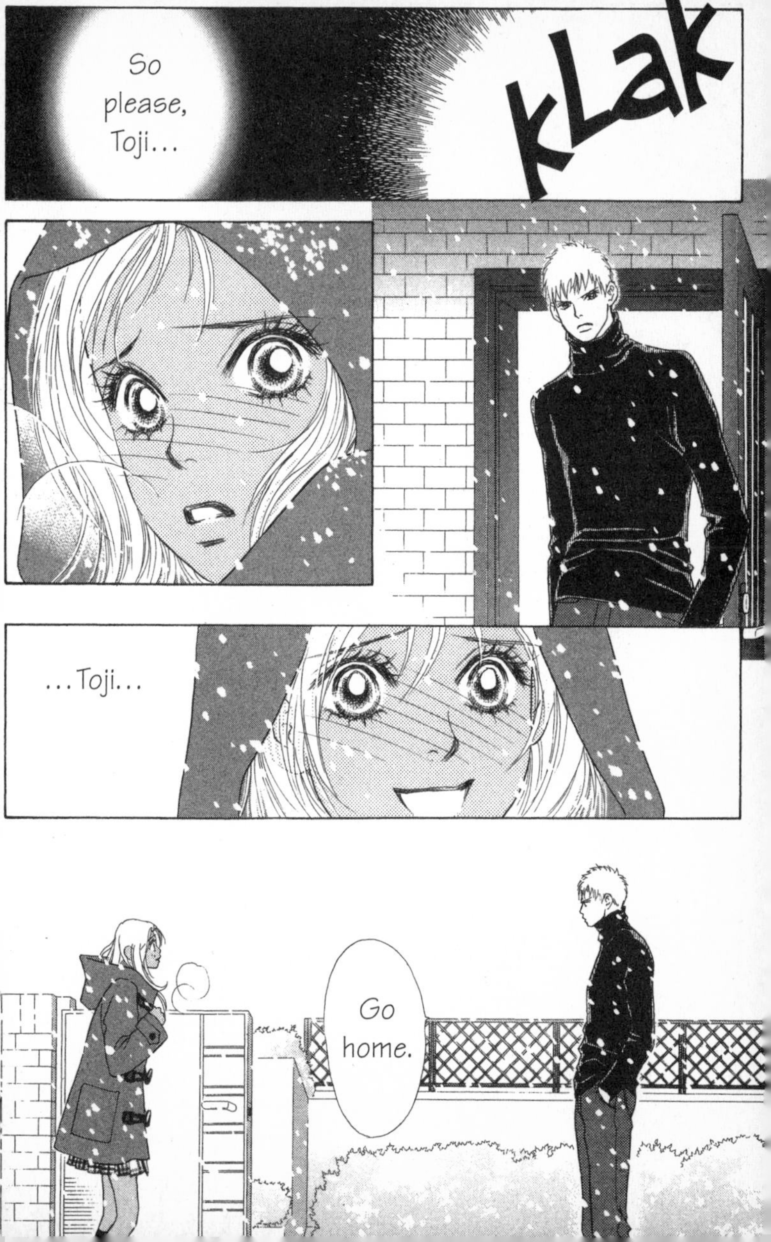
KLAK
So please, Toji...
...Toji...
Go home.

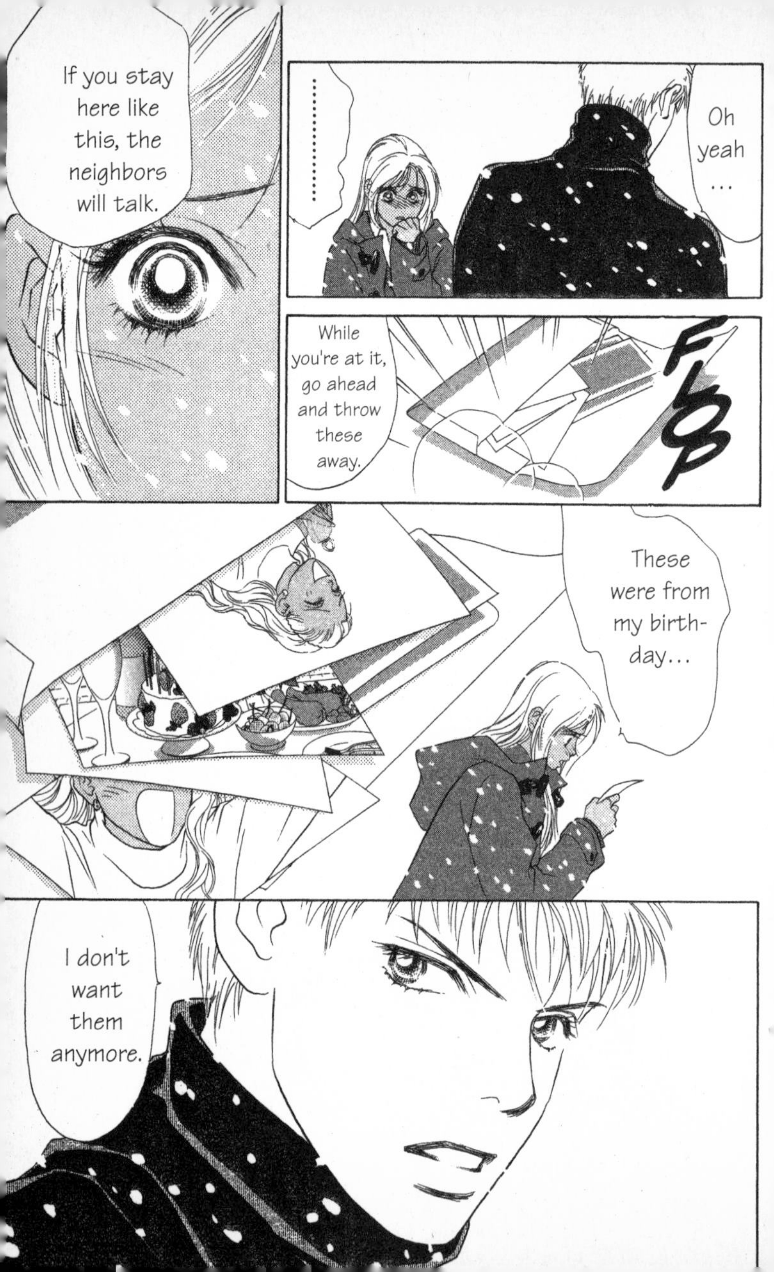
If you stay here like this, the neighbors will talk.
......
Oh yeah ...
While you're at it, go ahead and throw these away.
FLOP
These were from my birth-day...
I don't want them anymore.

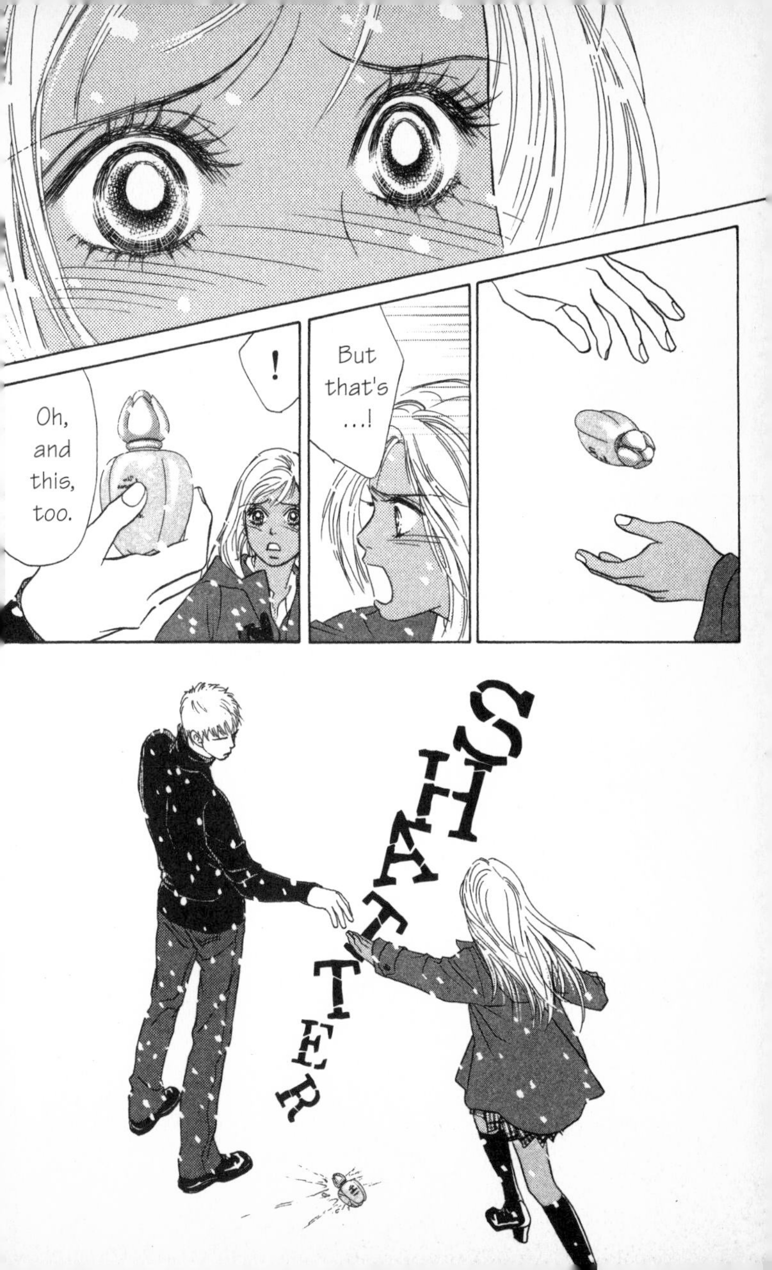
Oh, and this, too.
!
But that's ...!
SHATTER

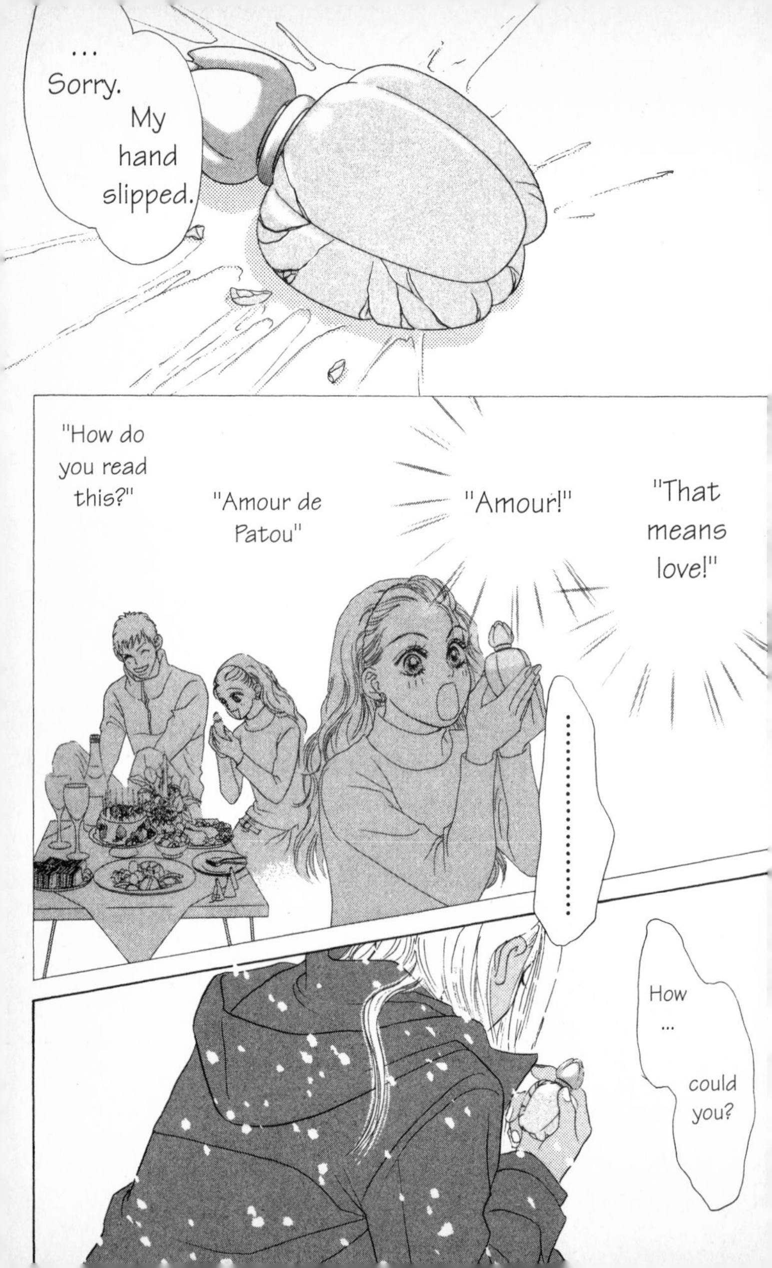
... Sorry. My hand slipped.
"How do you read this?"
"Amour de Patou"
"Amour!"
"That means love!"
....
How ... could you?

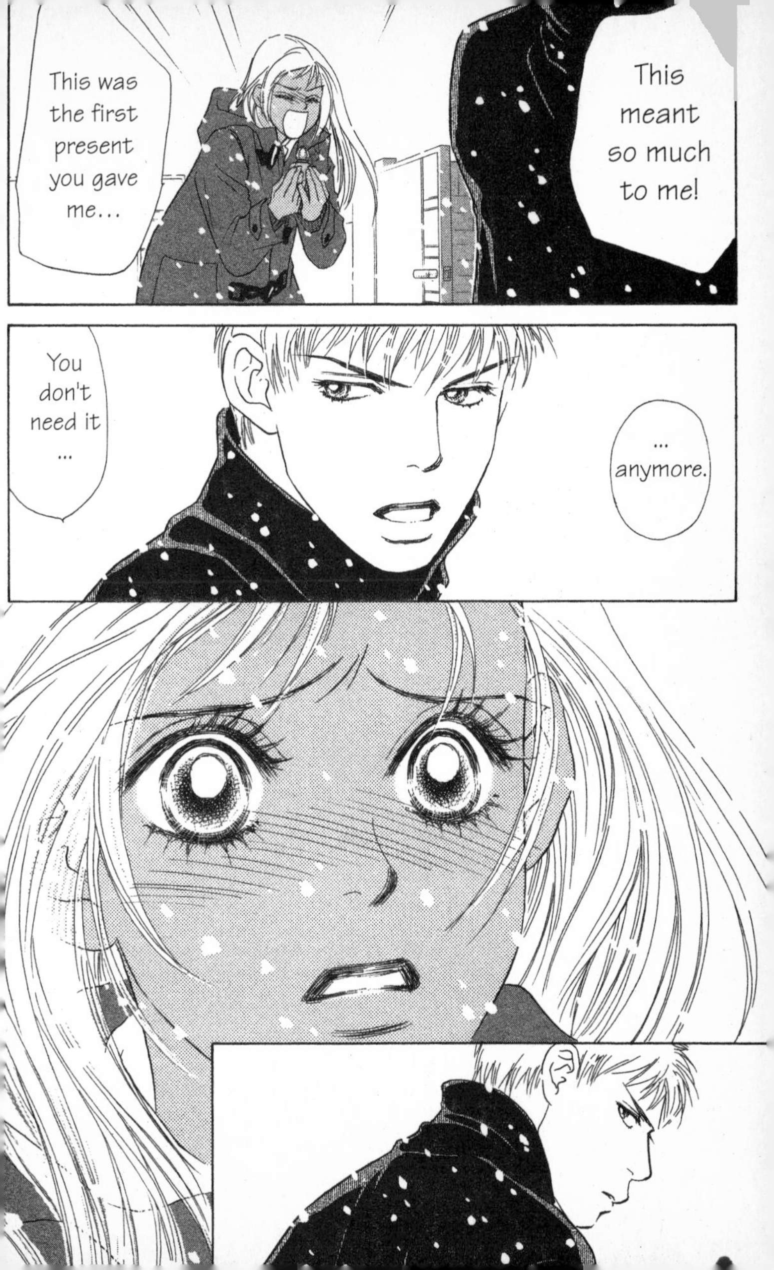
This was the first present you gave me…
This meant so much to me!
You don't need it …
… anymore.

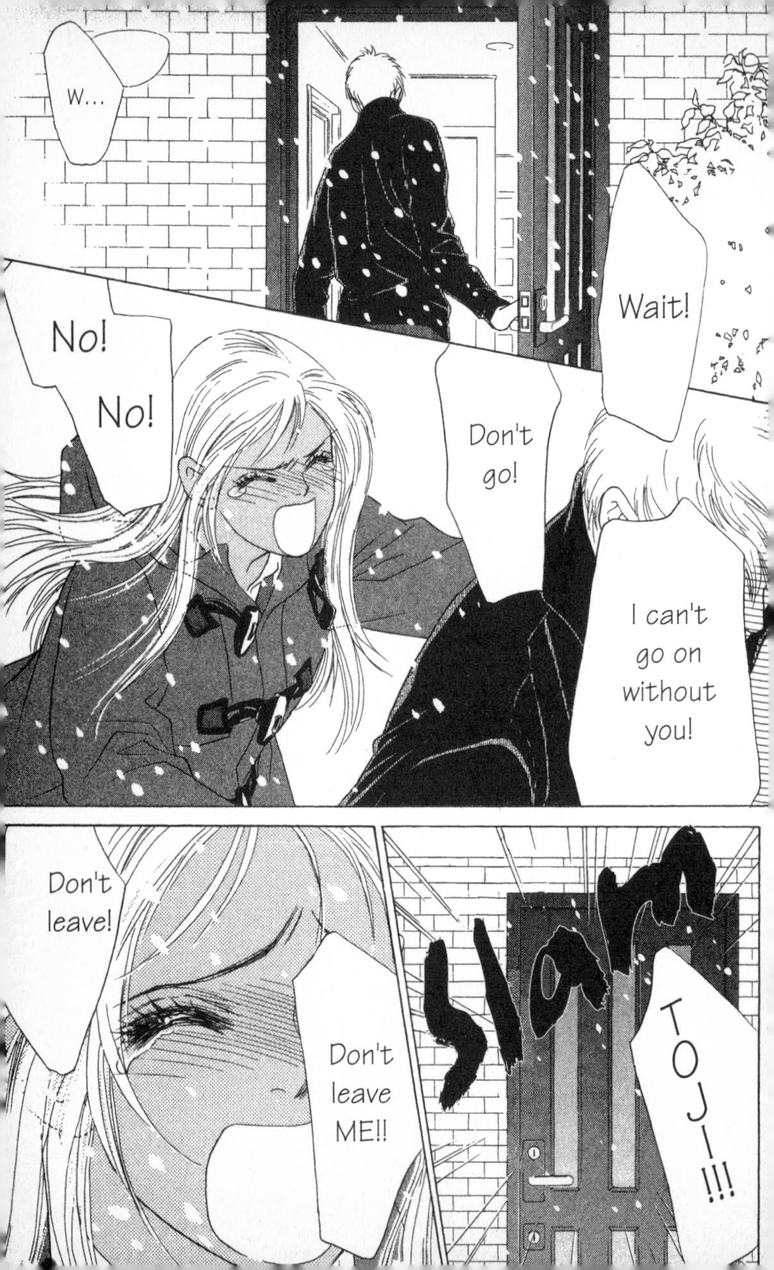
W...
Wait!
Don't go!
I can't go on without you!
No!
No!
slam
TOJI!!!
Don't leave!
Don't leave ME!!

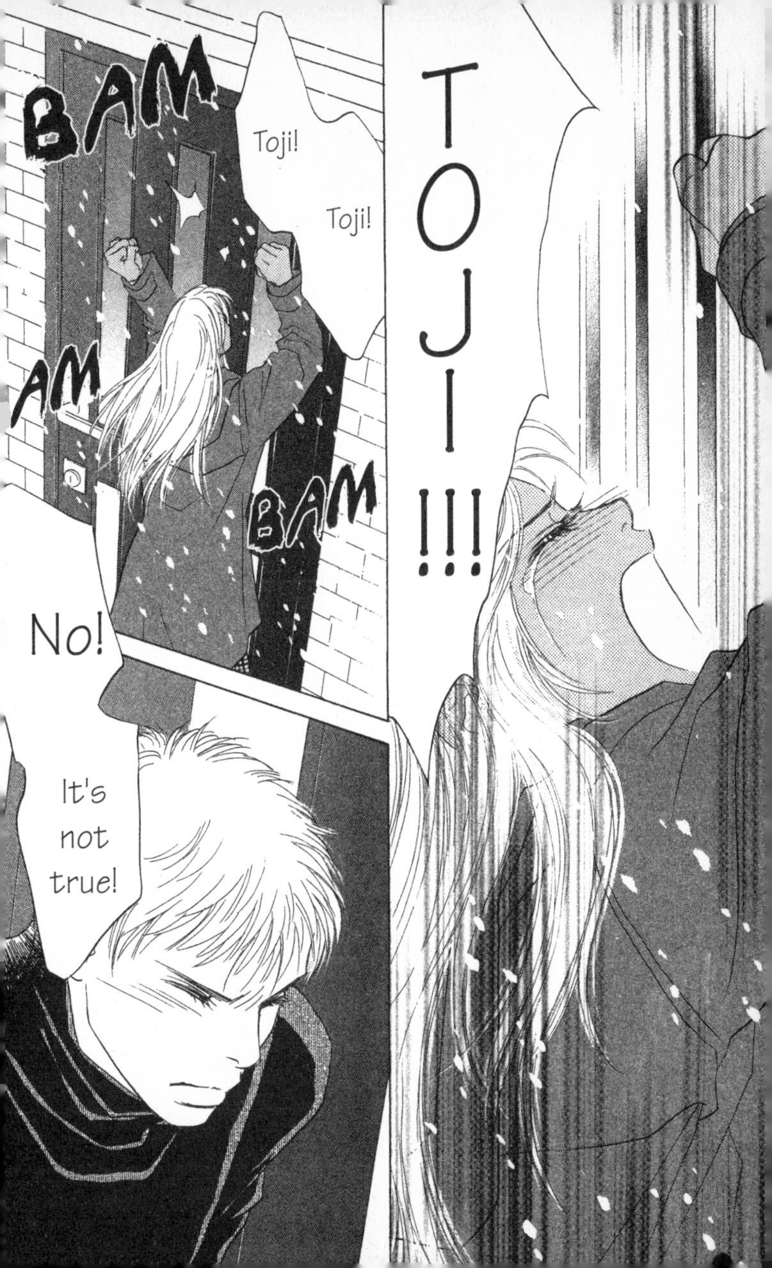
TOJI!!!
BAM
Toji!
Toji!
AM
BAM
No!
It's not true!

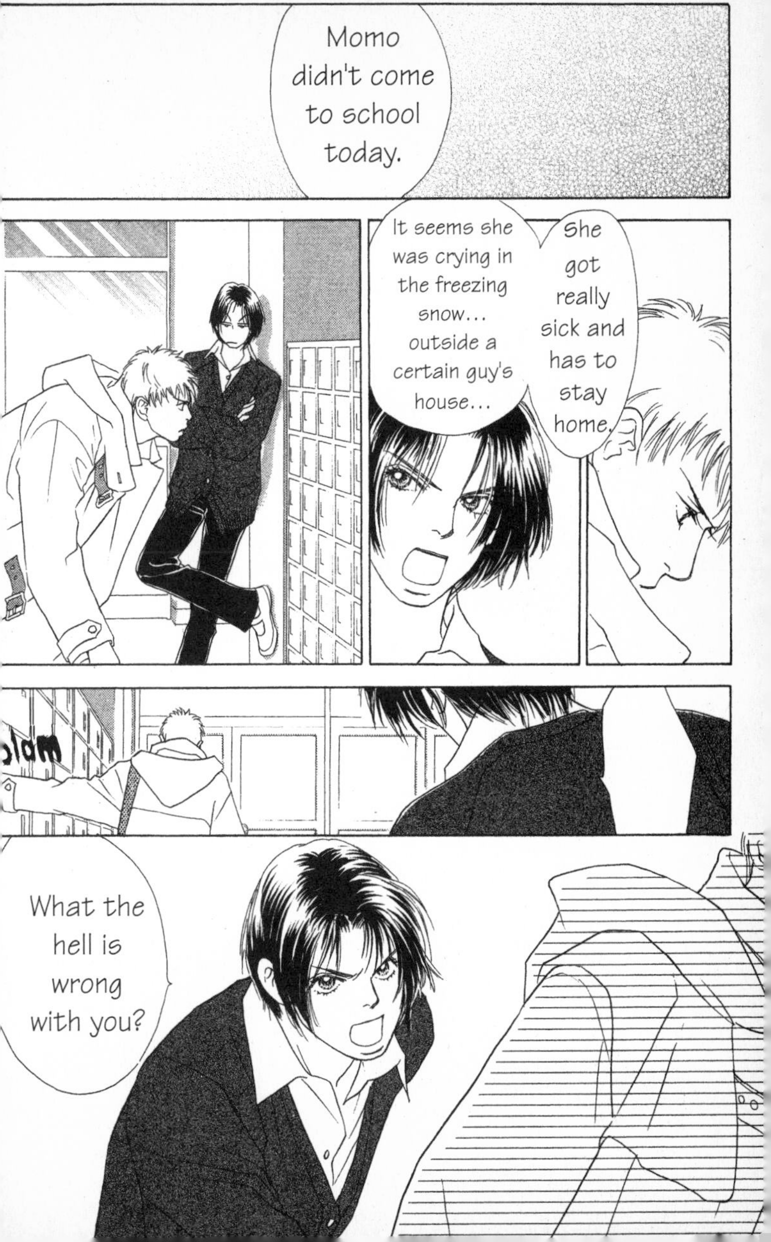
Momo didn't come to school today.
She got really sick and has to stay home.
It seems she was crying in the freezing snow... outside a certain guy's house...
slam
What the hell is wrong with you?

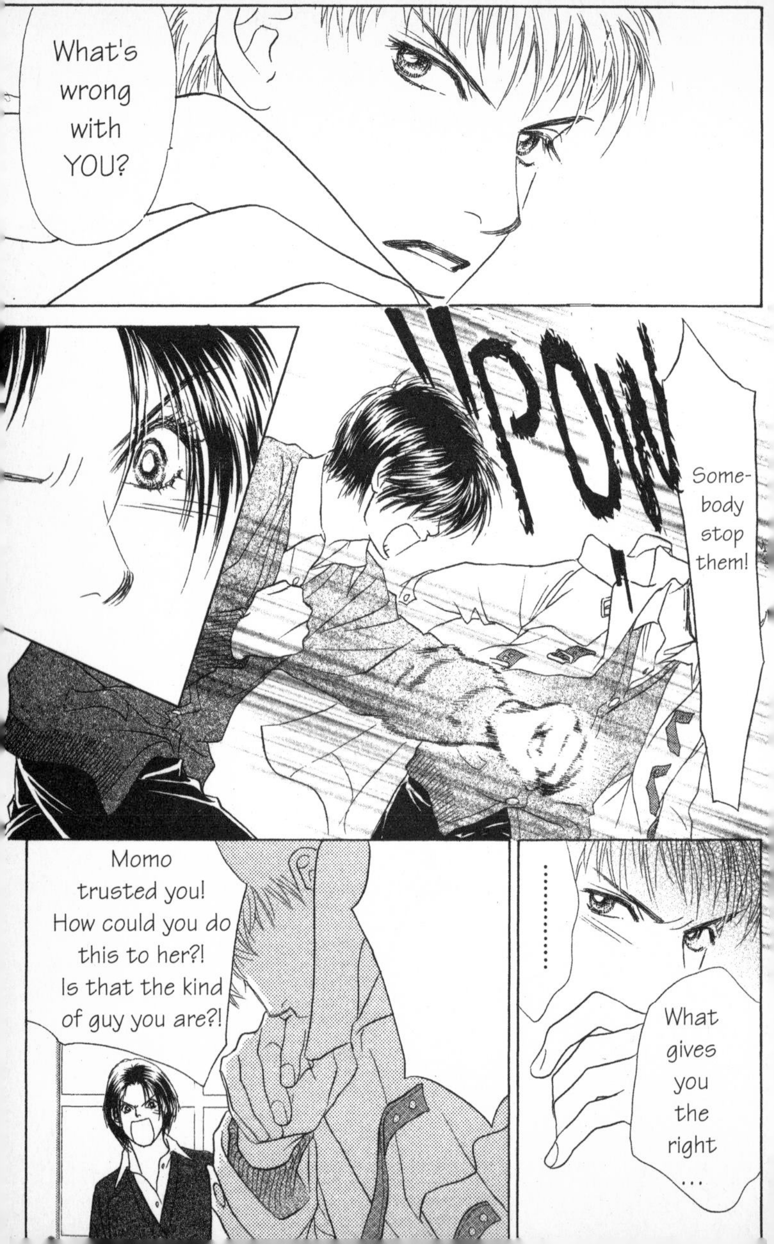
What's wrong with YOU?
POW
Somebody stop them!
Momo trusted you! How could you do this to her?! Is that the kind of guy you are?!
......
What gives you the right ...

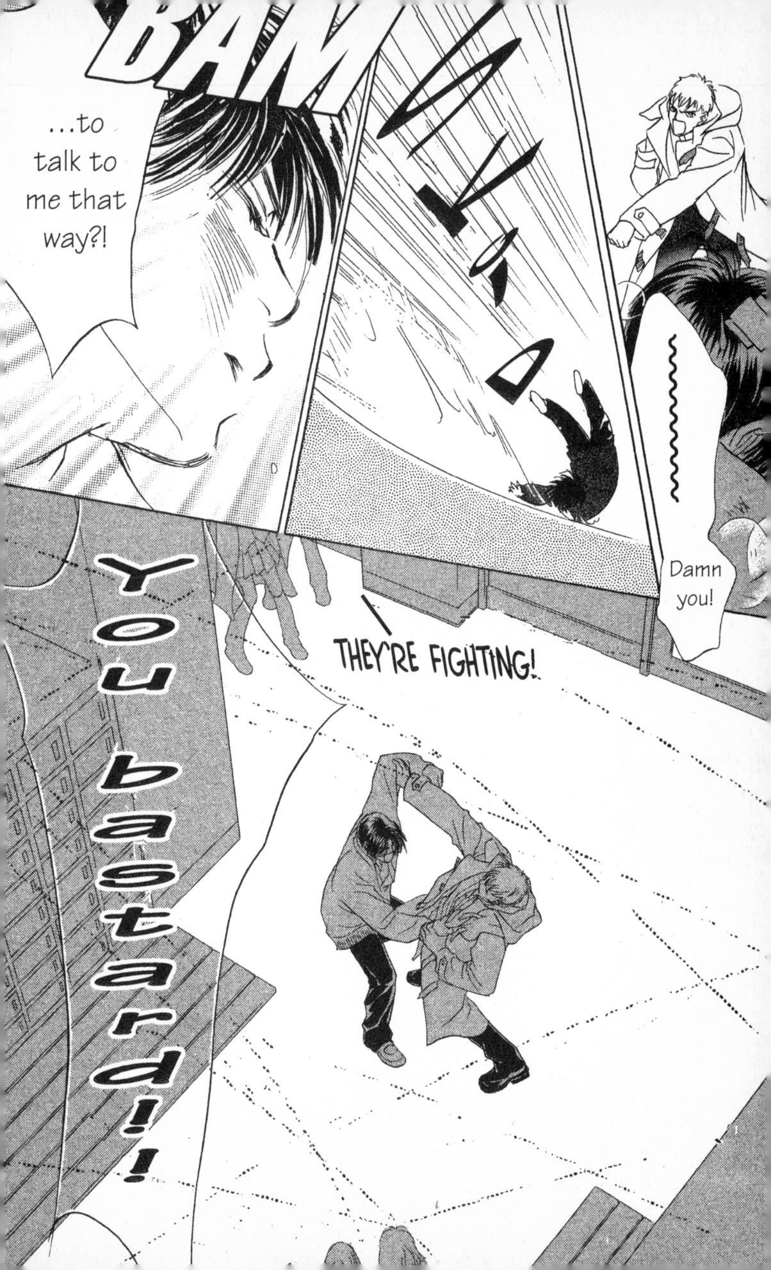
Damn you!
BAM
...to talk to me that way?!
THEY'RE FIGHTING!
You bastard!!

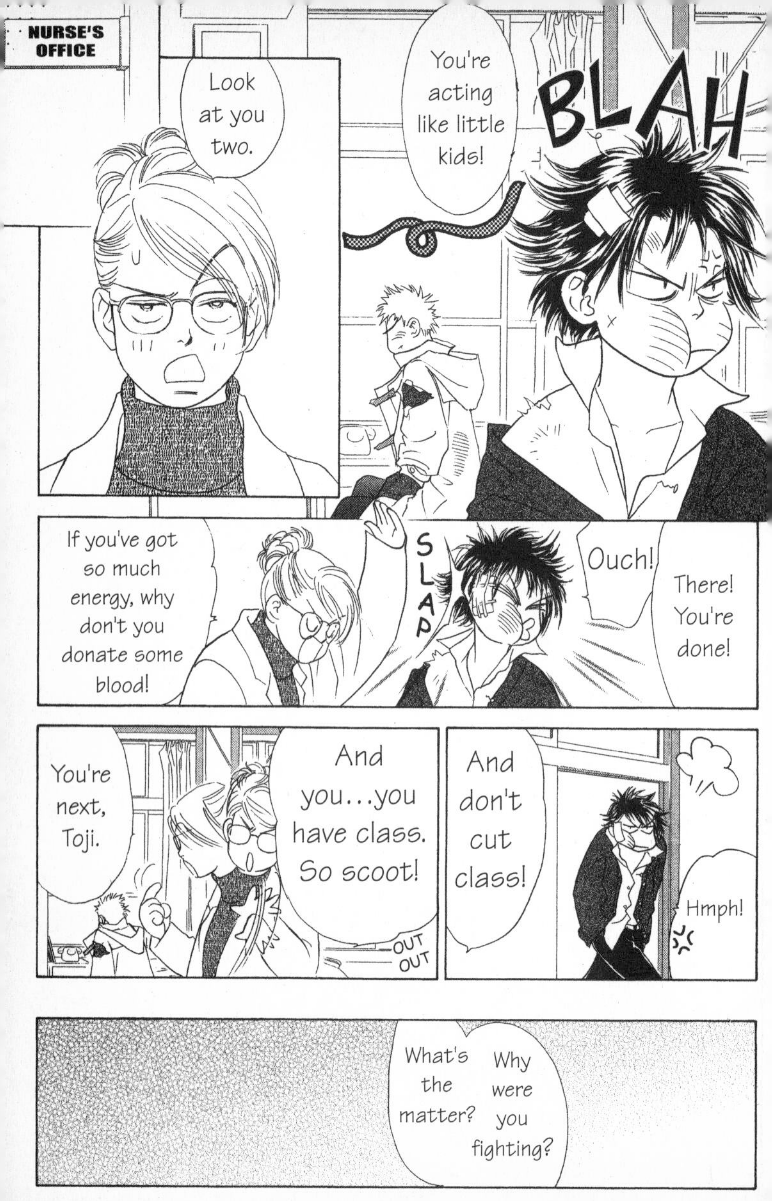
NURSE'S OFFICE
Look at you two.
You're acting like little kids!
BLAH
If you've got so much energy, why don't you donate some blood!
SLAP
Ouch!
There! You're done!
You're next, Toji.
And you...you have class. So scoot!
OUT OUT
And don't cut class!
Hmph!
What's the matter?
Why were you fighting?

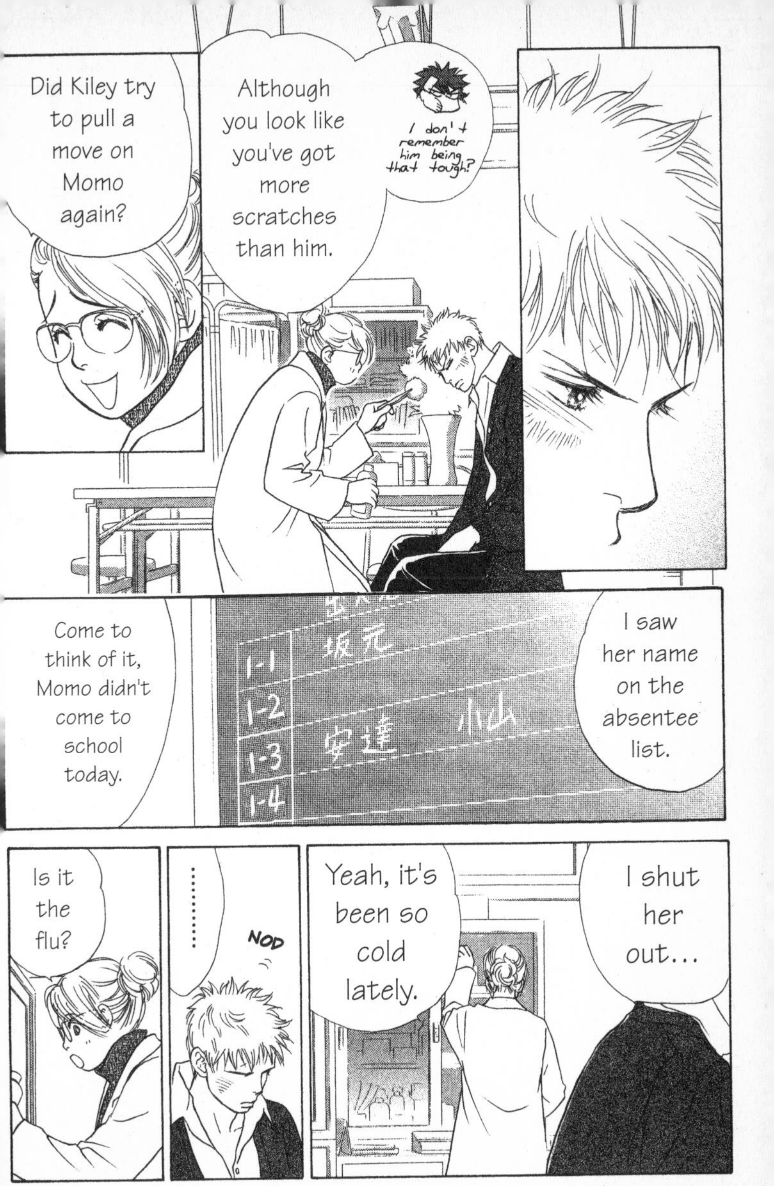

Did Kiley try to pull a move on Momo again?
Although you look like you've got more scratches than him.
I don't remember him being that tough?
Come to think of it, Momo didn't come to school today.
1-1 坂元
1-2
1-3 安達 小山
1-4
I saw her name on the absentee list.
Is it the flu?
....
NOD
Yeah, it's been so cold lately.
I shut her out...

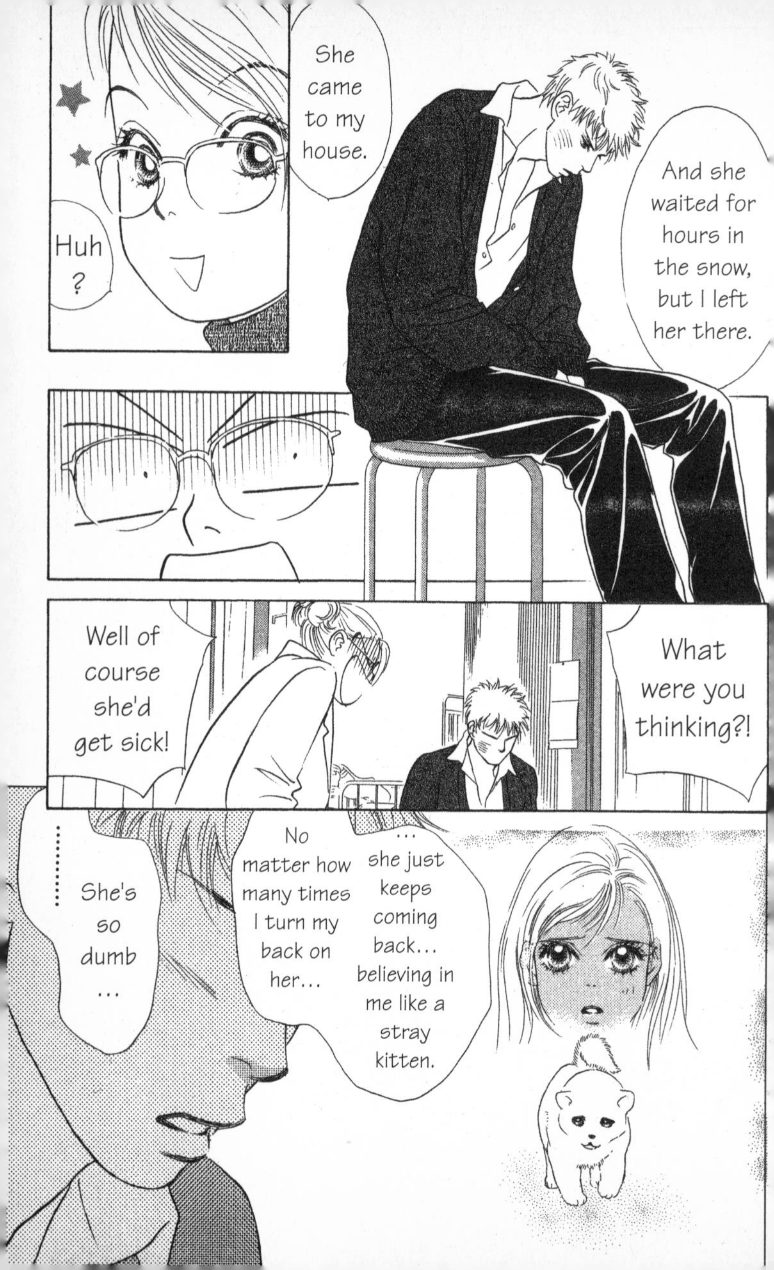
She came to my house.
Huh?
And she waited for hours in the snow, but I left her there.
What were you thinking?!
Well of course she'd get sick!
No matter how many times I turn my back on her…
… she just keeps coming back… believing in me like a stray kitten.
……… She's so dumb …

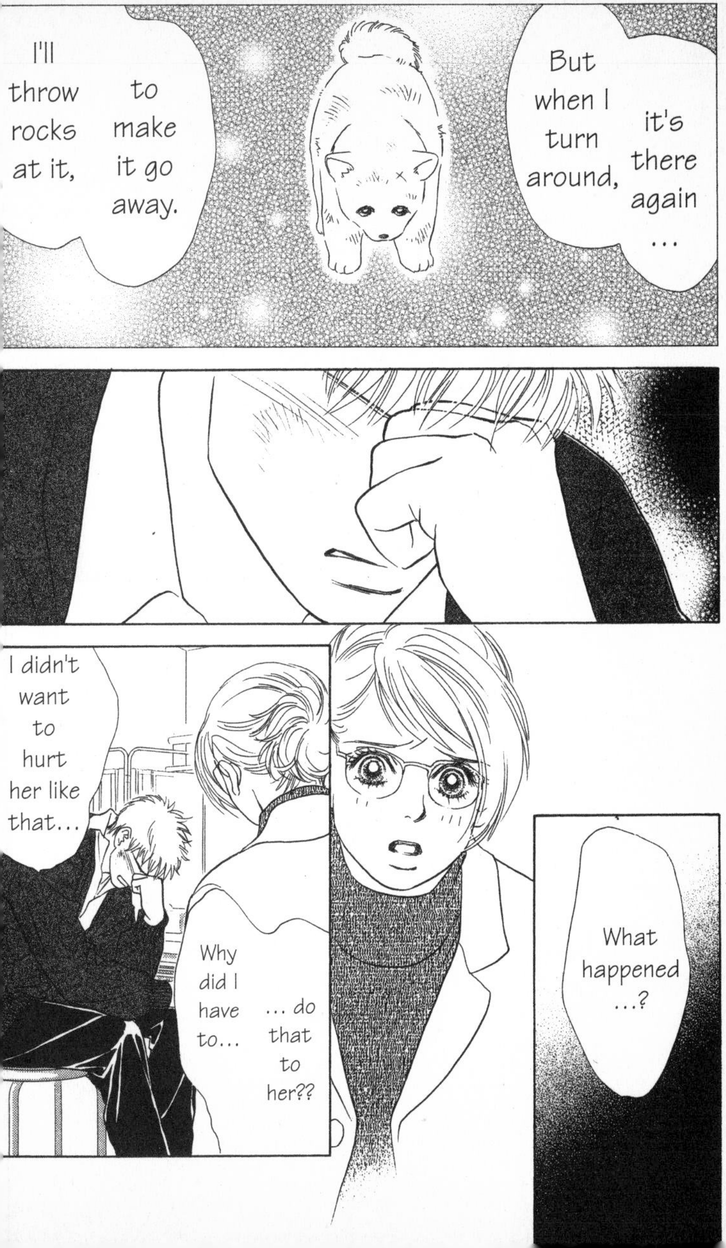
I'll throw rocks at it,
to make it go away.
But when I turn around,
it's there again ...
I didn't want to hurt her like that...
Why did I have to...
... do that to her??
What happened ...?

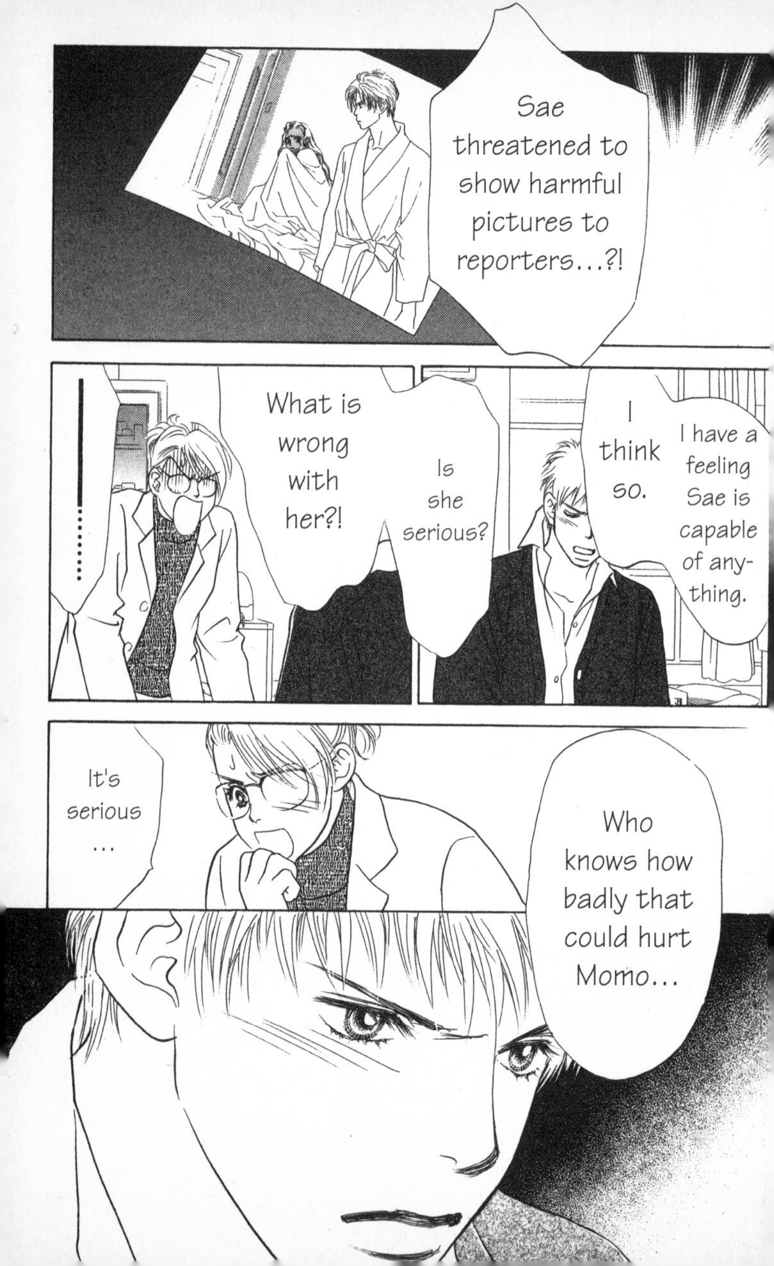
Sae threatened to show harmful pictures to reporters...?!
What is wrong with her?!
Is she serious?
I think so.
I have a feeling Sae is capable of anything.
It's serious ...
Who knows how badly that could hurt Momo...

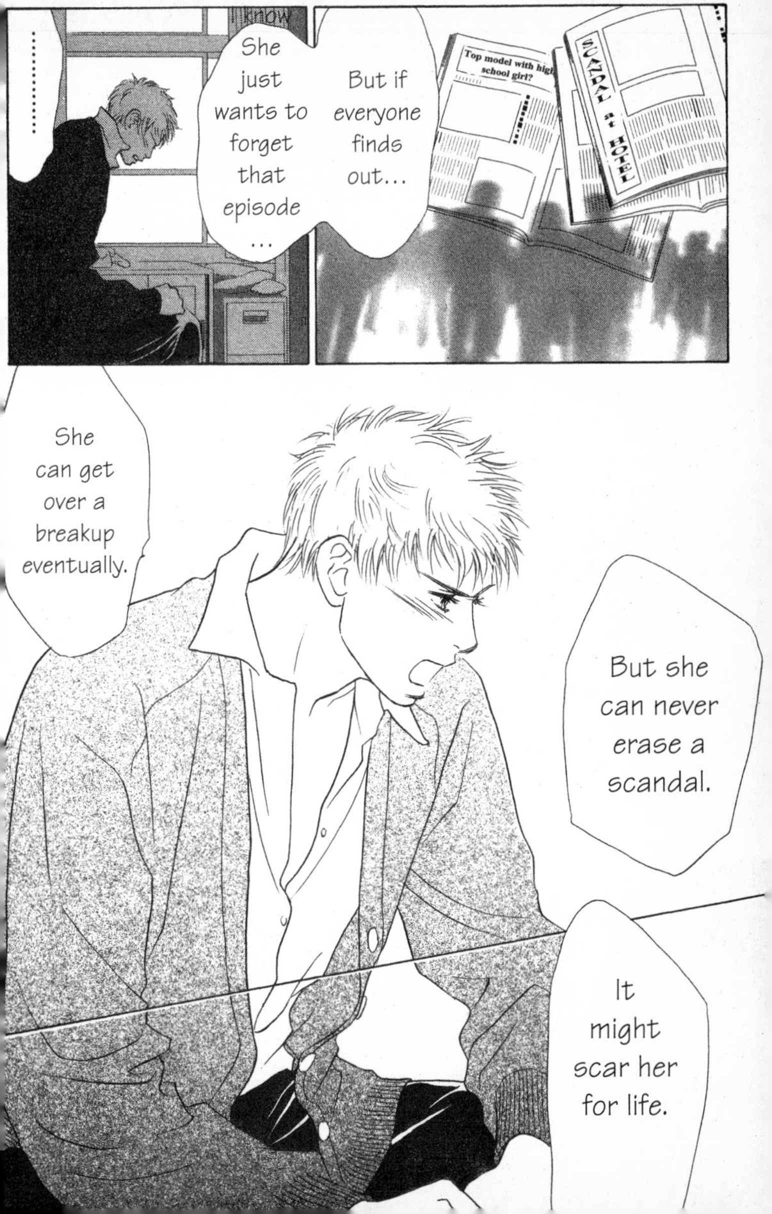

I know
......
She just wants to forget that episode...
But if everyone finds out...
Top model with hig school girl?
SCANDAL at HOTEL
She can get over a breakup eventually.
But she can never erase a scandal.
It might scar her for life.

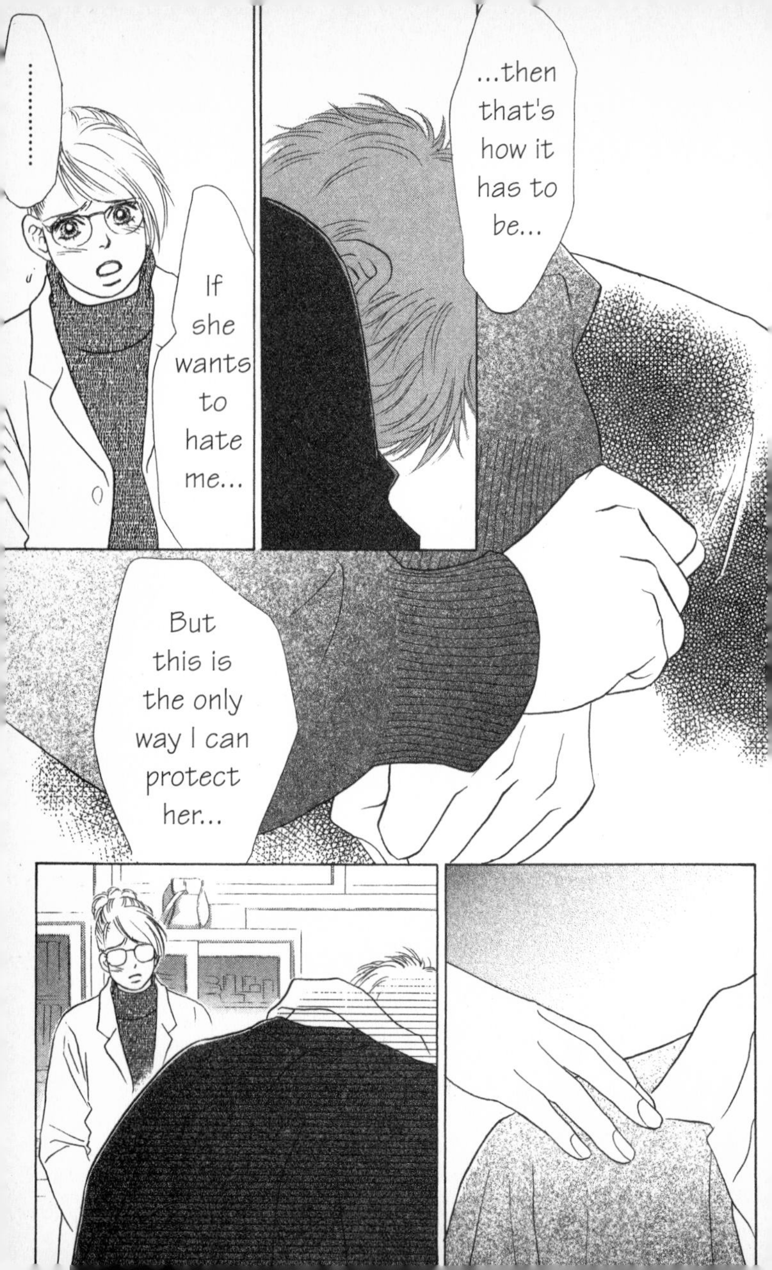
......
If she wants to hate me...
...then that's how it has to be...
But this is the only way I can protect her...

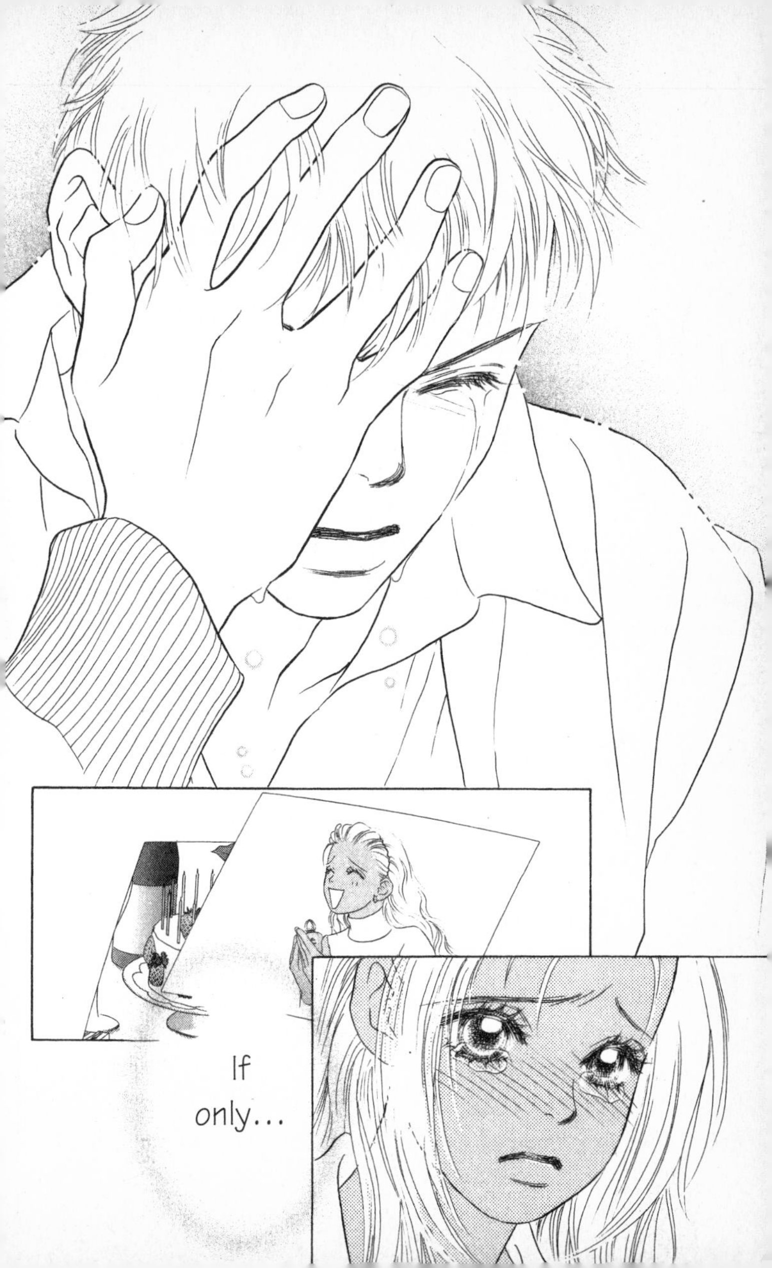
If only...

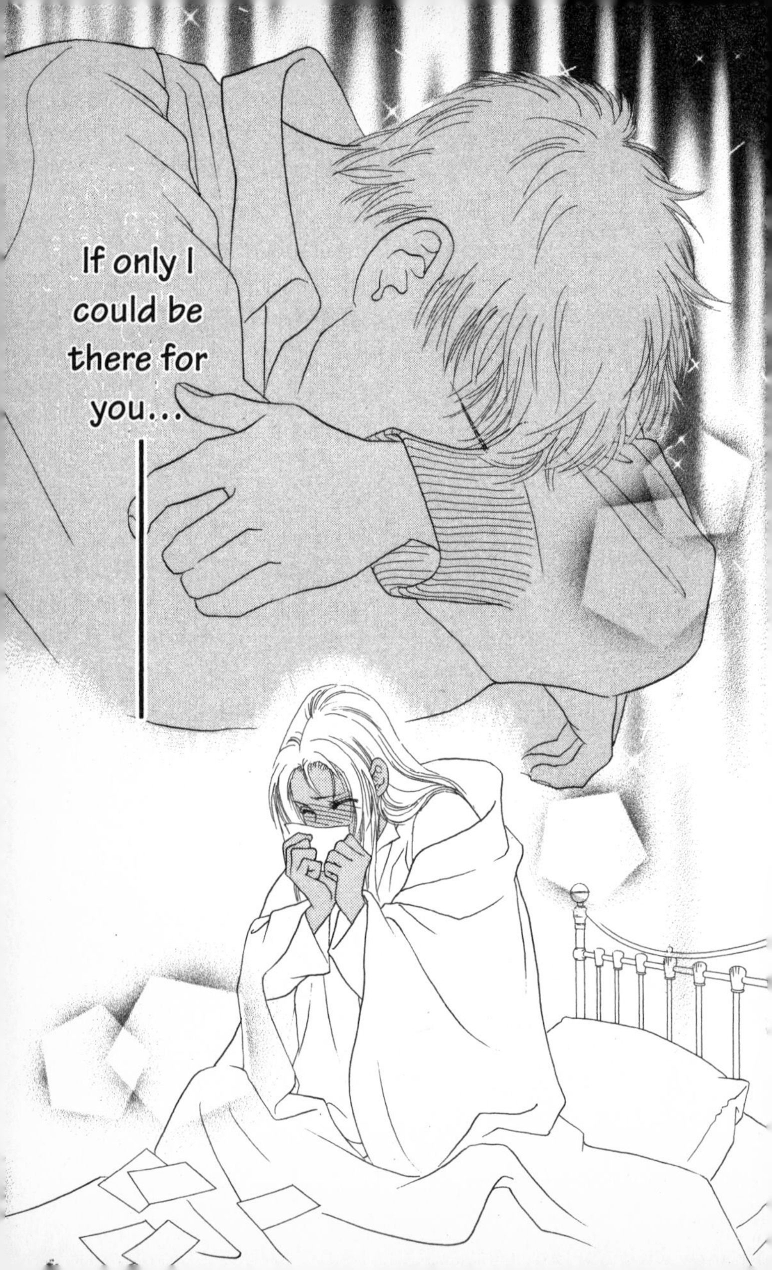
If only I could be there for you...

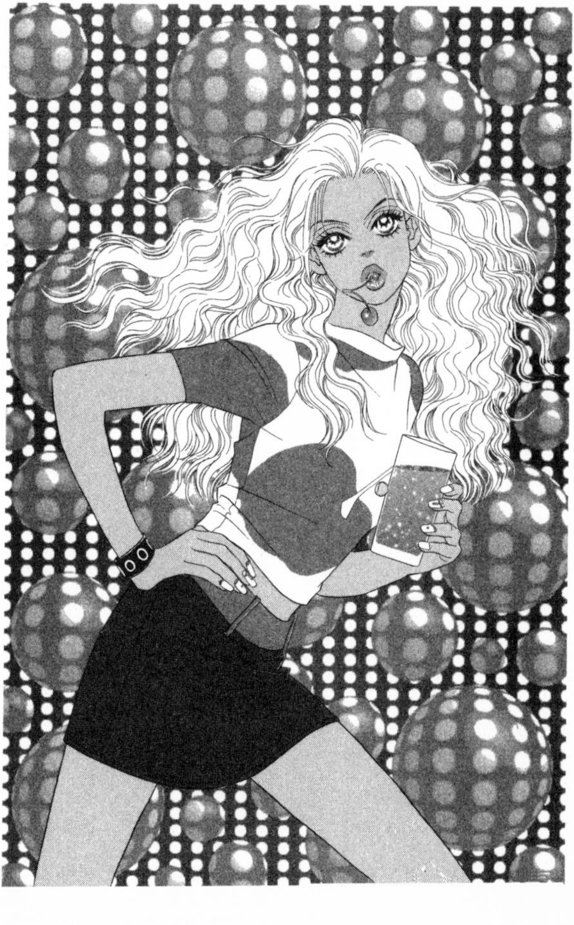

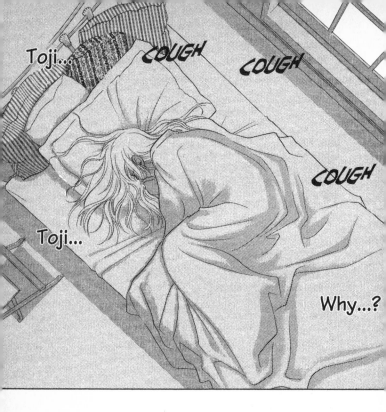

Toji...

COUGH COUGH

COUGH

Toji...

Why...?

PEACH CLUB

Hello, everybody! Welcome to *Peach Girl* 8.
This time around, with my illustration collection coming out, alternate cover illustrations, interviews, and the Bon festival, I haven't been able to deliver the end of book Bonus Pages. If you were looking forward to it, I'm sorry!
On the other hand, I feel I've overwritten a bit, and reading some of your letters, it seems that some of the subject matter is going a bit in circles. So I would like to end the "Sae vs. Momo" features. But if I get some more interesting letters, maybe I'll bring it back.
Oh, and for all of you who read Book 7, thank you for visiting my homepage! Of course, you may have bought Book 7 but never saw the web address, so here it is once again.
If you have a PC, please come by!
http://www.yomogi.sakura.ne.jp/~Peach/

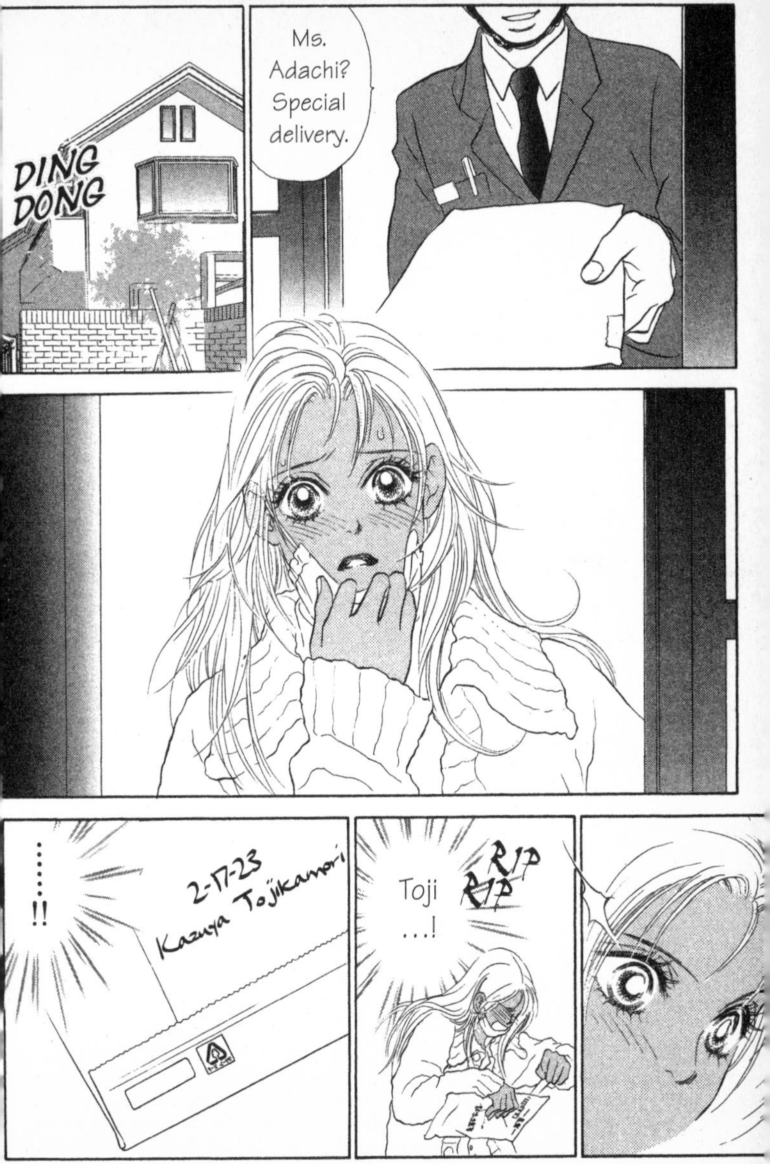
DING DONG
Ms. Adachi? Special delivery.
......!!
2-17-23 Kazuya Tojikamori
RIP RIP
Toji ...!

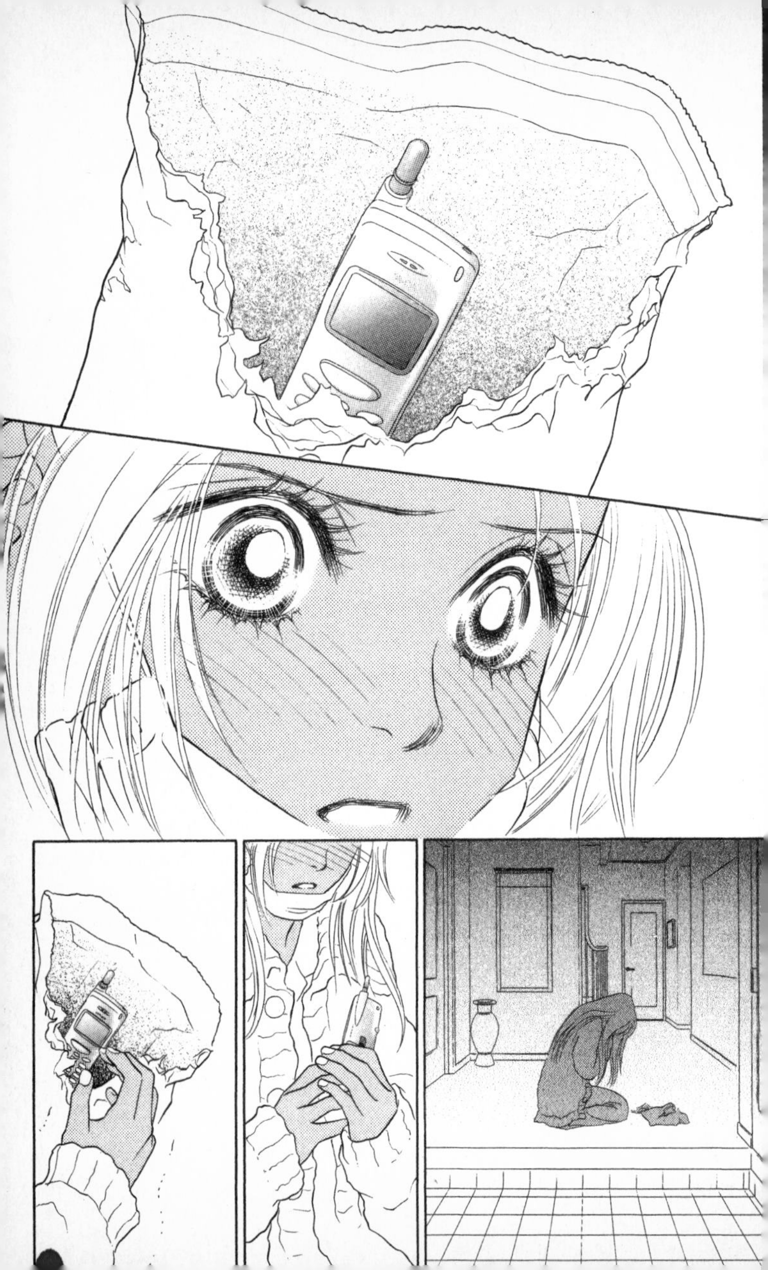

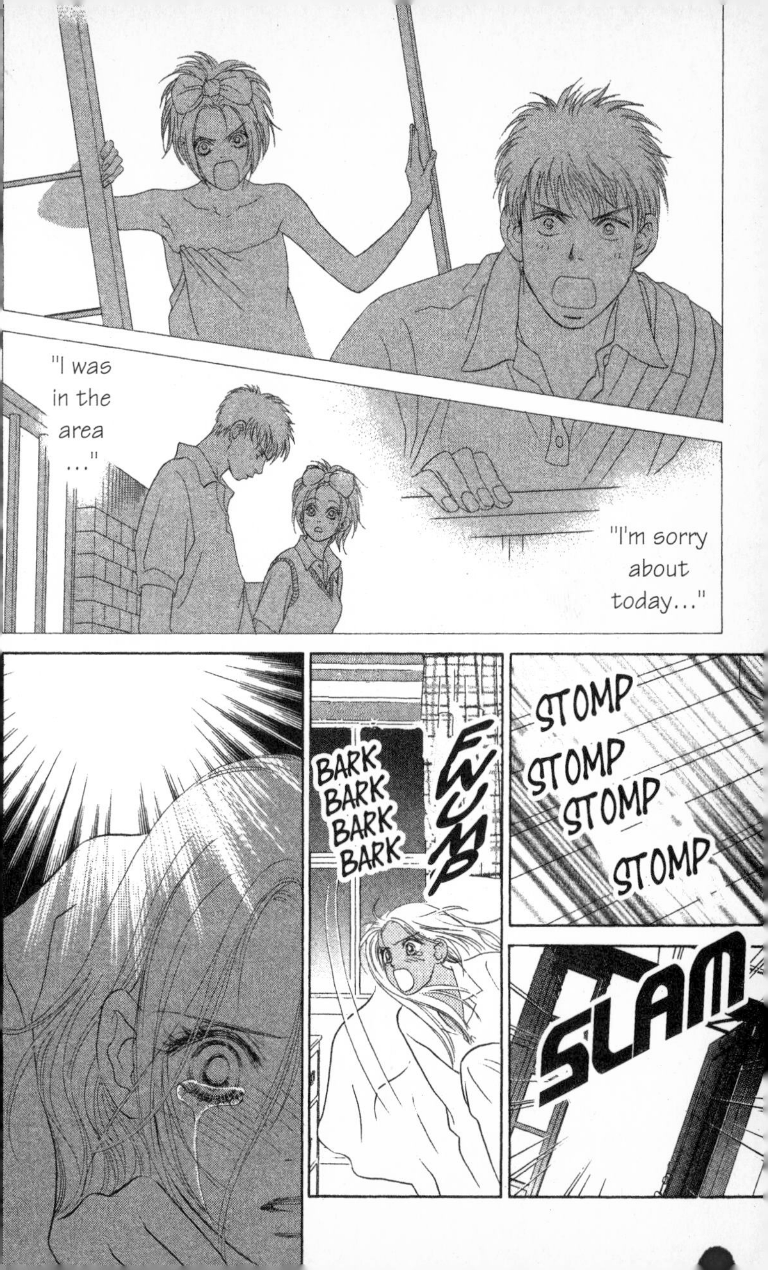
"I'm sorry about today..."
"I was in the area ..."
STOMP STOMP STOMP STOMP
SLAM
FWUMP
BARK BARK BARK BARK

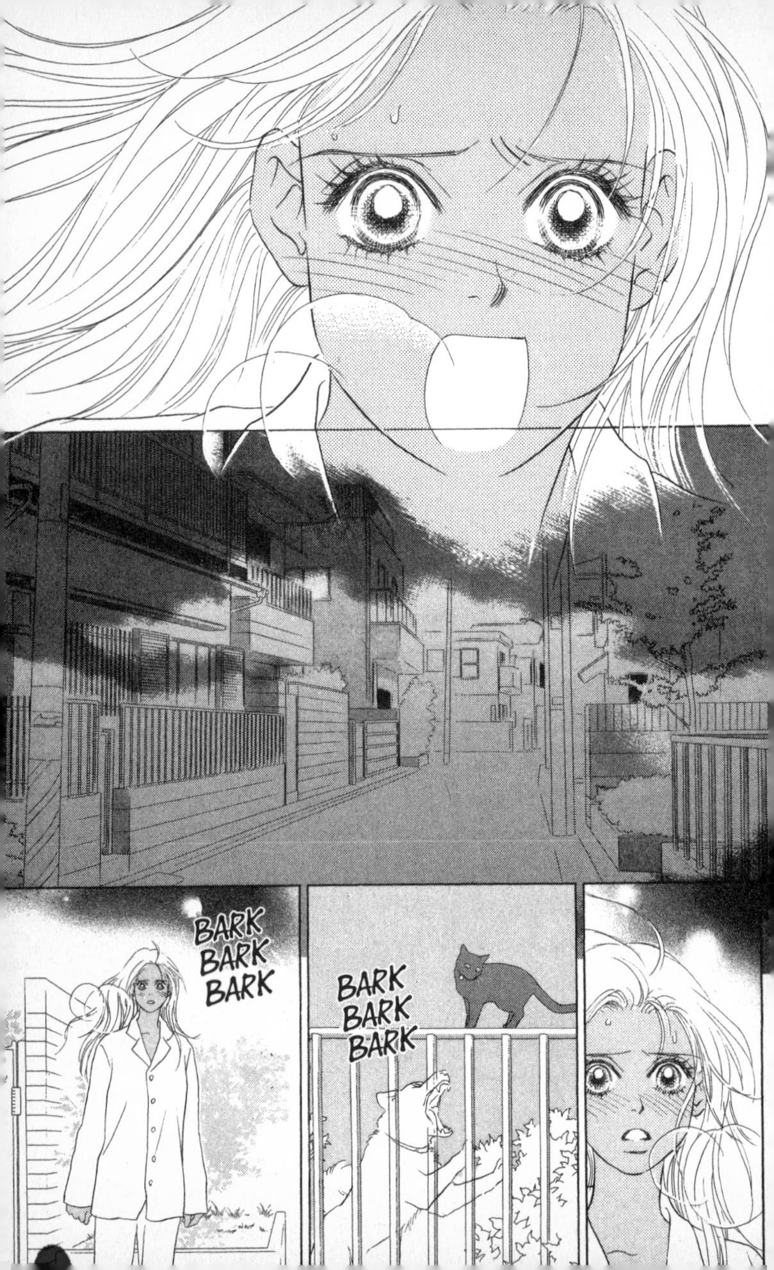
BARK
BARK
BARK
BARK
BARK
BARK

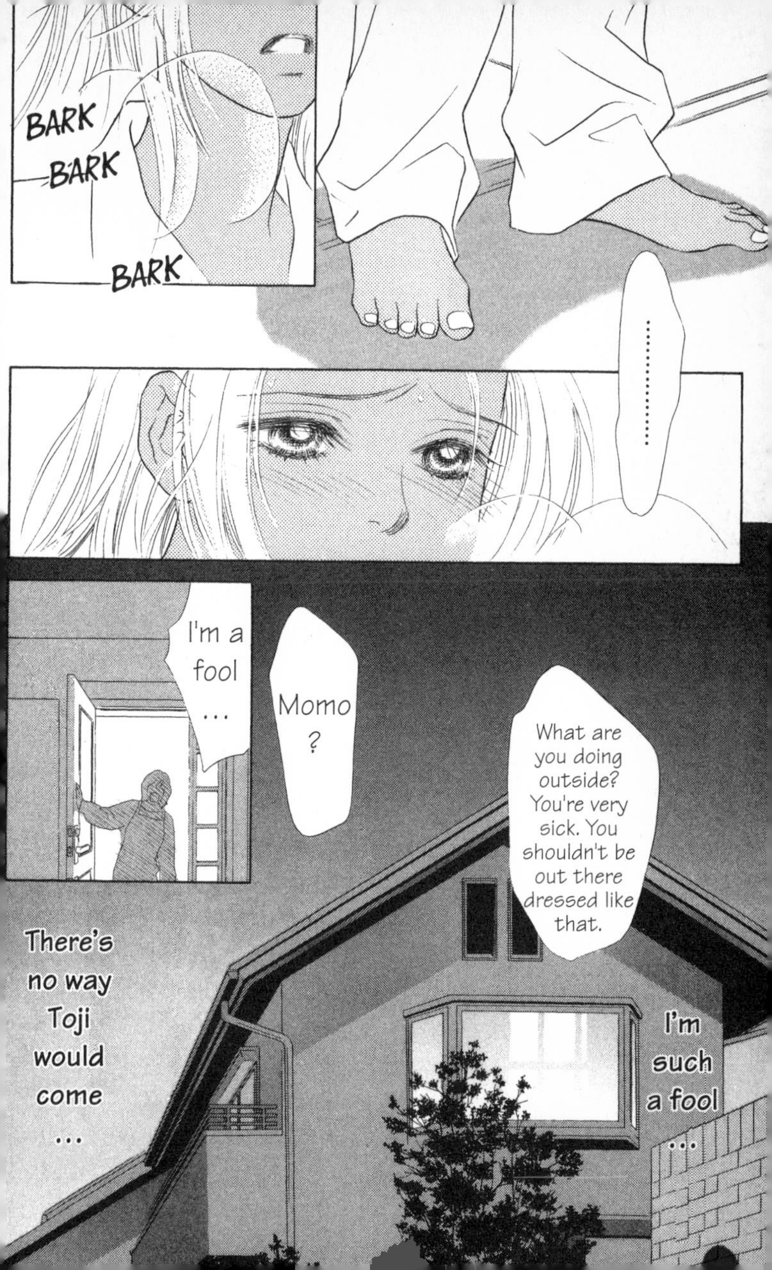

......
BARK
BARK
BARK
I'm such a fool ...
Momo ?
What are you doing outside? You're very sick. You shouldn't be out there dressed like that.
I'm a fool ...
There's no way Toji would come ...

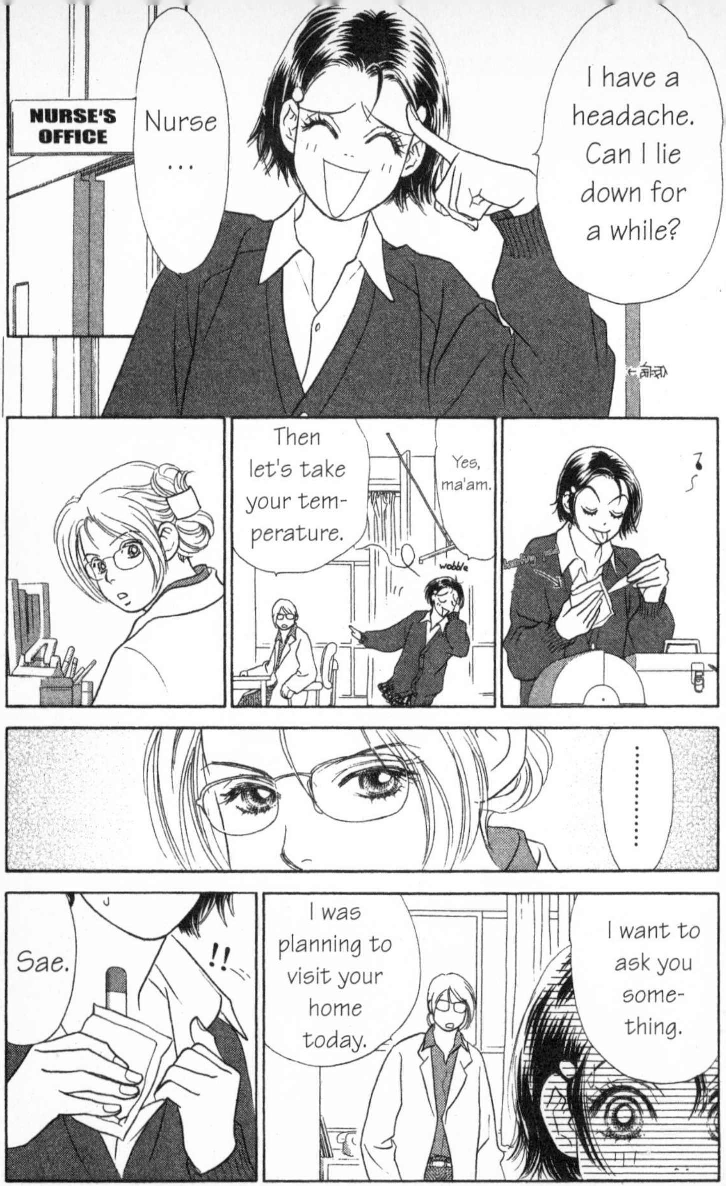
NURSE'S OFFICE
Nurse ...
I have a headache. Can I lie down for a while?
Then let's take your temperature.
Yes, ma'am.
wobble
......
Sae.
!!
I was planning to visit your home today.
I want to ask you something.

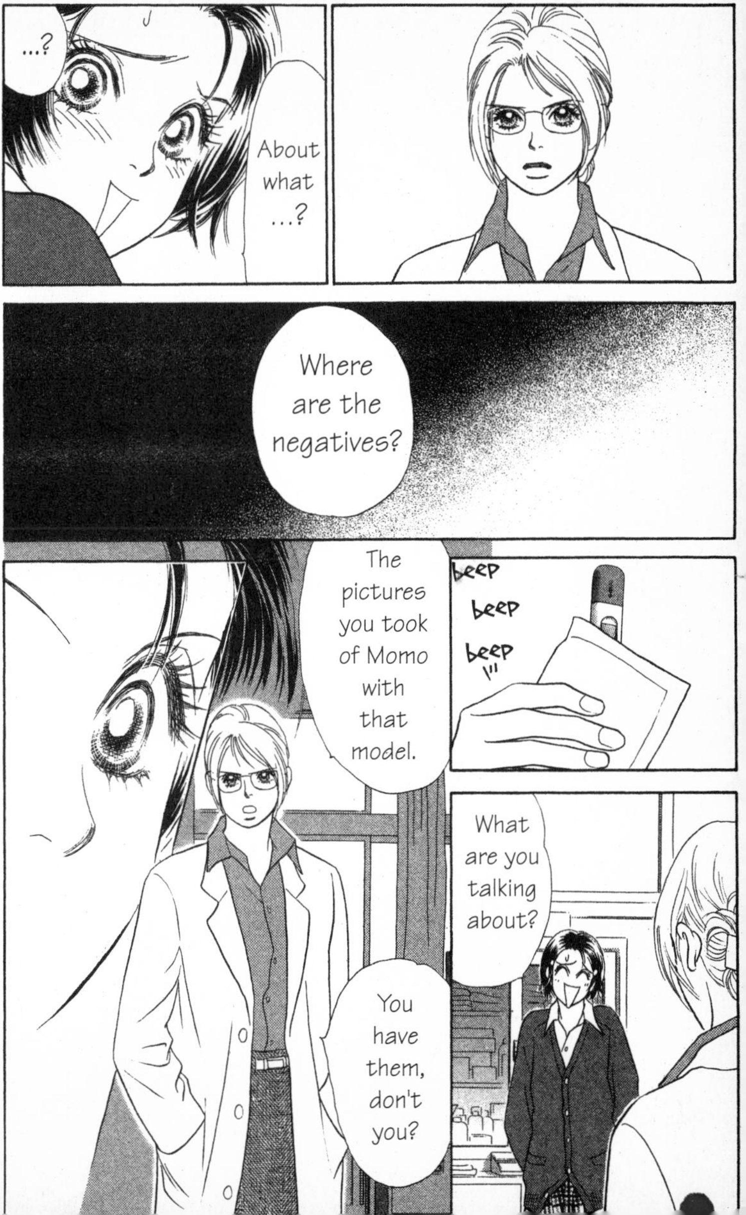
...?
About what ...?
Where are the negatives?
beep beep beep
What are you talking about?
The pictures you took of Momo with that model.
You have them, don't you?

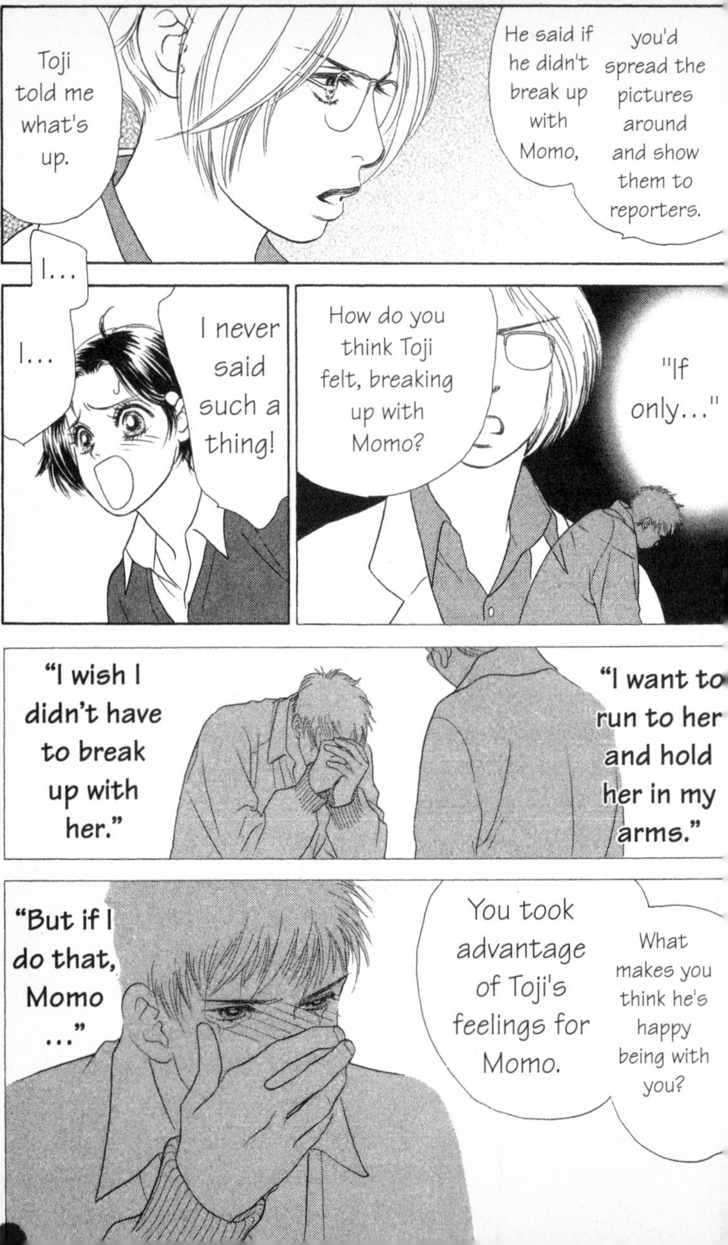
Toji told me what's up.
He said if he didn't break up with Momo, you'd spread the pictures around and show them to reporters.
I...
I...
I never said such a thing!
How do you think Toji felt, breaking up with Momo?
"If only..."
"I wish I didn't have to break up with her."
"I want to run to her and hold her in my arms."
"But if I do that, Momo..."
You took advantage of Toji's feelings for Momo.
What makes you think he's happy being with you?

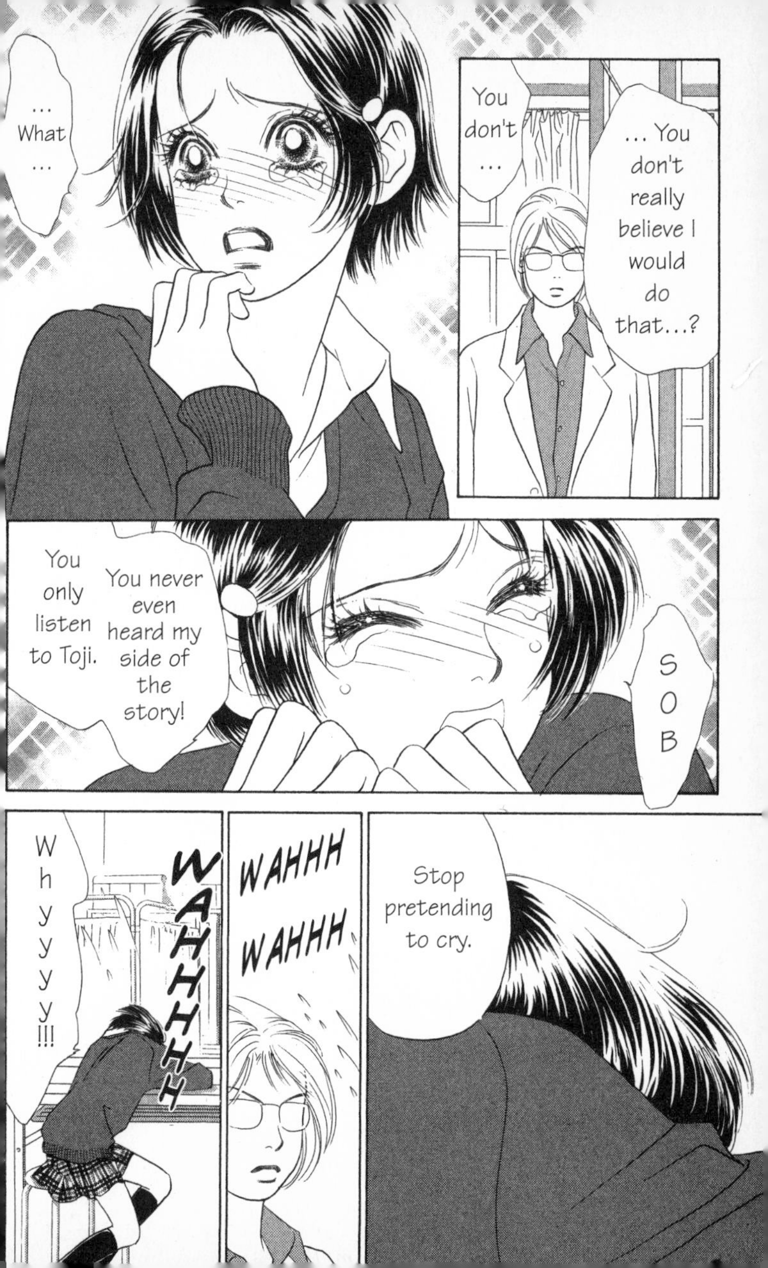
You don't ...
... You don't really believe I would do that...?
... What ...
SOB
You never even heard my side of the story!
You only listen to Toji.
Stop pretending to cry.
WAHHH WAHHH
WAHHHHHH
Whyyyyy!!!

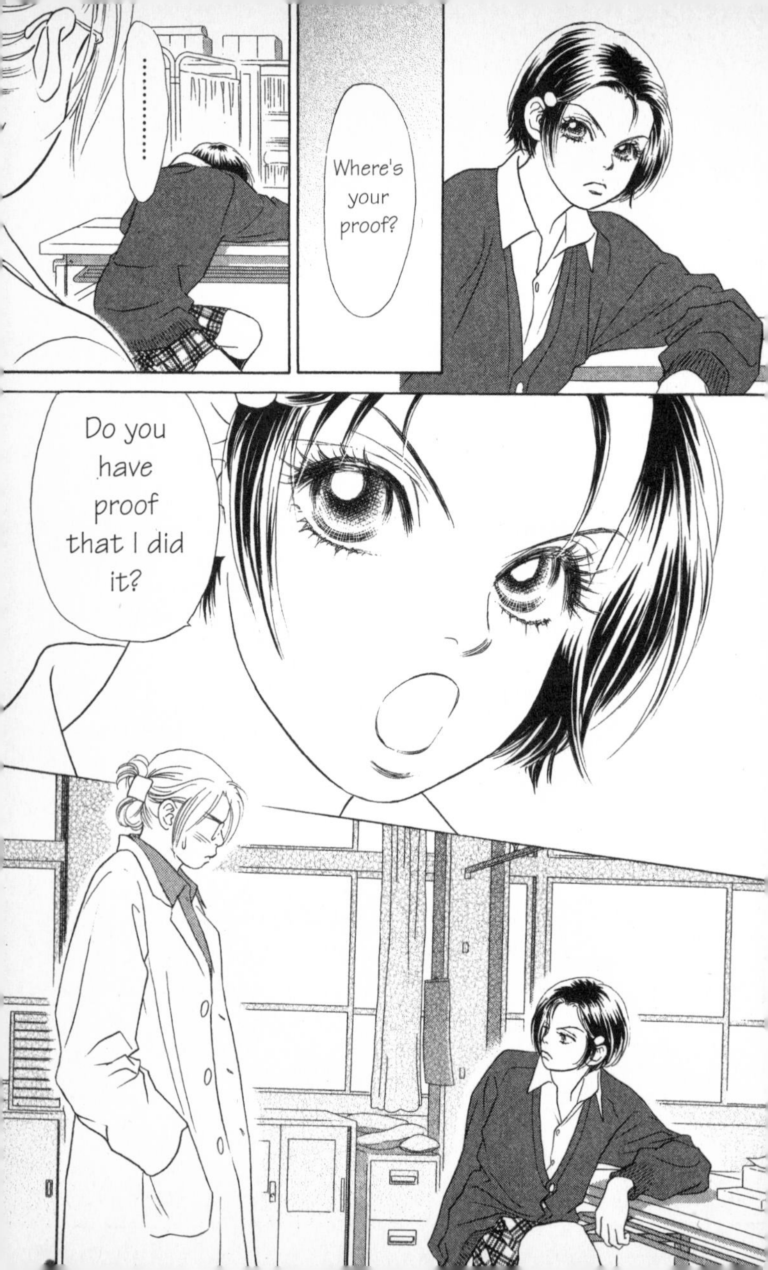
Where's your proof?
......
Do you have proof that I did it?

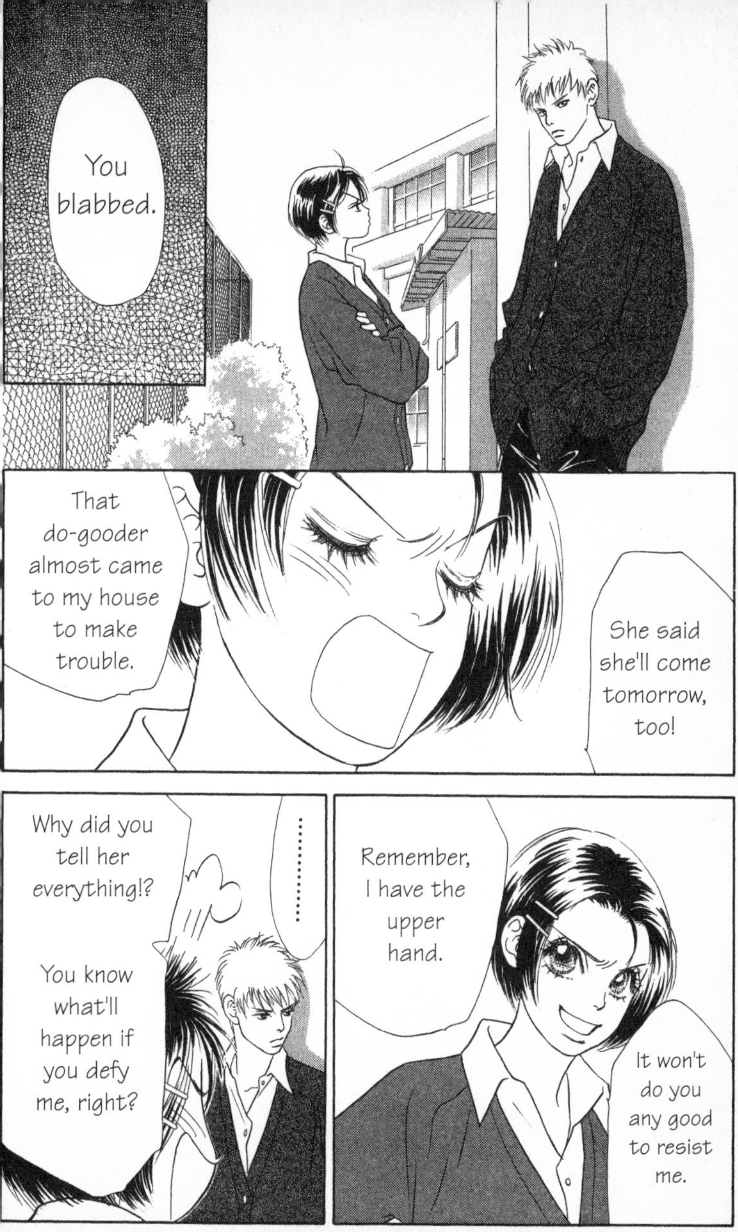
You blabbed.
That do-gooder almost came to my house to make trouble.
She said she'll come tomorrow, too!
Why did you tell her everything!?
......
You know what'll happen if you defy me, right?
Remember, I have the upper hand.
It won't do you any good to resist me.

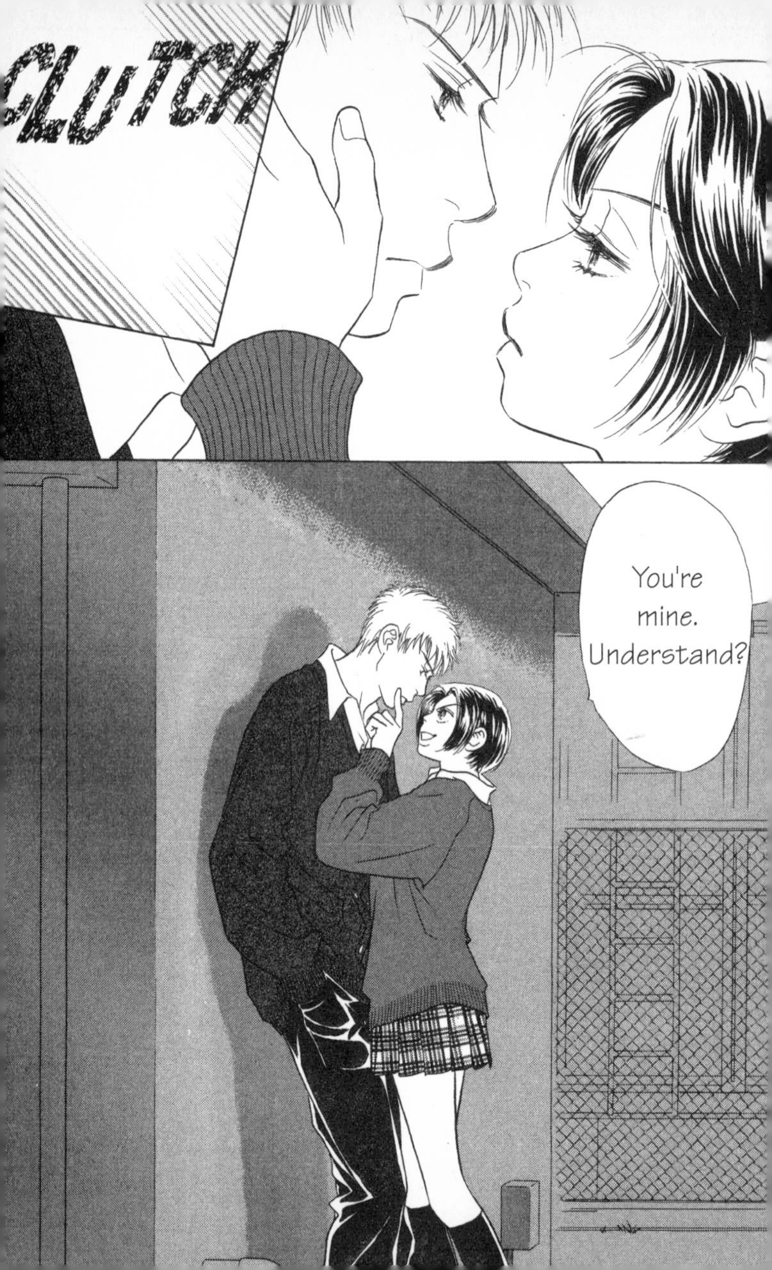
CLUTCH
You're mine. Understand?

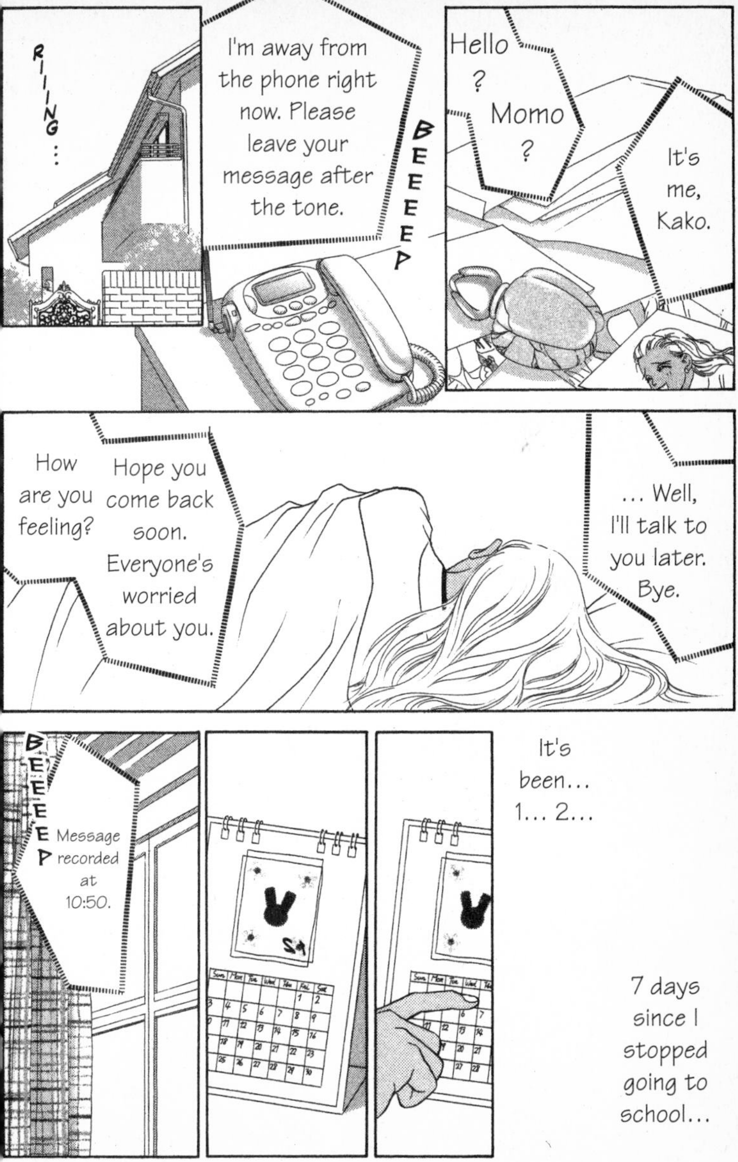
RIIIING...
I'm away from the phone right now. Please leave your message after the tone.
BEEEEP
Hello? Momo?
It's me, Kako.
How are you feeling?
Hope you come back soon. Everyone's worried about you.
... Well, I'll talk to you later. Bye.
BEEEEP
Message recorded at 10:50.
It's been... 1... 2...
7 days since I stopped going to school...

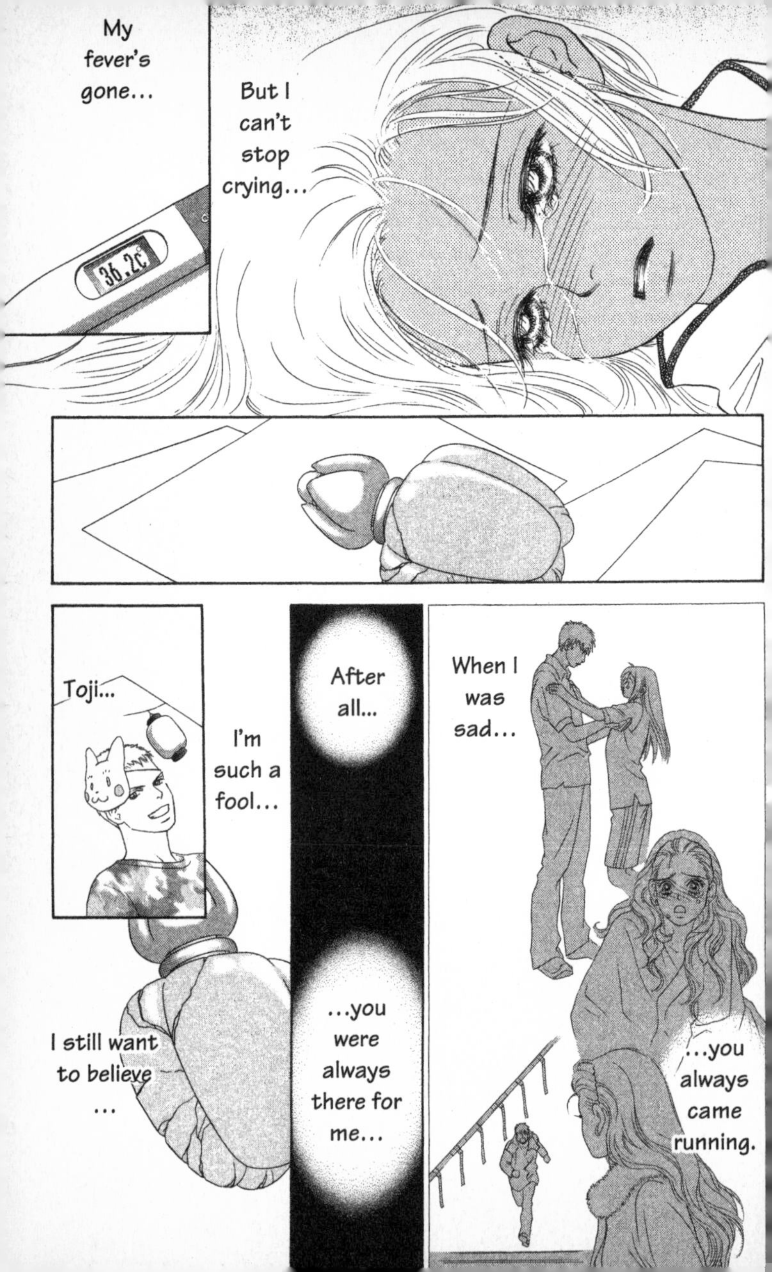
My fever's gone...
36.2c
But I can't stop crying...
When I was sad...
...you always came running.
After all...
...you were always there for me...
Toji...
I'm such a fool...
I still want to believe ...

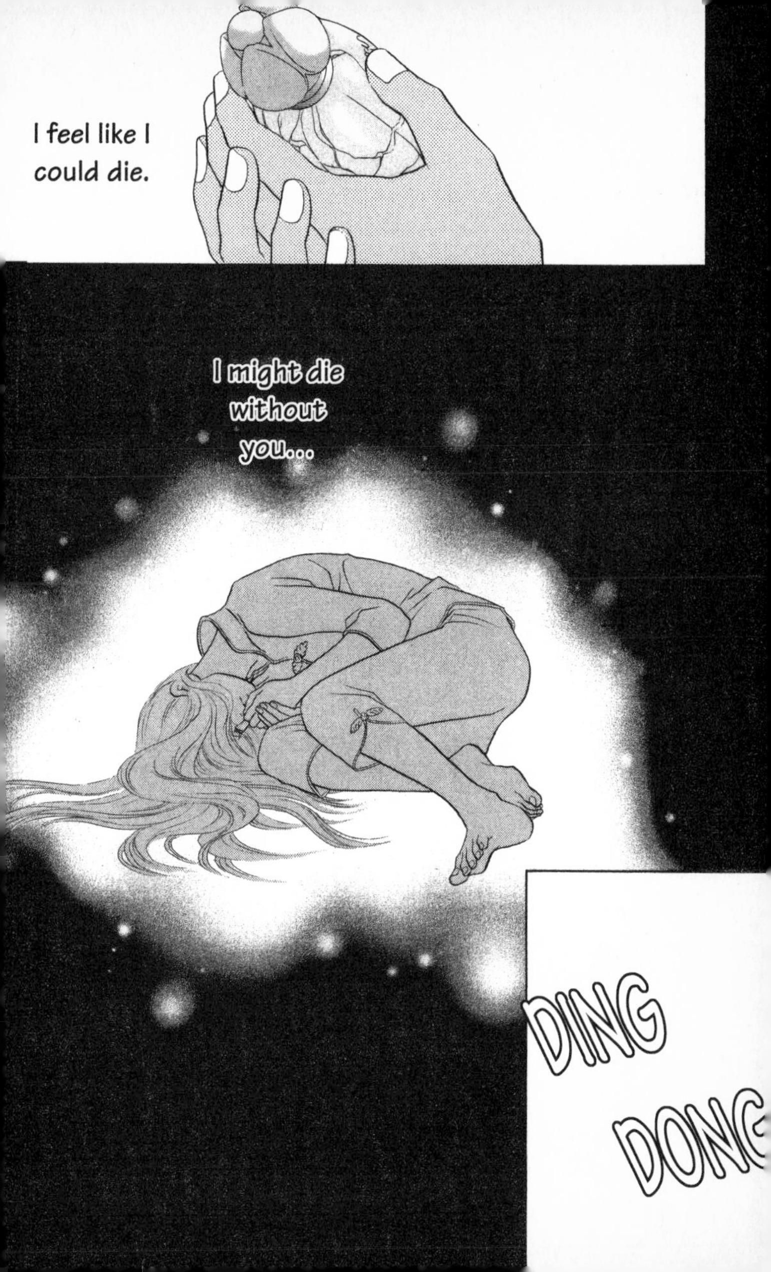
I feel like I could die.
I might die without you...
DING
DONG

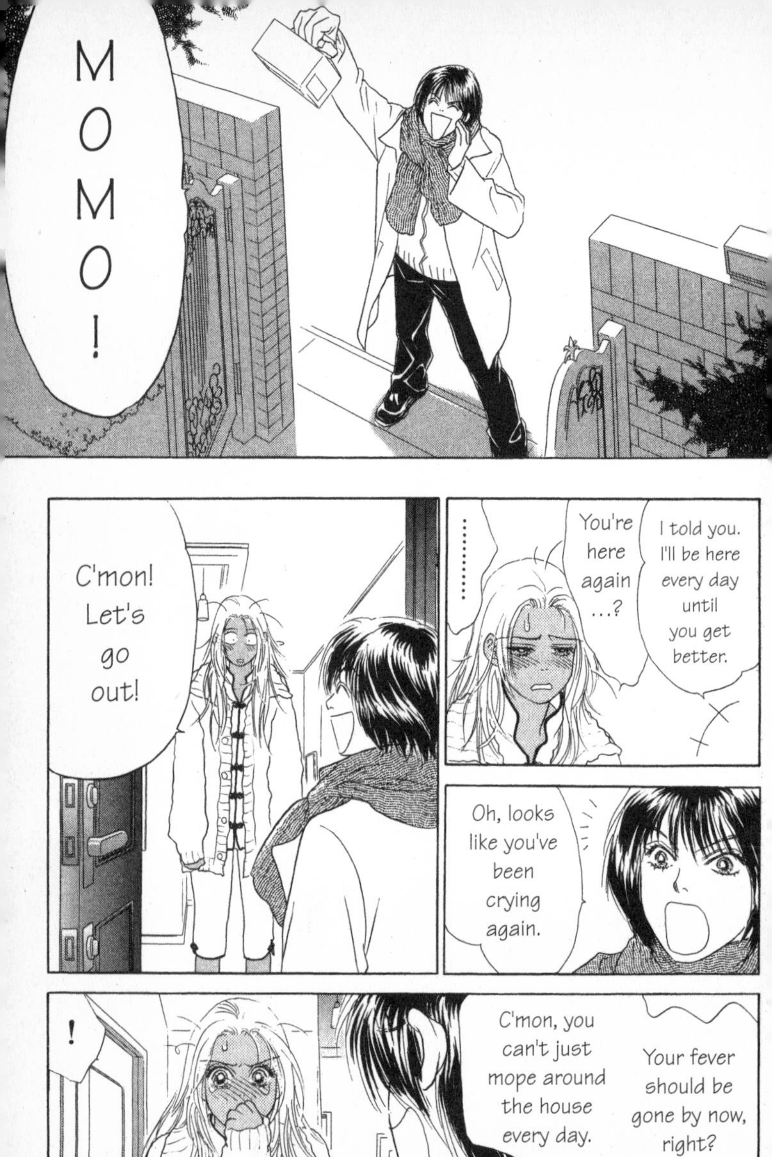
MOMO!
C'mon! Let's go out!
....
You're here again ...?
I told you. I'll be here every day until you get better.
Oh, looks like you've been crying again.
!
C'mon, you can't just mope around the house every day.
Your fever should be gone by now, right?

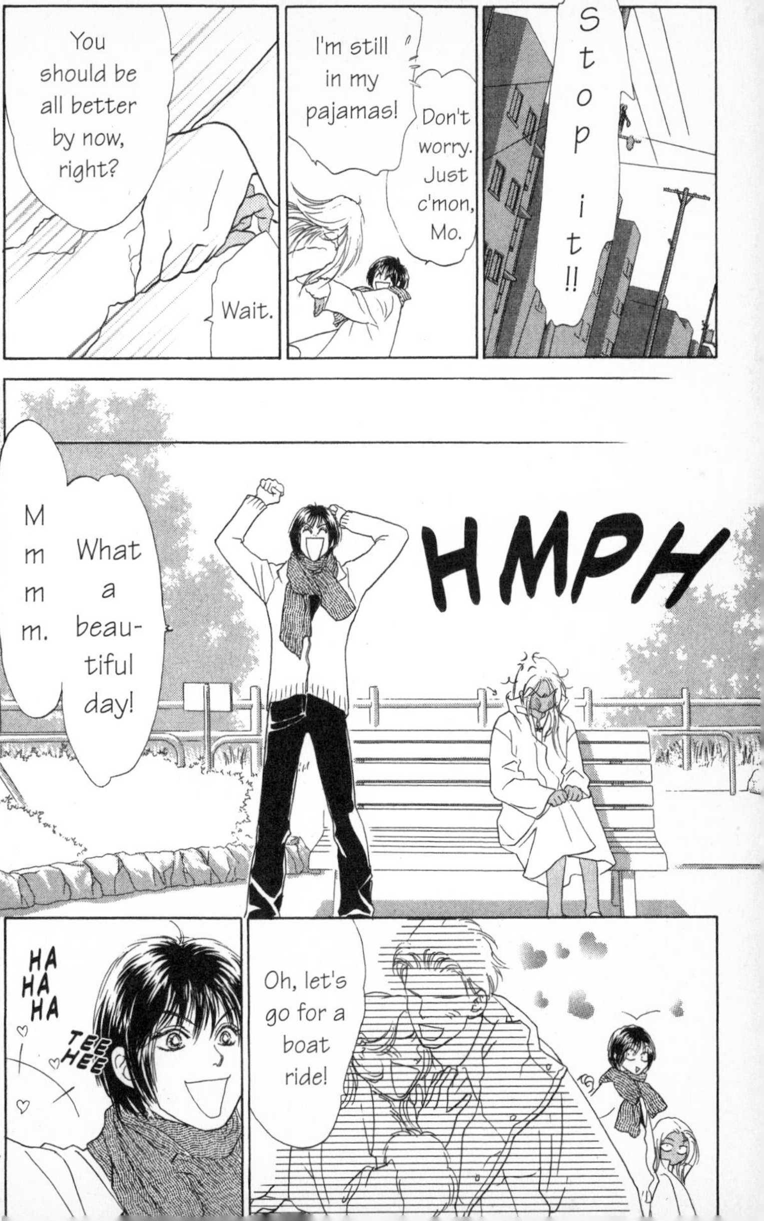
Stop it!!
I'm still in my pajamas!
Don't worry. Just c'mon, Mo.
You should be all better by now, right?
Wait.
HMPH
What a beau-tiful day!
Mmmm.
Oh, let's go for a boat ride!
HA HA HA
TEE HEE

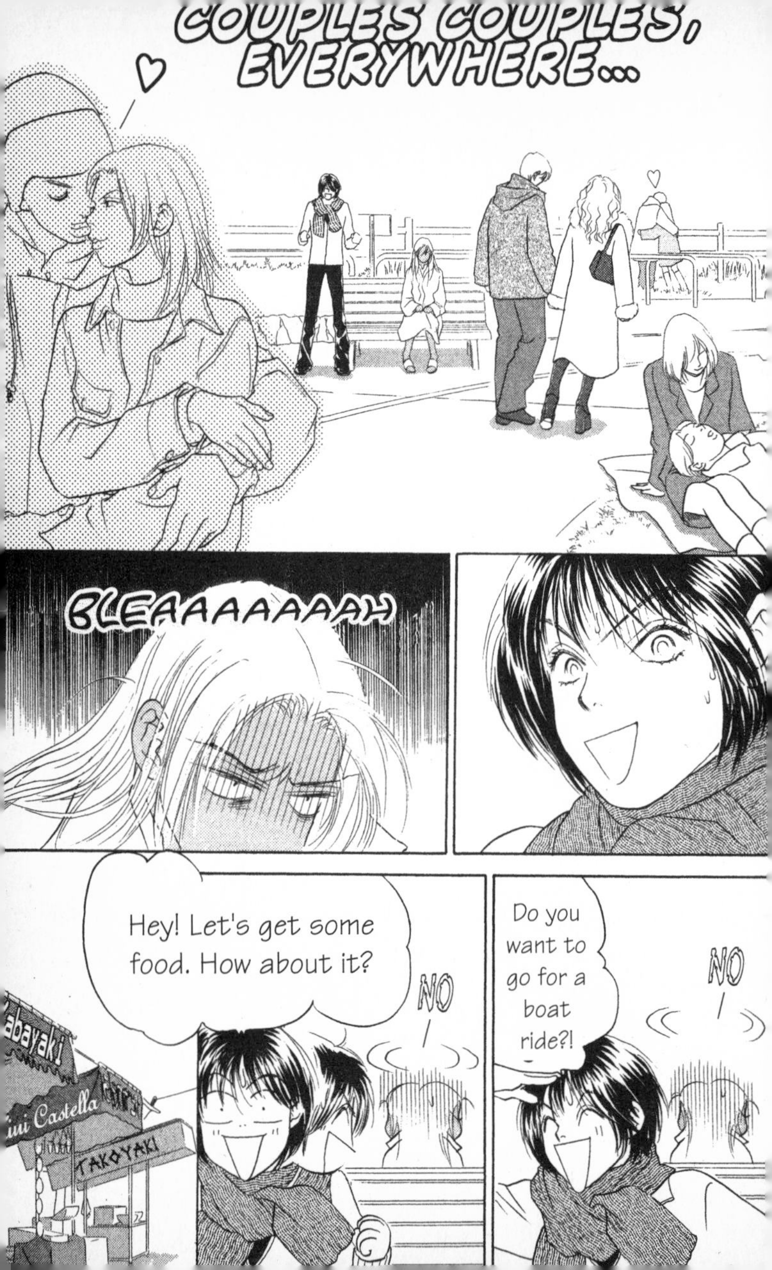
COUPLES COUPLES, EVERYWHERE...
BLEAAAAAAAAH
Do you want to go for a boat ride?!
NO
Hey! Let's get some food. How about it?
NO
Castella
TAKOYAKI

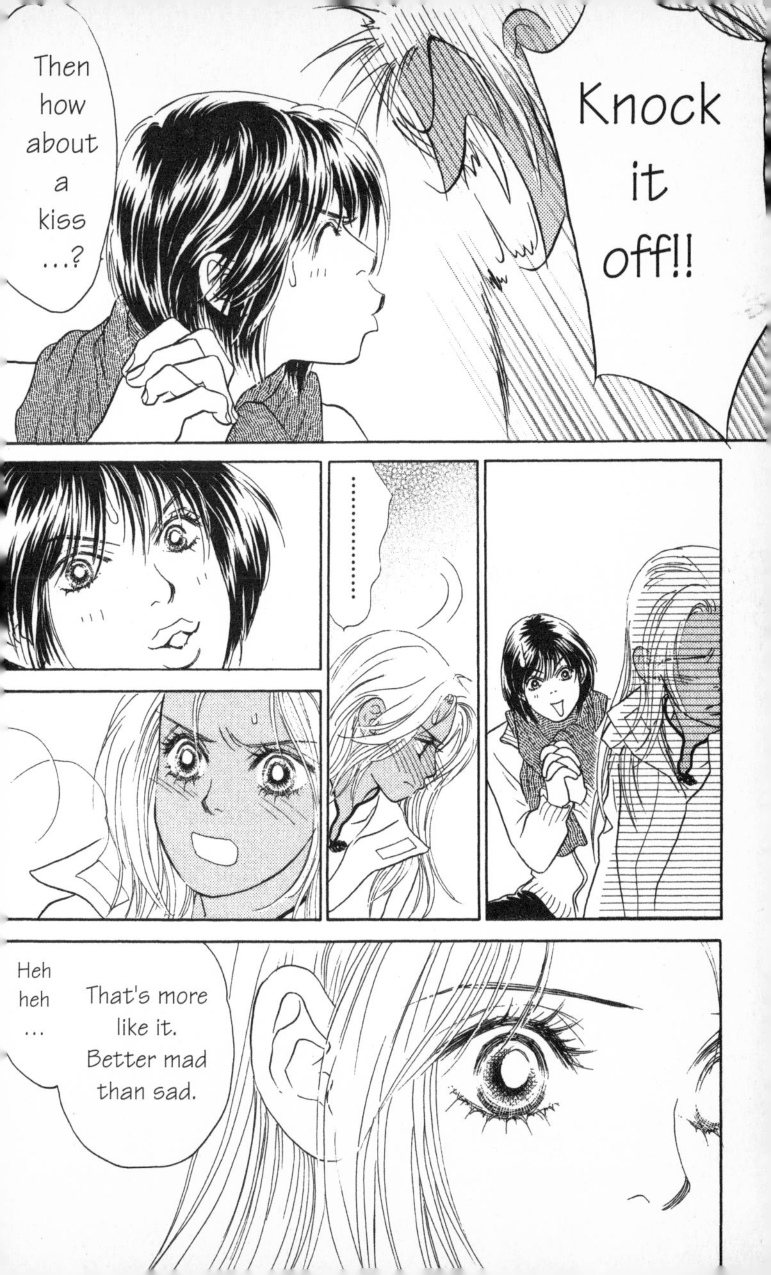
Then how about a kiss ...?
Knock it off!!
......
Heh heh ...
That's more like it. Better mad than sad.

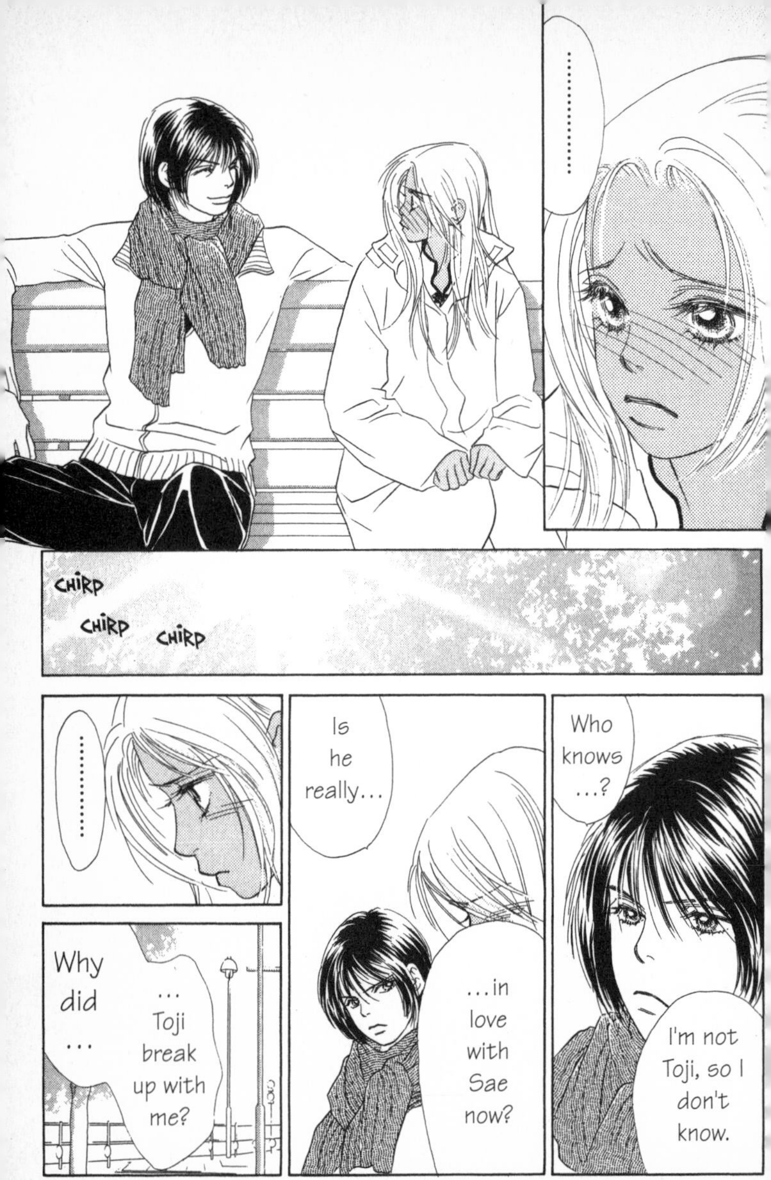

......
CHIRP
CHIRP
CHIRP
......
Why did ...
... Toji break up with me?
Is he really...
...in love with Sae now?
Who knows ...?
I'm not Toji, so I don't know.

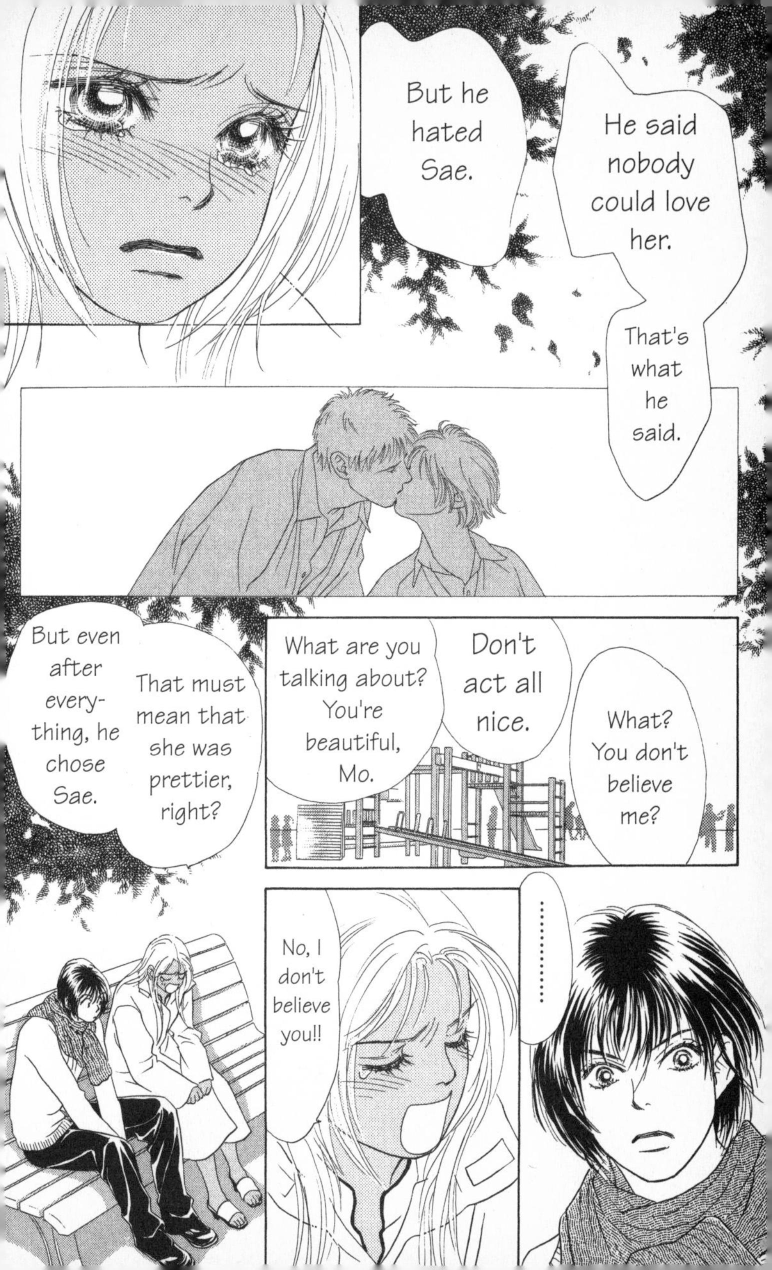
But he hated Sae.
He said nobody could love her.
That's what he said.
But even after every-thing, he chose Sae.
That must mean that she was prettier, right?
What are you talking about? You're beautiful, Mo.
Don't act all nice.
What? You don't believe me?
No, I don't believe you!!
....

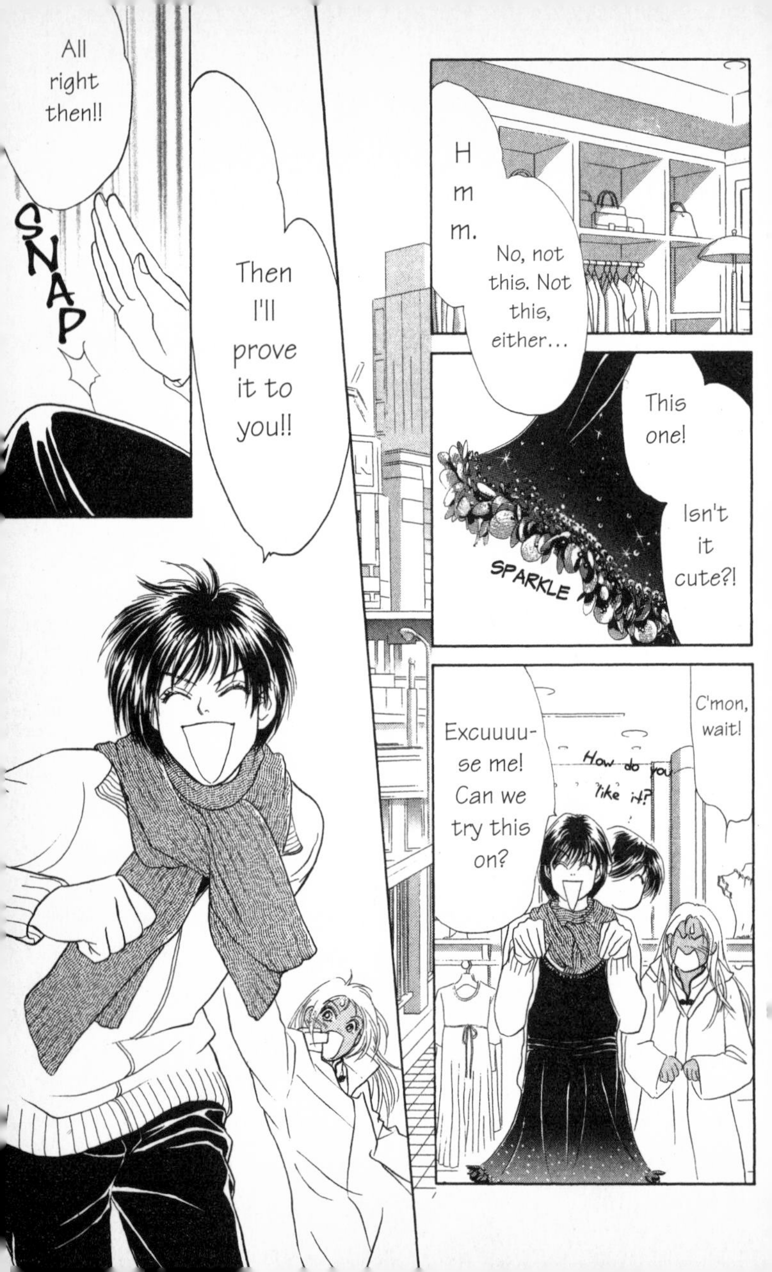
All right then!!
SNAP
Then I'll prove it to you!!
Hmm.
No, not this. Not this, either...
This one!
Isn't it cute?!
SPARKLE
Excuuuu-se me! Can we try this on?
How do you like it?
C'mon, wait!

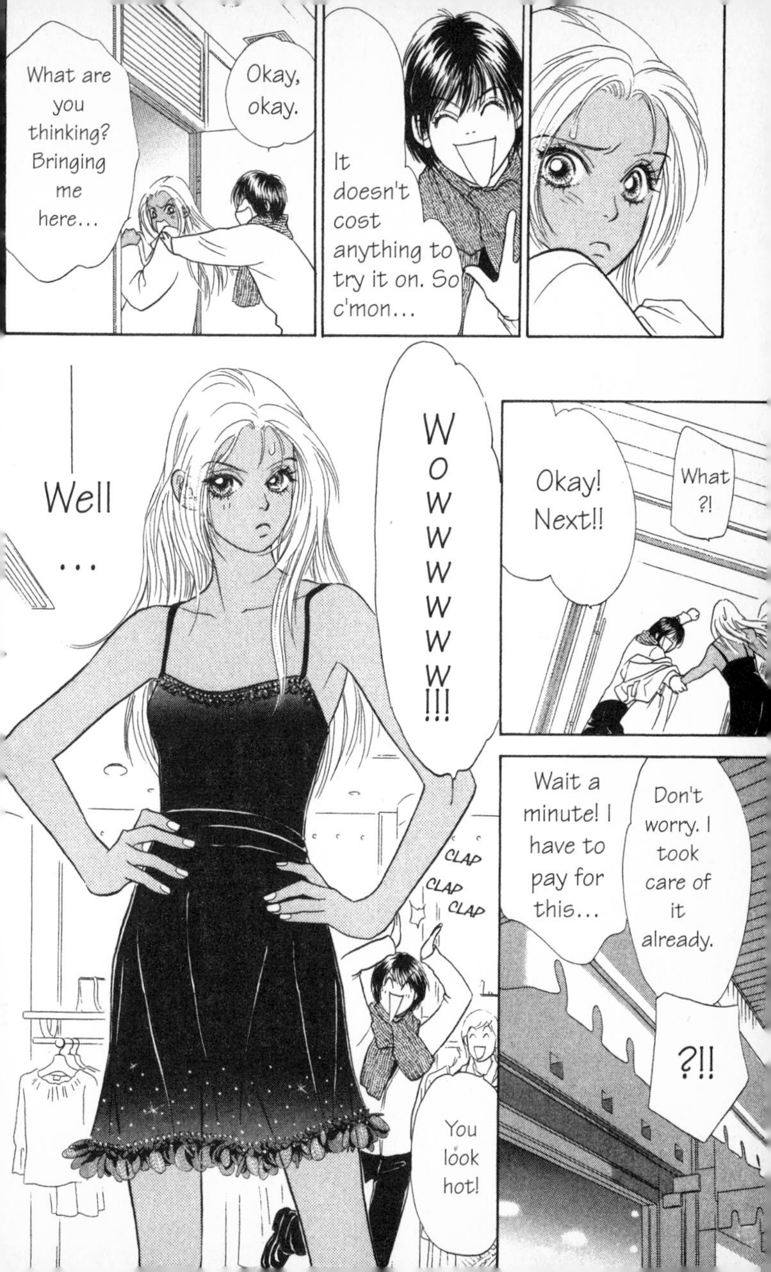
What are you thinking? Bringing me here…
Okay, okay.
It doesn't cost anything to try it on. So c'mon…
Well…
WOWWWWWWW!!!
CLAP CLAP CLAP
You look hot!
Okay! Next!!
What?!
Wait a minute! I have to pay for this…
Don't worry. I took care of it already.
?!!

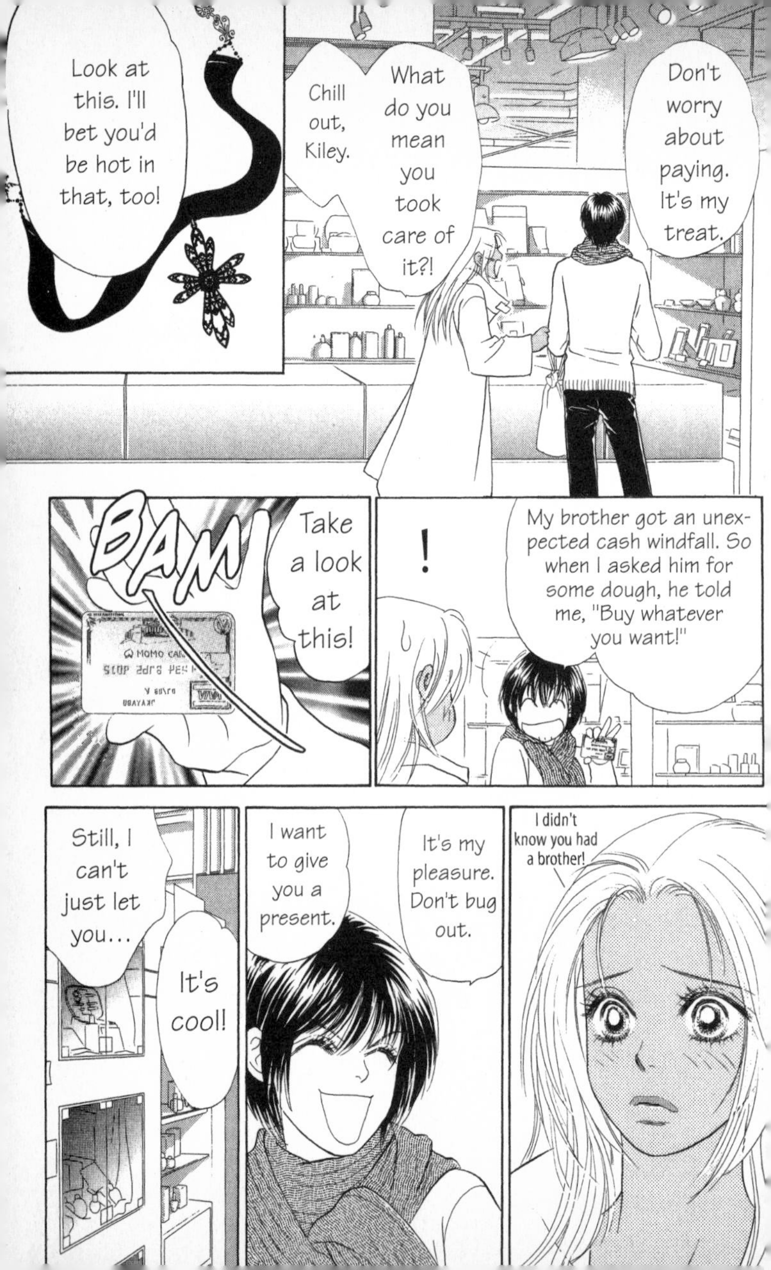
Don't worry about paying. It's my treat.
What do you mean you took care of it?!
Chill out, Kiley.
Look at this. I'll bet you'd be hot in that, too!
!
My brother got an unexpected cash windfall. So when I asked him for some dough, he told me, "Buy whatever you want!"
BAM
Take a look at this!
I didn't know you had a brother!
It's my pleasure. Don't bug out.
I want to give you a present.
Still, I can't just let you...
It's cool!

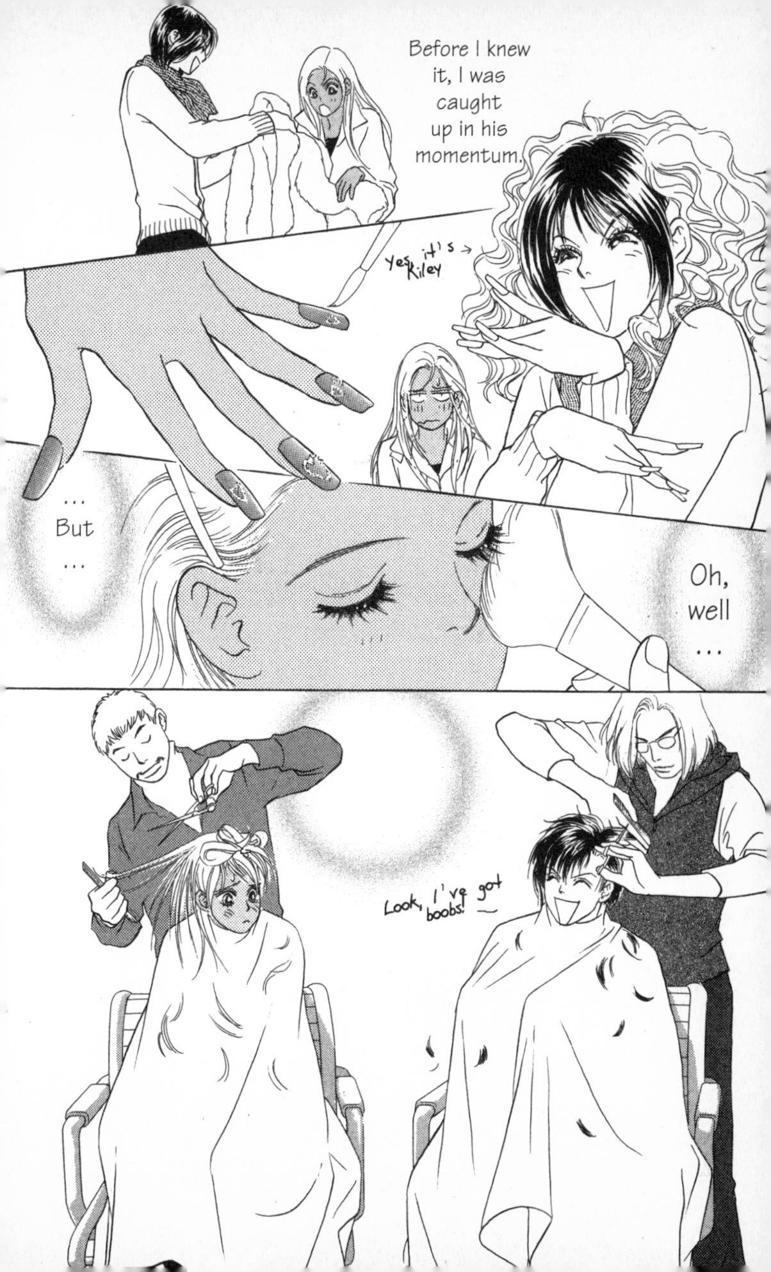
Before I knew it, I was caught up in his momentum.
Yes, it's Kiley →
Oh, well ...
... But ...
Look, I've got boobs! —

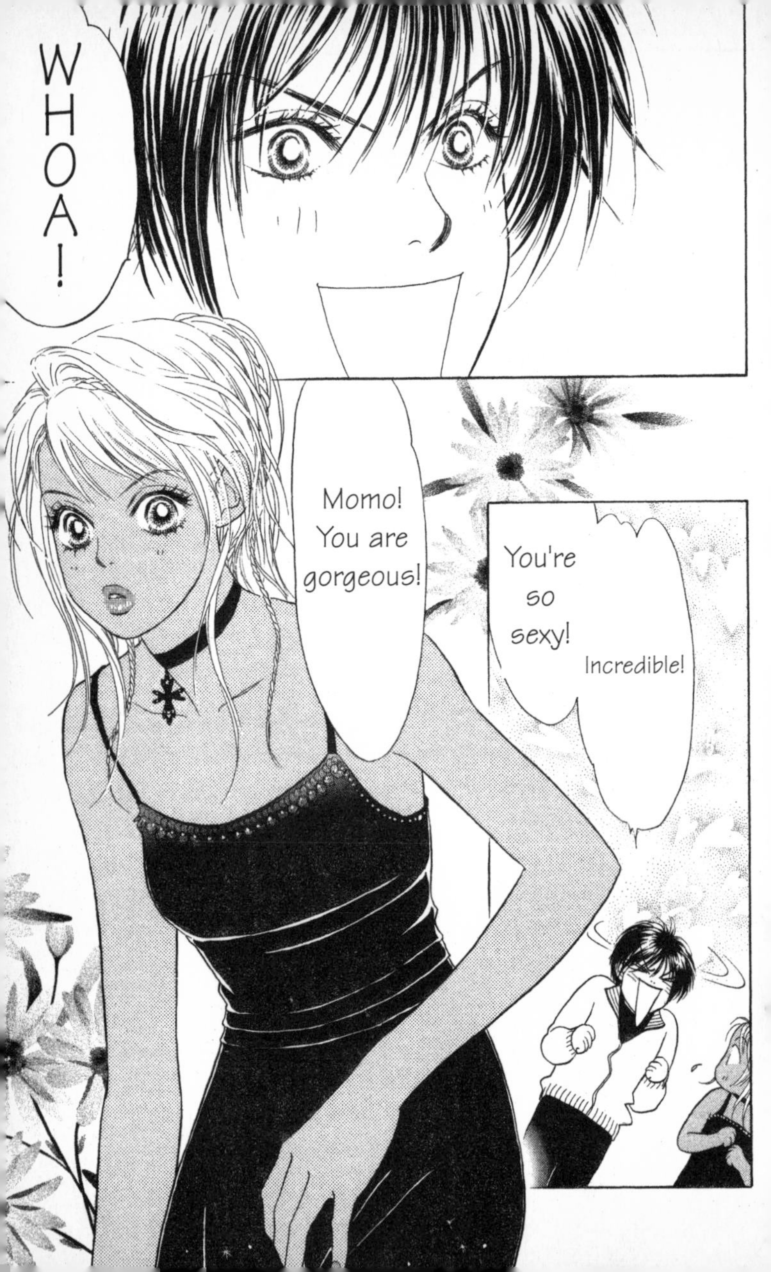
WHOA!
Momo! You are gorgeous!
You're so sexy!
Incredible!

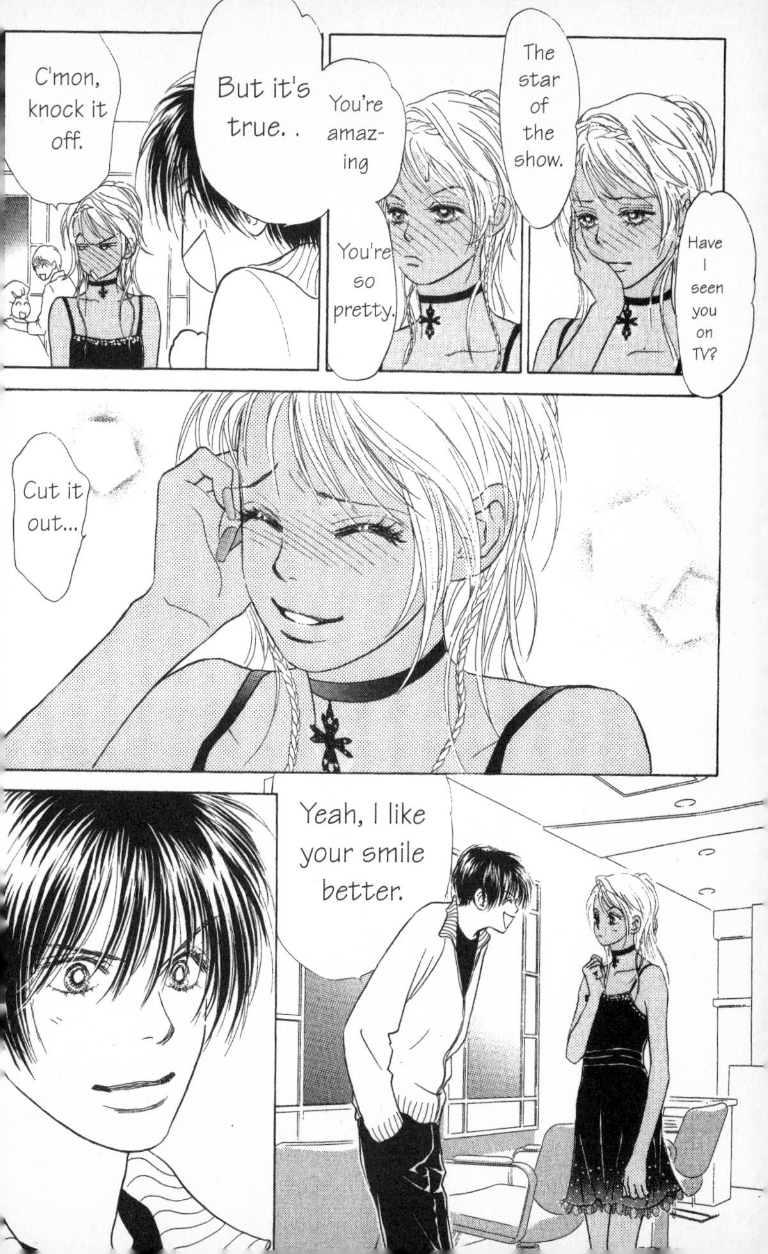
The star of the show.
Have I seen you on TV?
You're amazing
You're so pretty.
C'mon, knock it off.
But it's true. .
Cut it out...
Yeah, I like your smile better.

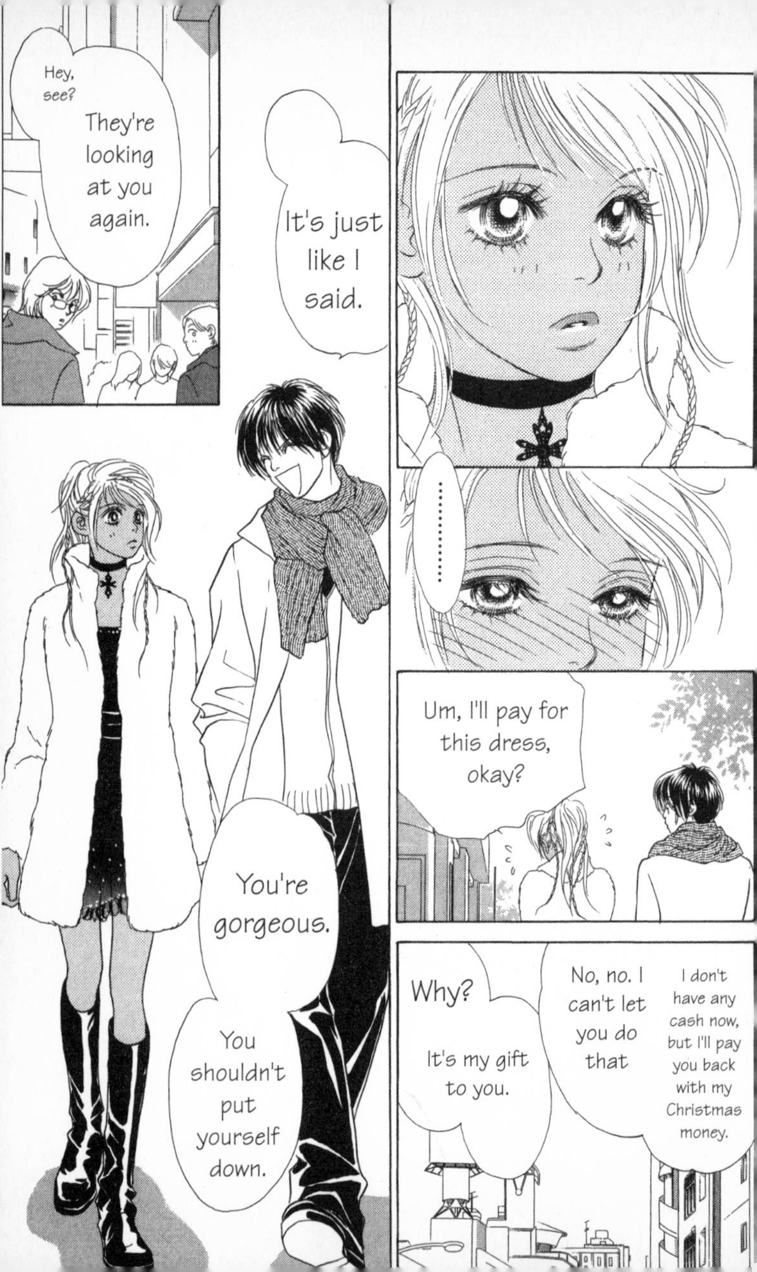
Hey, see? They're looking at you again.
It's just like I said.
You're gorgeous.
You shouldn't put yourself down.
......
Um, I'll pay for this dress, okay?
Why?
It's my gift to you.
No, no. I can't let you do that
I don't have any cash now, but I'll pay you back with my Christmas money.

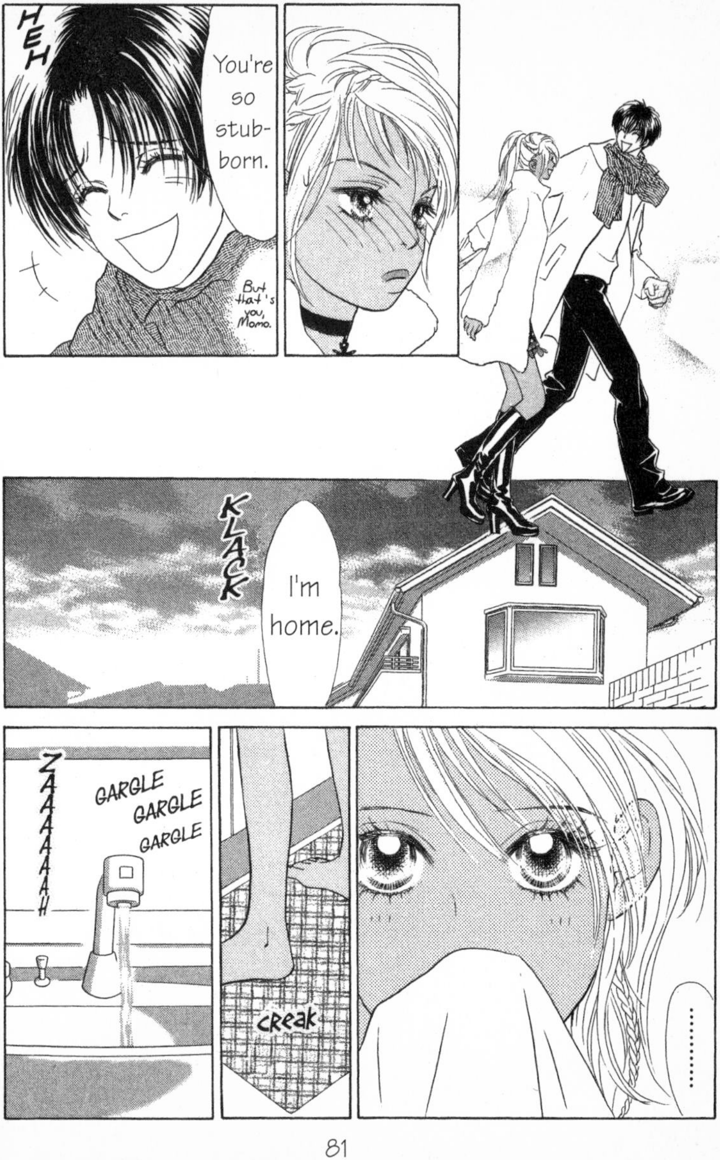
You're so stubborn.
HEH
But that's you, Momo.
I'm home.
KLACK
......
creak
GARGLE GARGLE GARGLE
ZAAAAAAAH

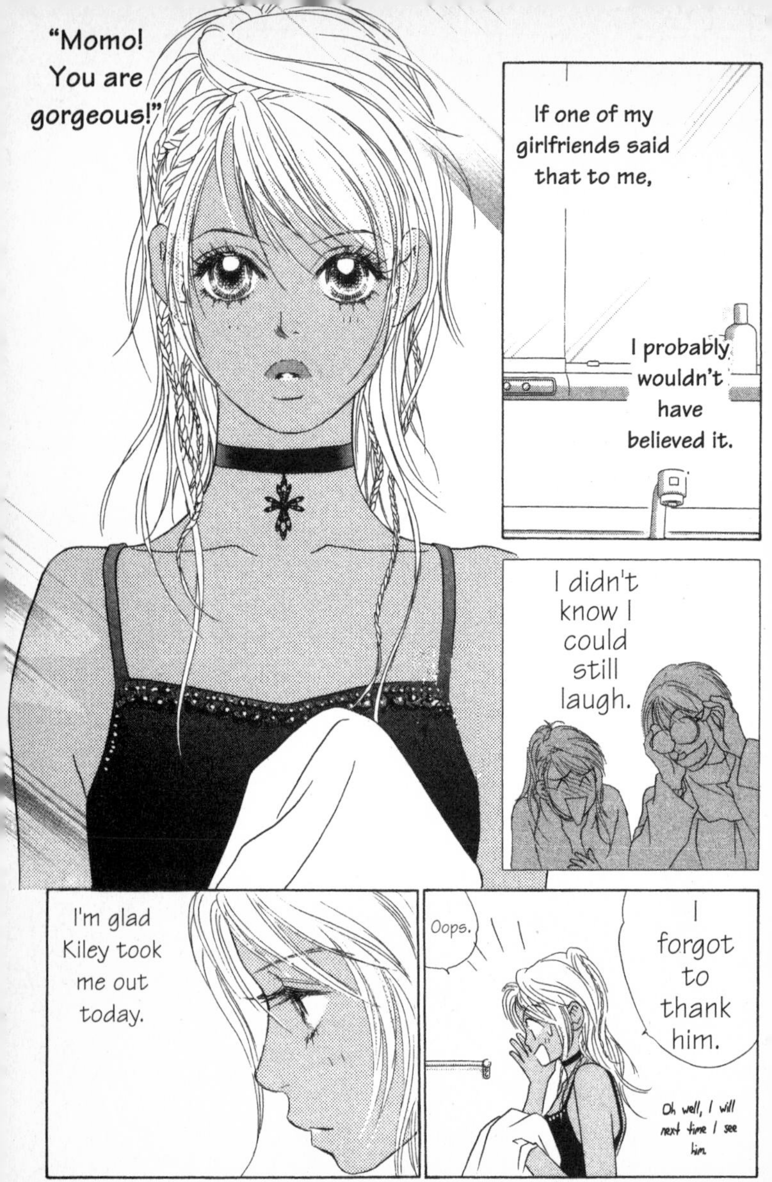
"Momo! You are gorgeous!"
If one of my girlfriends said that to me,
I probably wouldn't have believed it.
I didn't know I could still laugh.
I'm glad Kiley took me out today.
Oops.
I forgot to thank him.
Oh well, I will next time I see him.

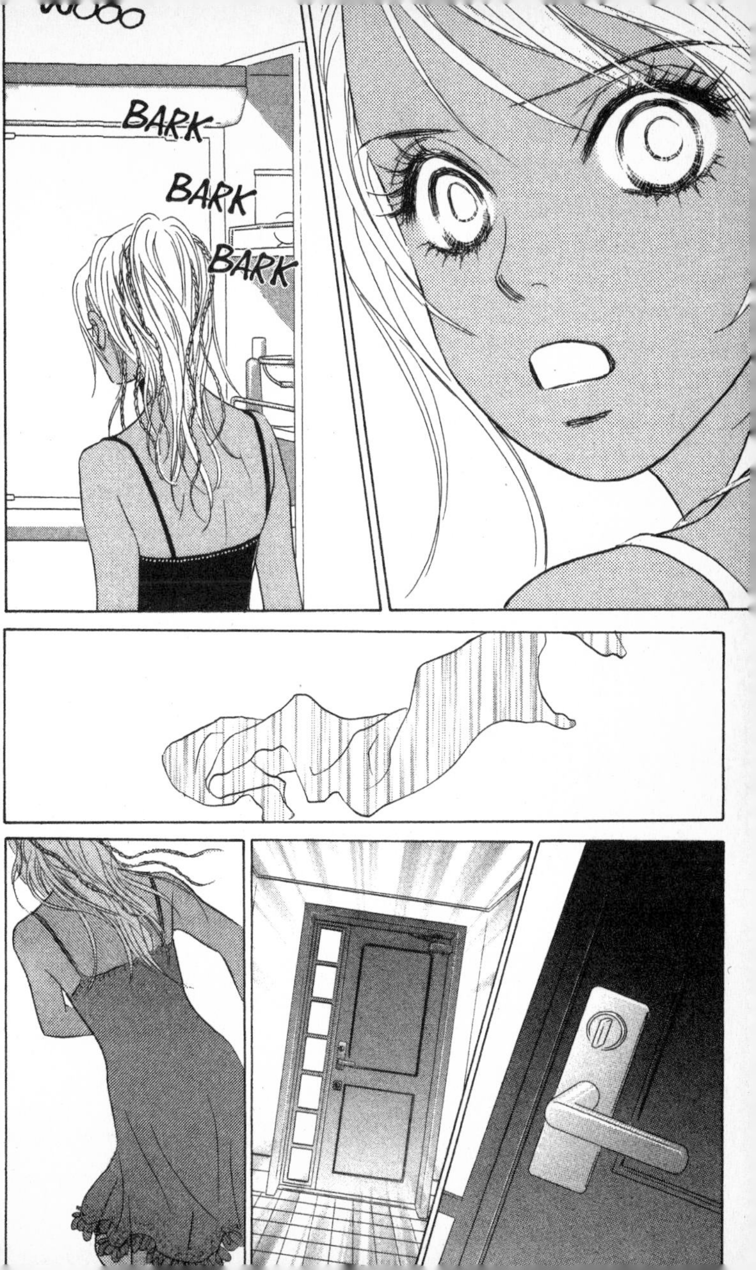
BARK
BARK
BARK

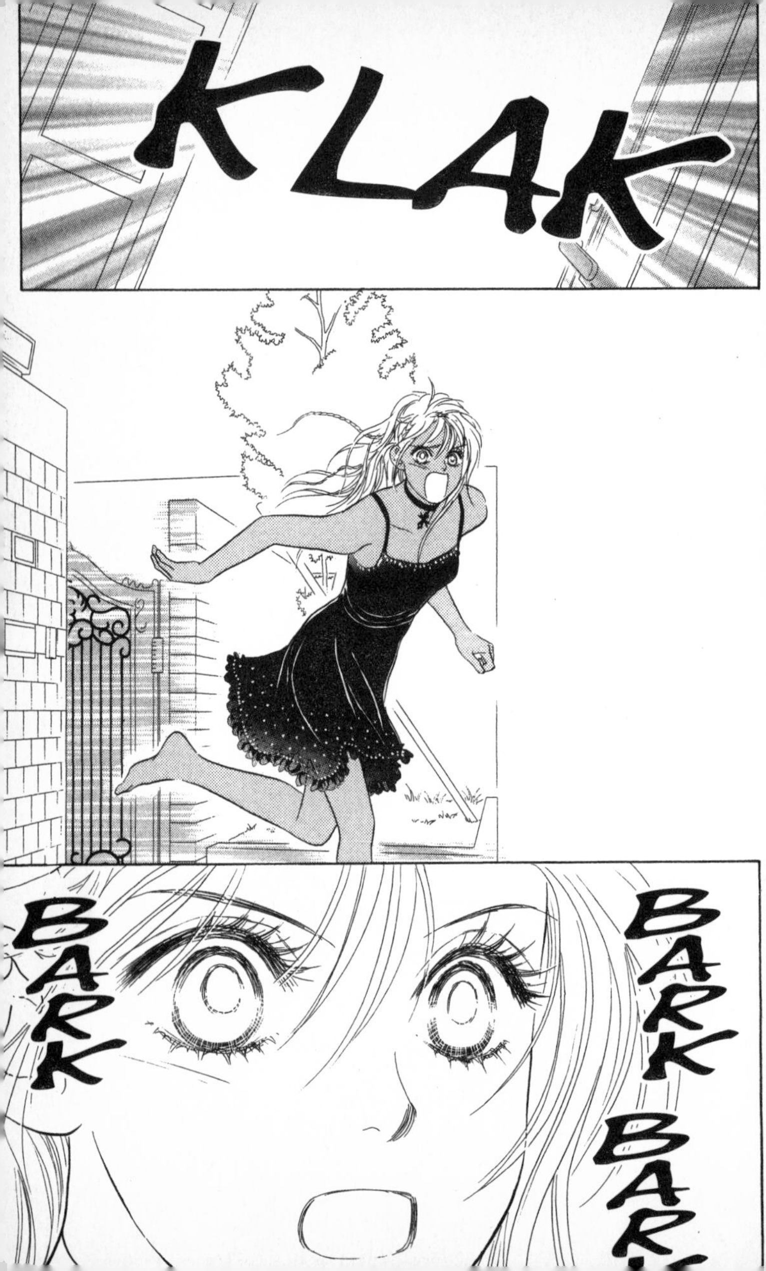
KLAK
BARK
BARK

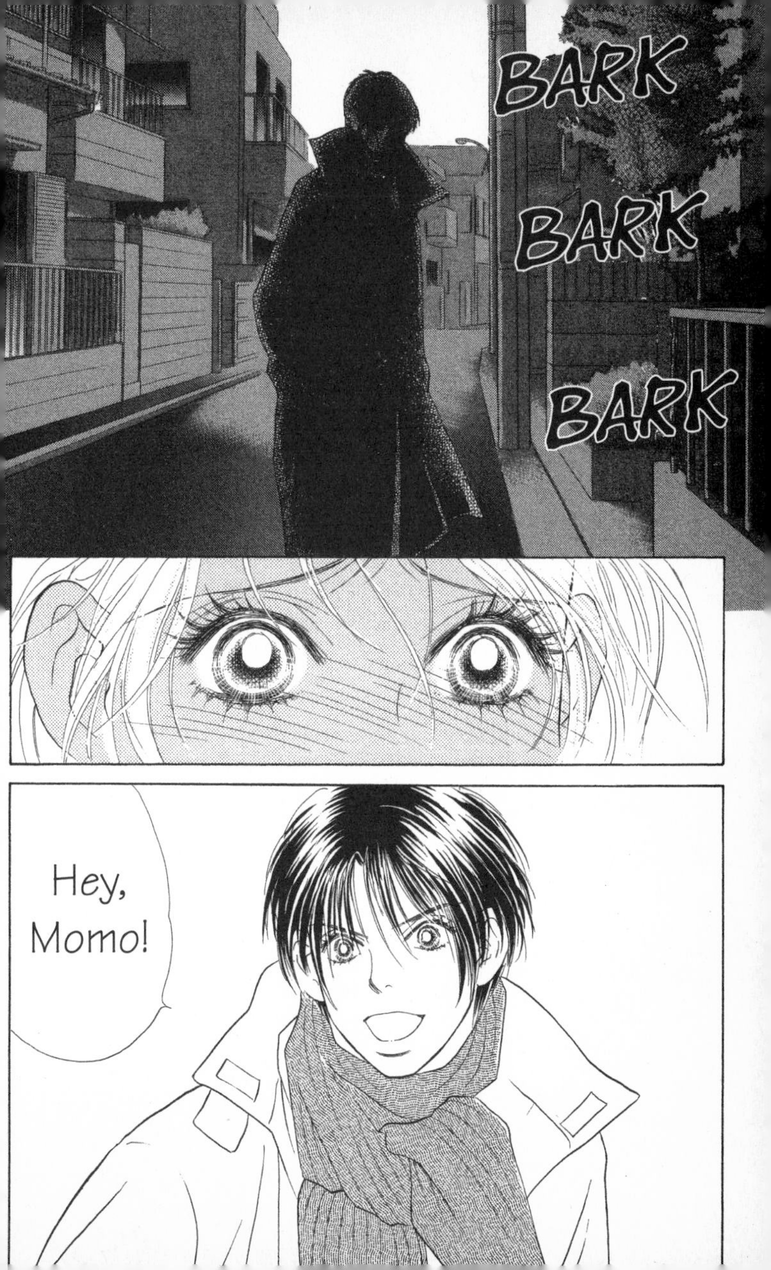
BARK
BARK
BARK
Hey, Momo!

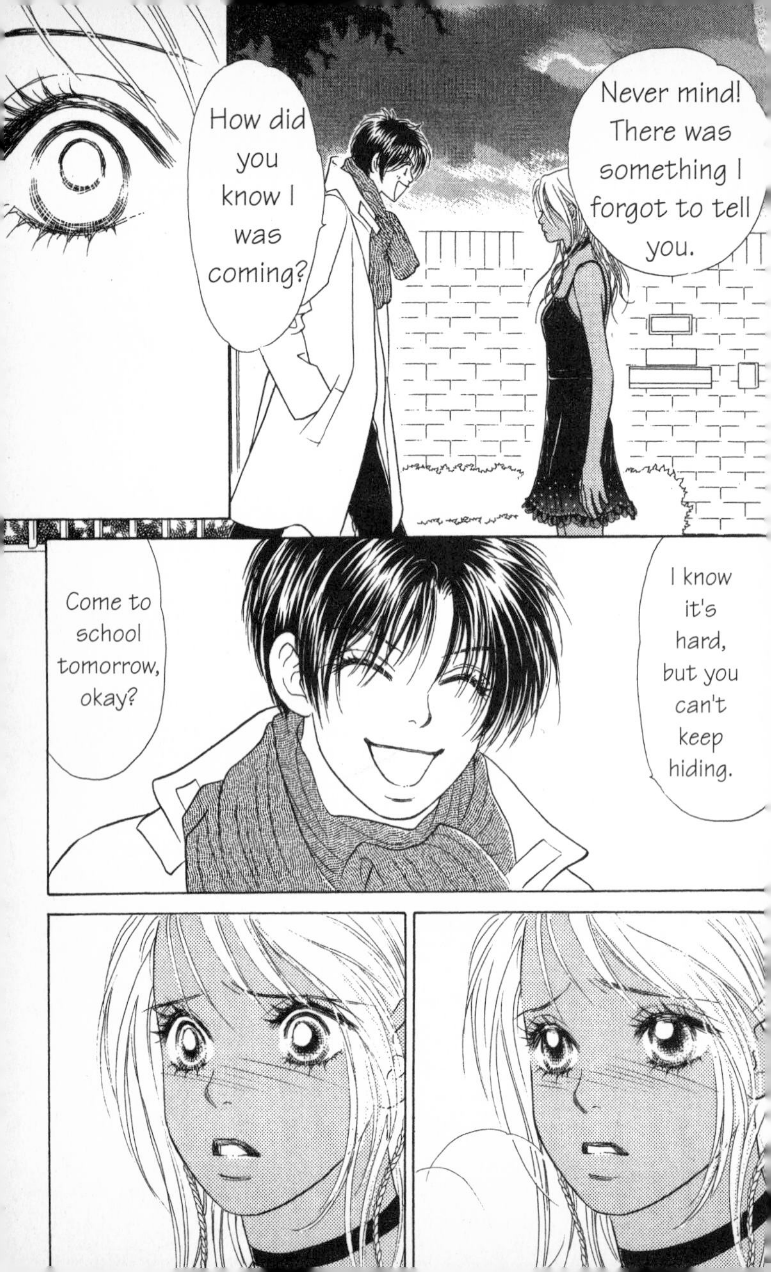
How did you know I was coming?
Never mind! There was something I forgot to tell you.
I know it's hard, but you can't keep hiding.
Come to school tomorrow, okay?

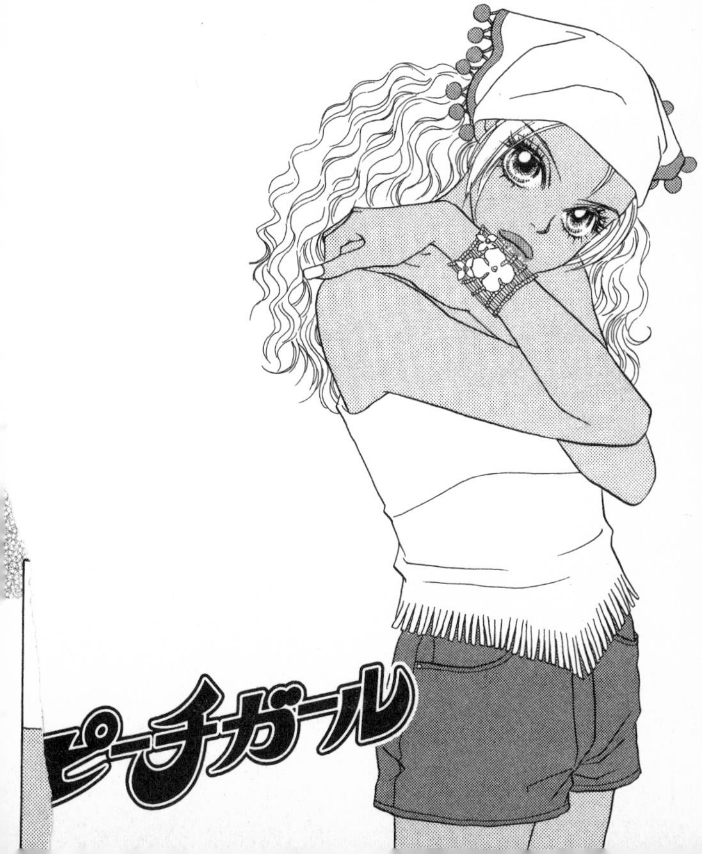
ピーチガール

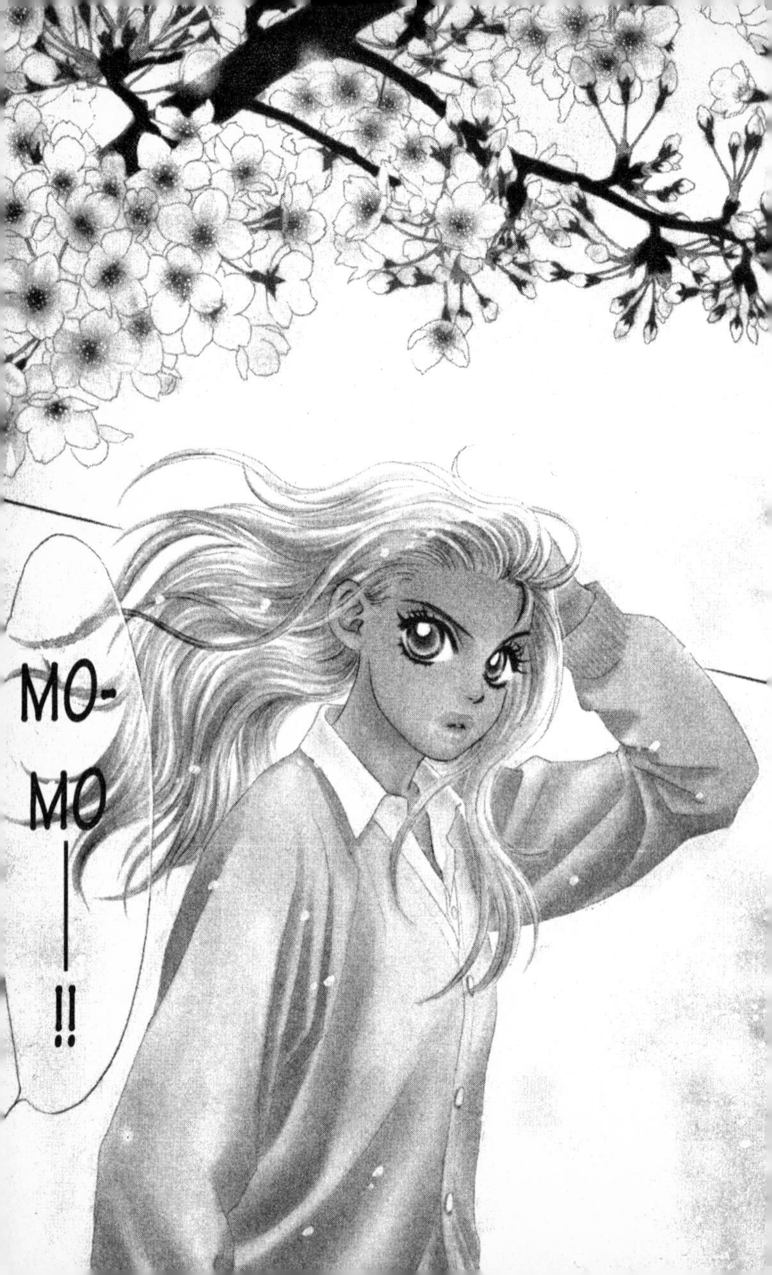
MO-MO——!!

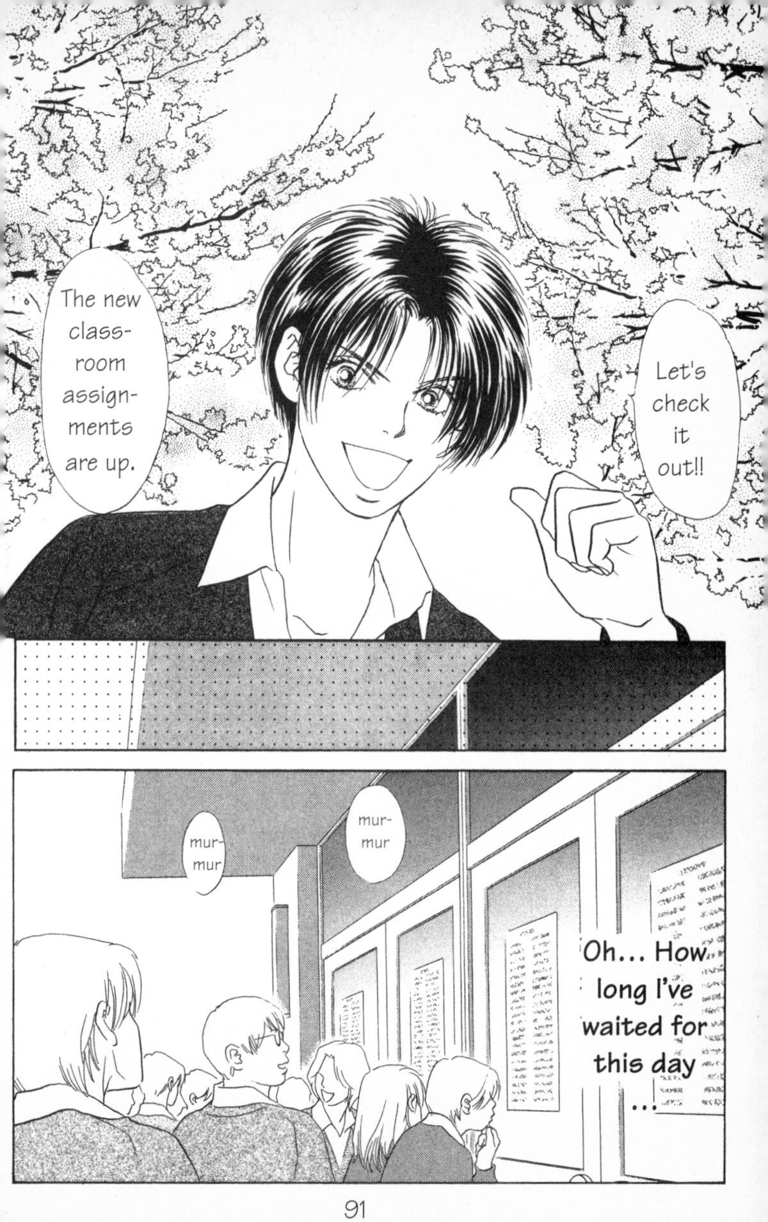
The new class-room assign-ments are up.
Let's check it out!!
mur-mur
mur-mur
Oh... How long I've waited for this day ...!

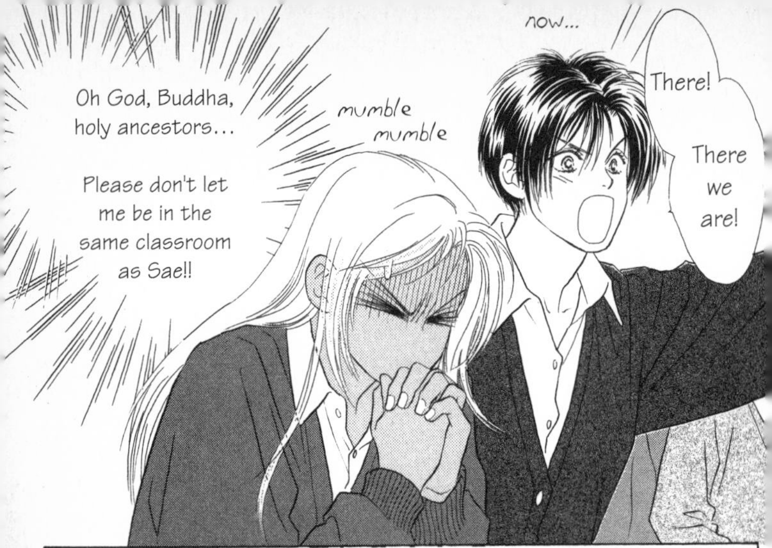
now...
There!
There we are!
mumble mumble
Oh God, Buddha, holy ancestors...
Please don't let me be in the same classroom as Sae!!

Junior Class
Homeroom 3

Kazu Uehara **Momo Adachi**
Kiley Okayasu **Shinya Kato**
Yoko Ito **Kei Uno**

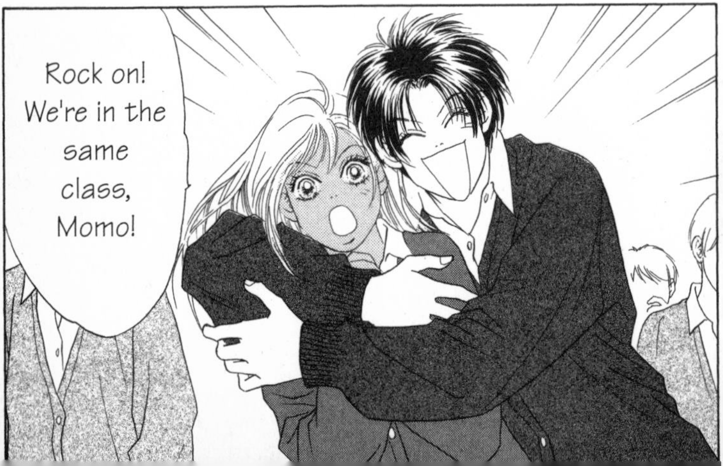
Rock on! We're in the same class, Momo!

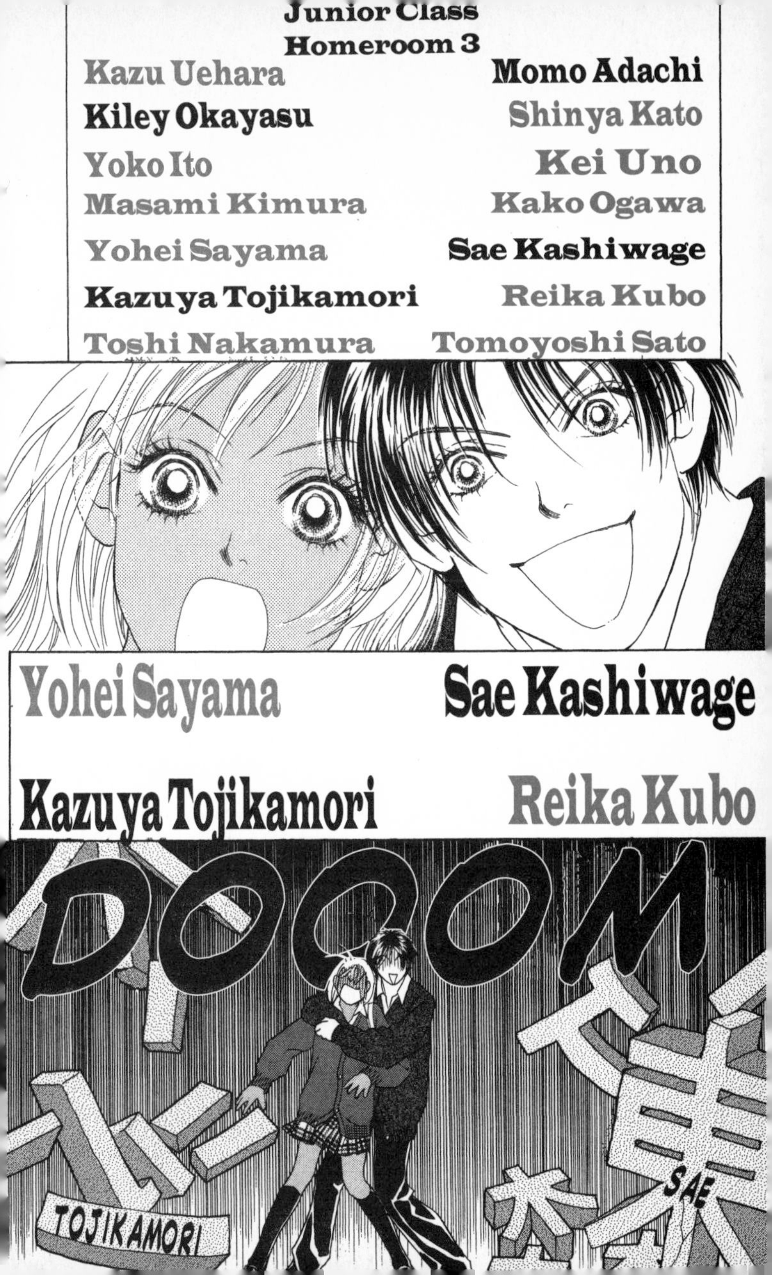
Junior Class
Homeroom 3
Kazu Uehara
Momo Adachi
Kiley Okayasu
Shinya Kato
Yoko Ito
Kei Uno
Masami Kimura
Kako Ogawa
Yohei Sayama
Sae Kashiwage
Kazuya Tojikamori
Reika Kubo
Toshi Nakamura
Tomoyoshi Sato
Yohei Sayama
Sae Kashiwage
Kazuya Tojikamori
Reika Kubo
DOOOM
SAE
TOJIKAMORI

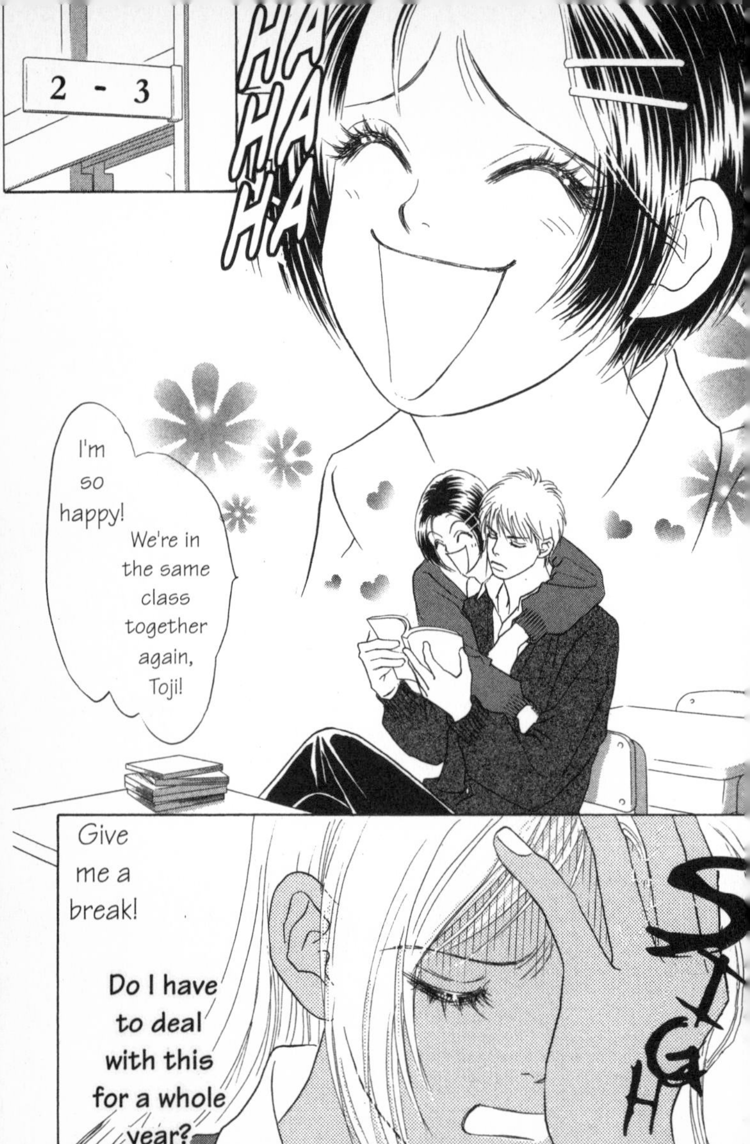
HA HA HA HA
2 - 3
I'm so happy! We're in the same class together again, Toji!
SIGH
Give me a break!
Do I have to deal with this for a whole year?

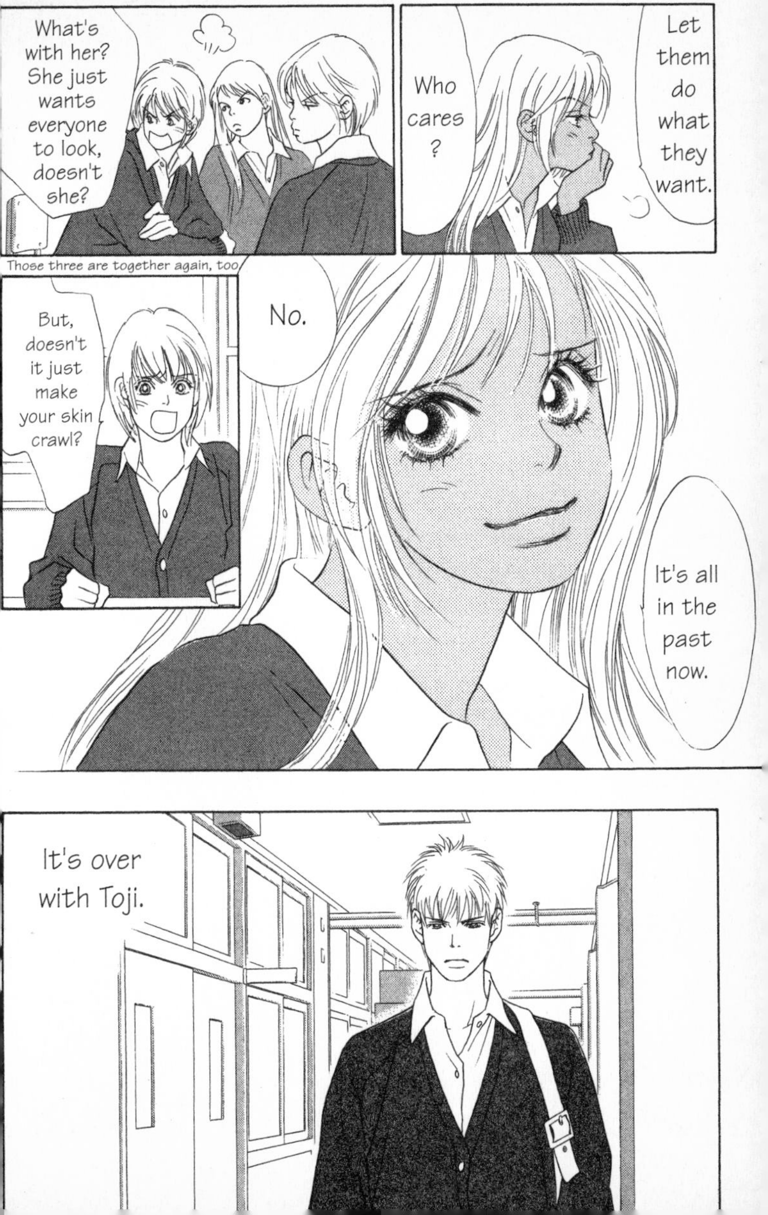
What's with her? She just wants everyone to look, doesn't she?
Those three are together again, too
Who cares?
Let them do what they want.
But, doesn't it just make your skin crawl?
No.
It's all in the past now.
It's over with Toji.

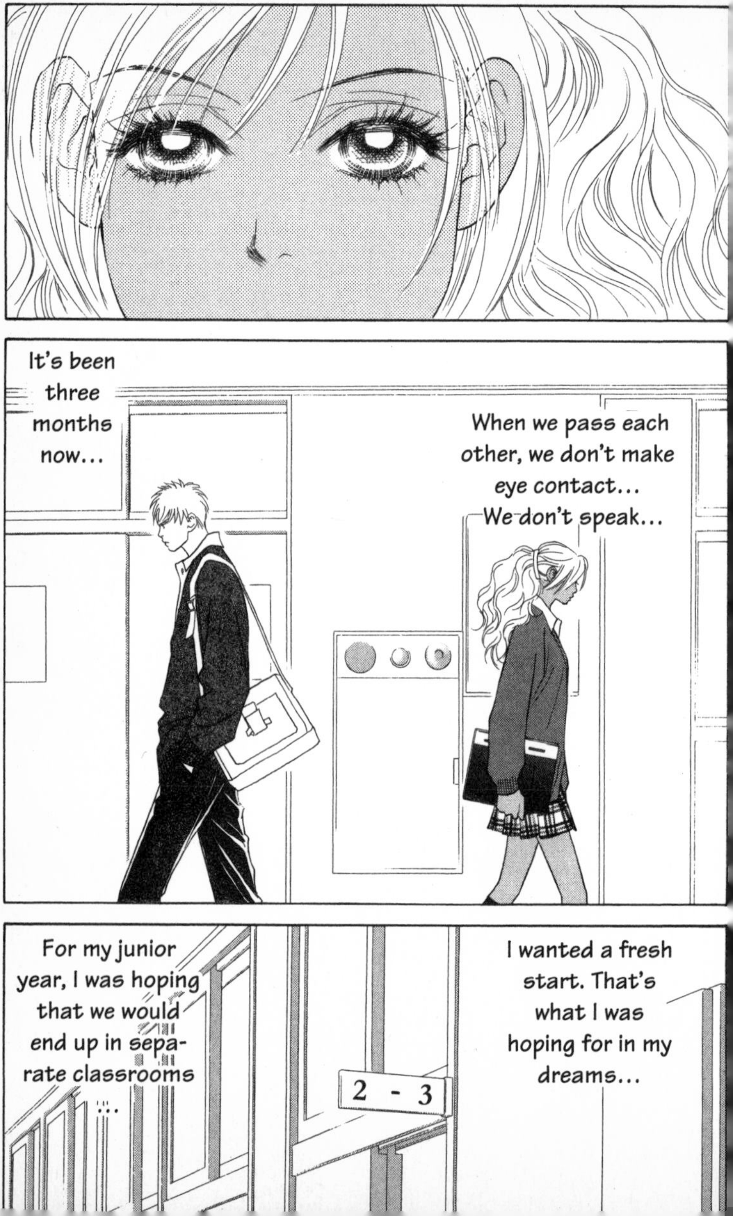
It's been three months now...
When we pass each other, we don't make eye contact...
We don't speak...
For my junior year, I was hoping that we would end up in separate classrooms ...
2 - 3
I wanted a fresh start. That's what I was hoping for in my dreams...

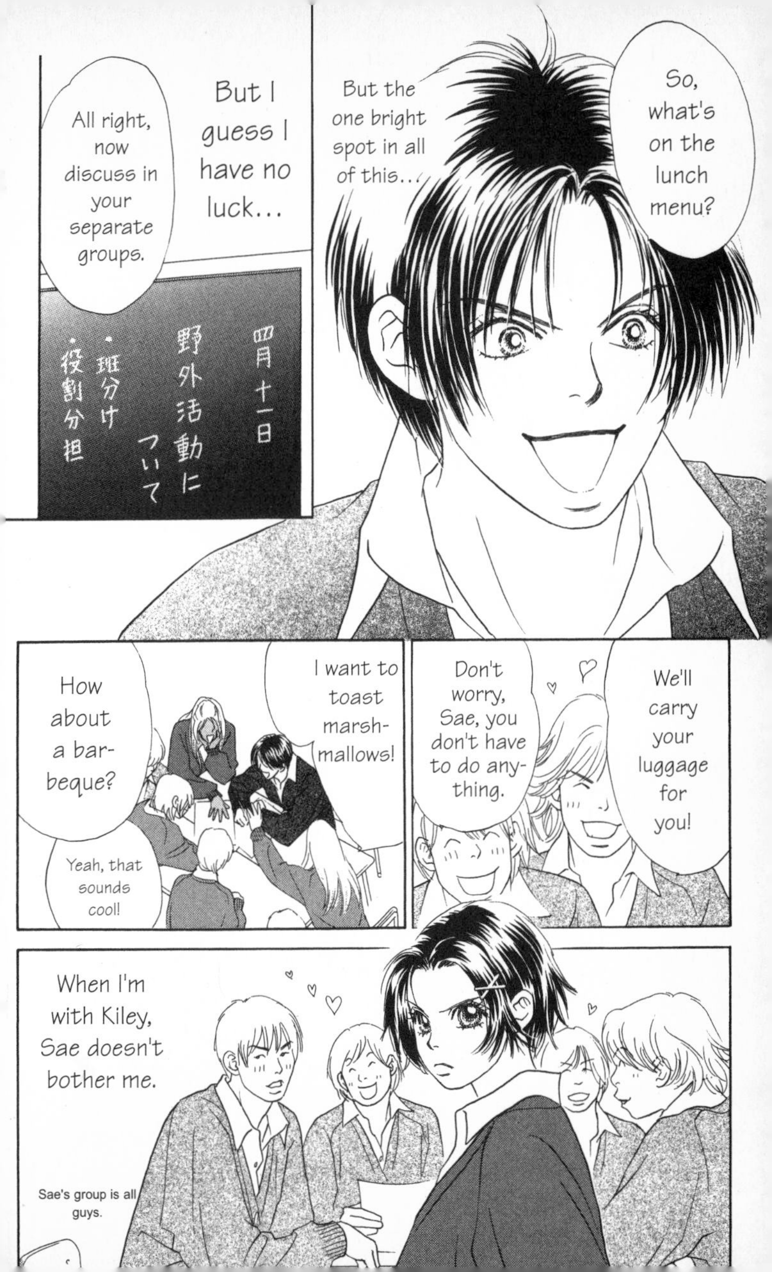
All right, now discuss in your separate groups.
四月十一日
野外活動について
・班分け
・役割分担
But I guess I have no luck...
But the one bright spot in all of this...
So, what's on the lunch menu?
How about a barbeque?
I want to toast marshmallows!
Yeah, that sounds cool!
Don't worry, Sae, you don't have to do anything.
We'll carry your luggage for you!
When I'm with Kiley, Sae doesn't bother me.
Sae's group is all guys.

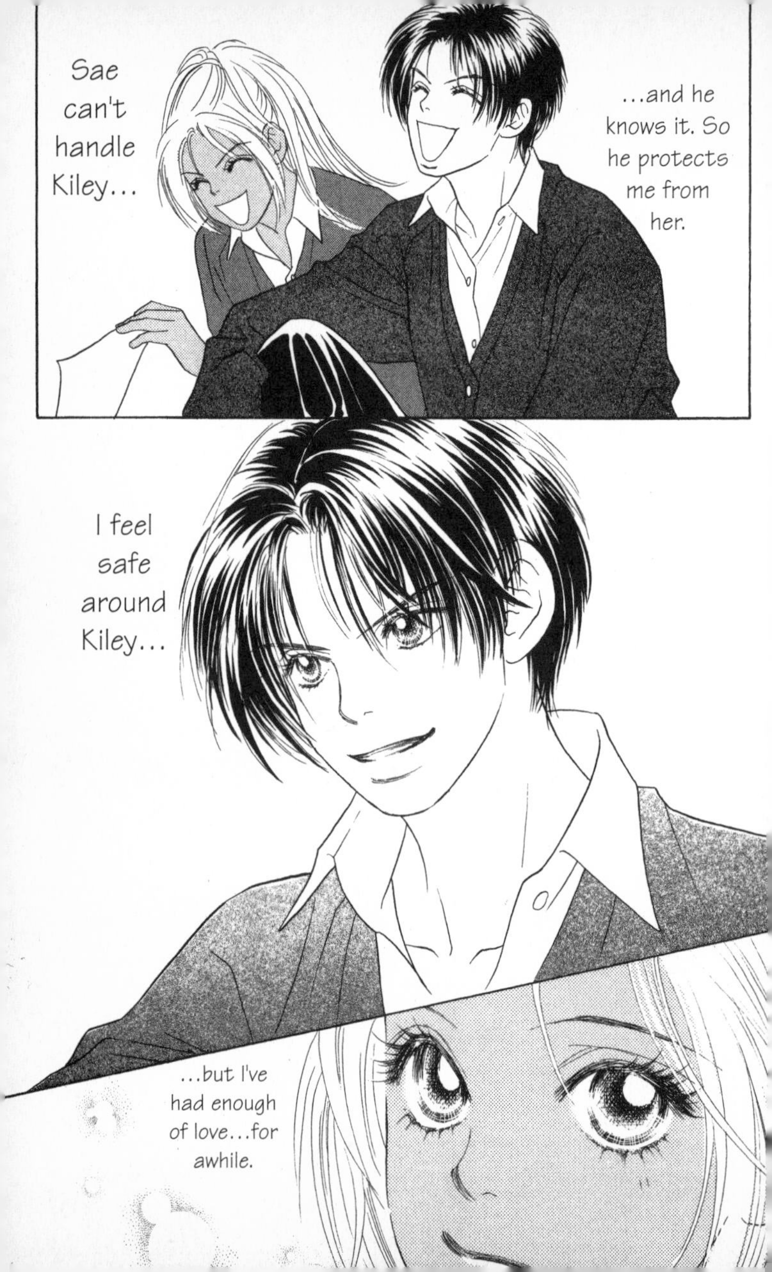
Sae can't handle Kiley...
...and he knows it. So he protects me from her.
I feel safe around Kiley...
...but I've had enough of love...for awhile.

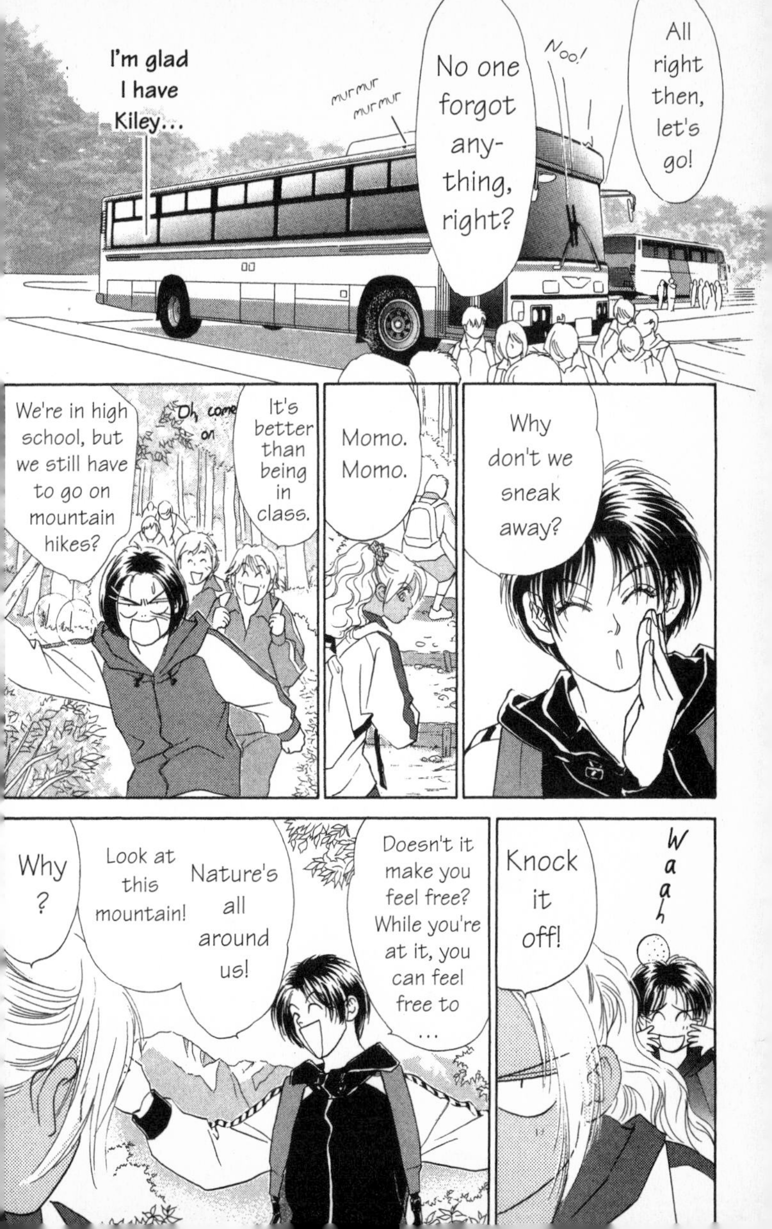
I'm glad I have Kiley...
murmur murmur
No one forgot anything, right?
Noo!
All right then, let's go!
We're in high school, but we still have to go on mountain hikes?
Oh, come on
It's better than being in class.
Momo. Momo.
Why don't we sneak away?
Why?
Look at this mountain!
Nature's all around us!
Doesn't it make you feel free? While you're at it, you can feel free to ...
Knock it off!
Waah

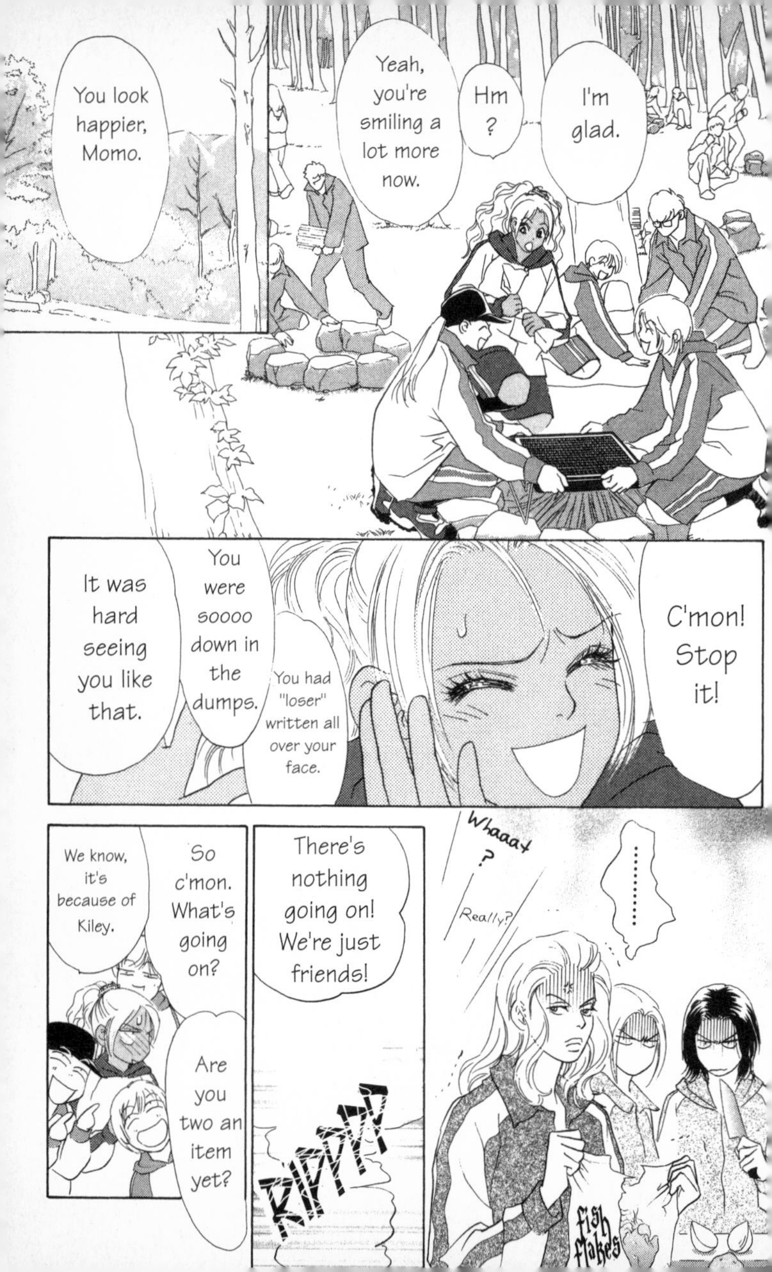
You look happier, Momo.
Yeah, you're smiling a lot more now.
Hm?
I'm glad.
It was hard seeing you like that.
You were soooo down in the dumps.
You had "loser" written all over your face.
C'mon! Stop it!
We know, it's because of Kiley.
So c'mon. What's going on?
Are you two an item yet?
There's nothing going on! We're just friends!
RIPPP
Whaaat?
Really?
....
fish flakes

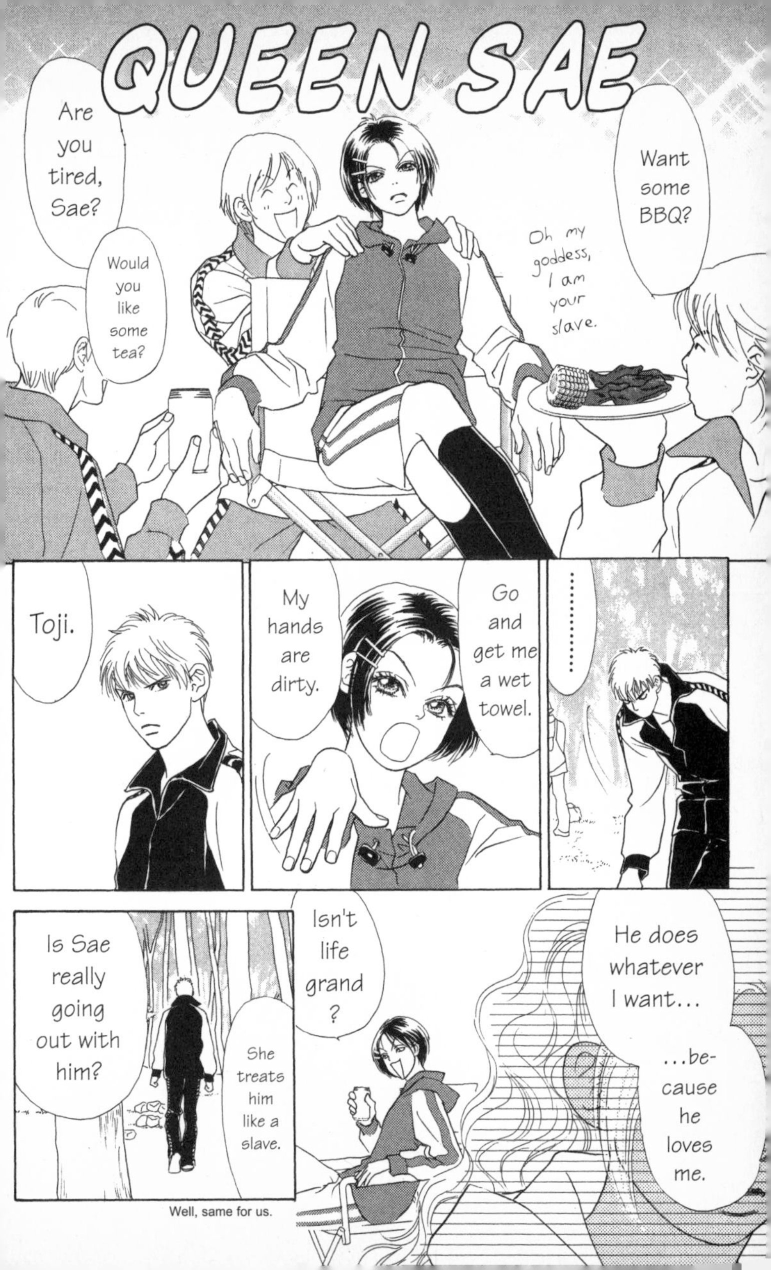
QUEEN SAE
Are you tired, Sae?
Would you like some tea?
Oh my goddess, I am your slave.
Want some BBQ?
Toji.
My hands are dirty.
Go and get me a wet towel.
......
Is Sae really going out with him?
She treats him like a slave.
Isn't life grand?
He does whatever I want...
...be-cause he loves me.
Well, same for us.

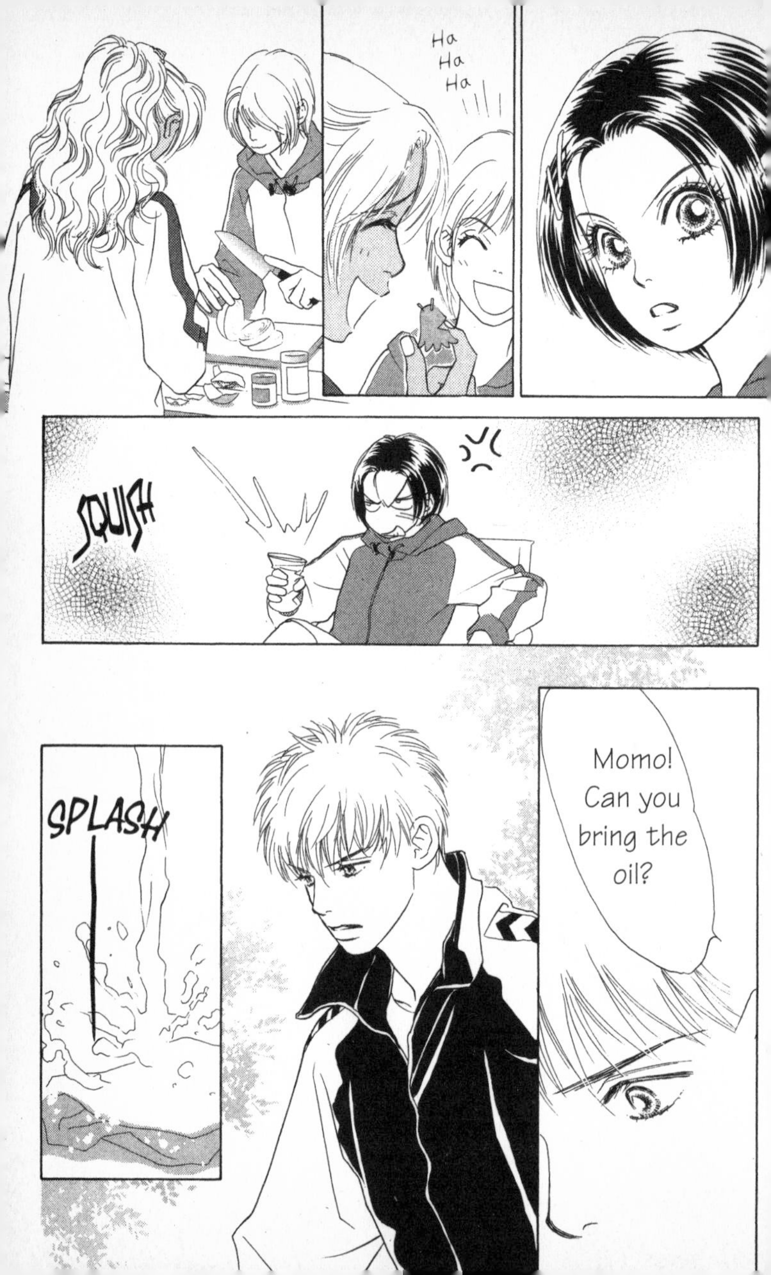
Ha Ha Ha
SQUISH
Momo! Can you bring the oil?
SPLASH

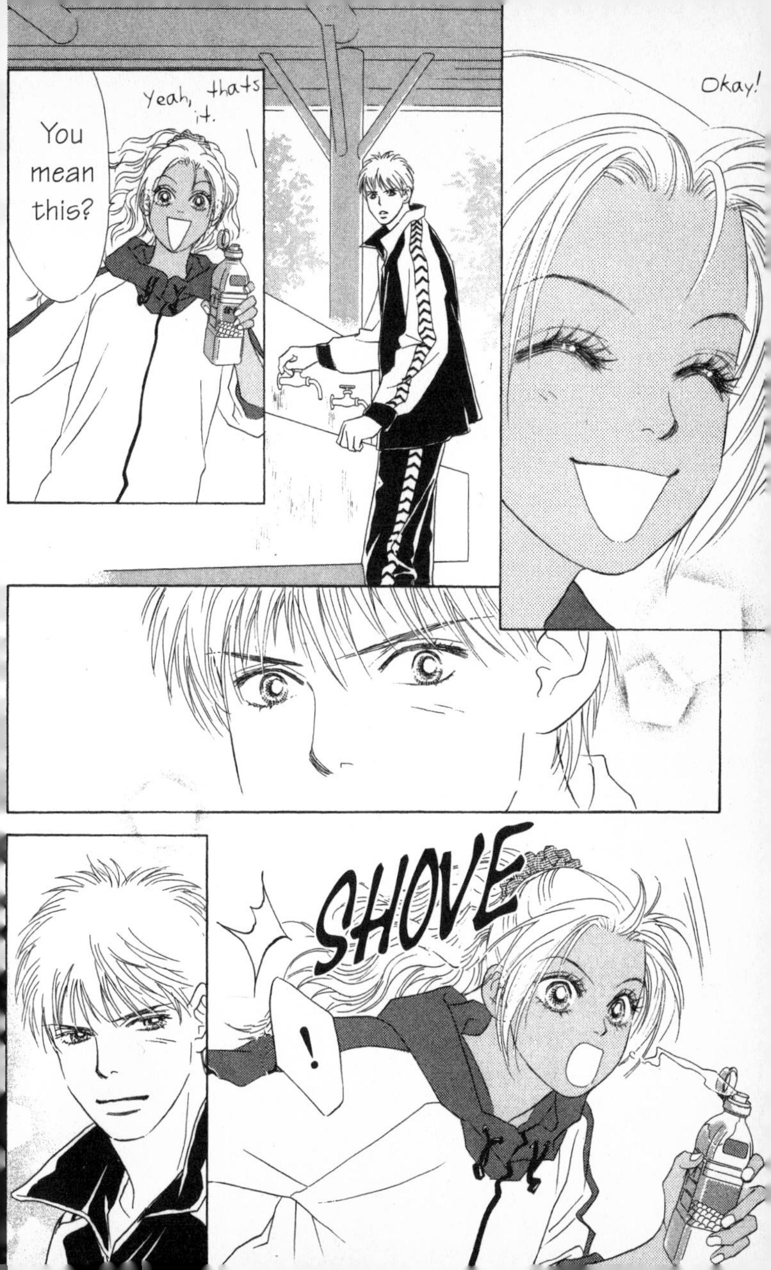
You mean this?
Yeah, thats it.
Okay!
SHOVE
!

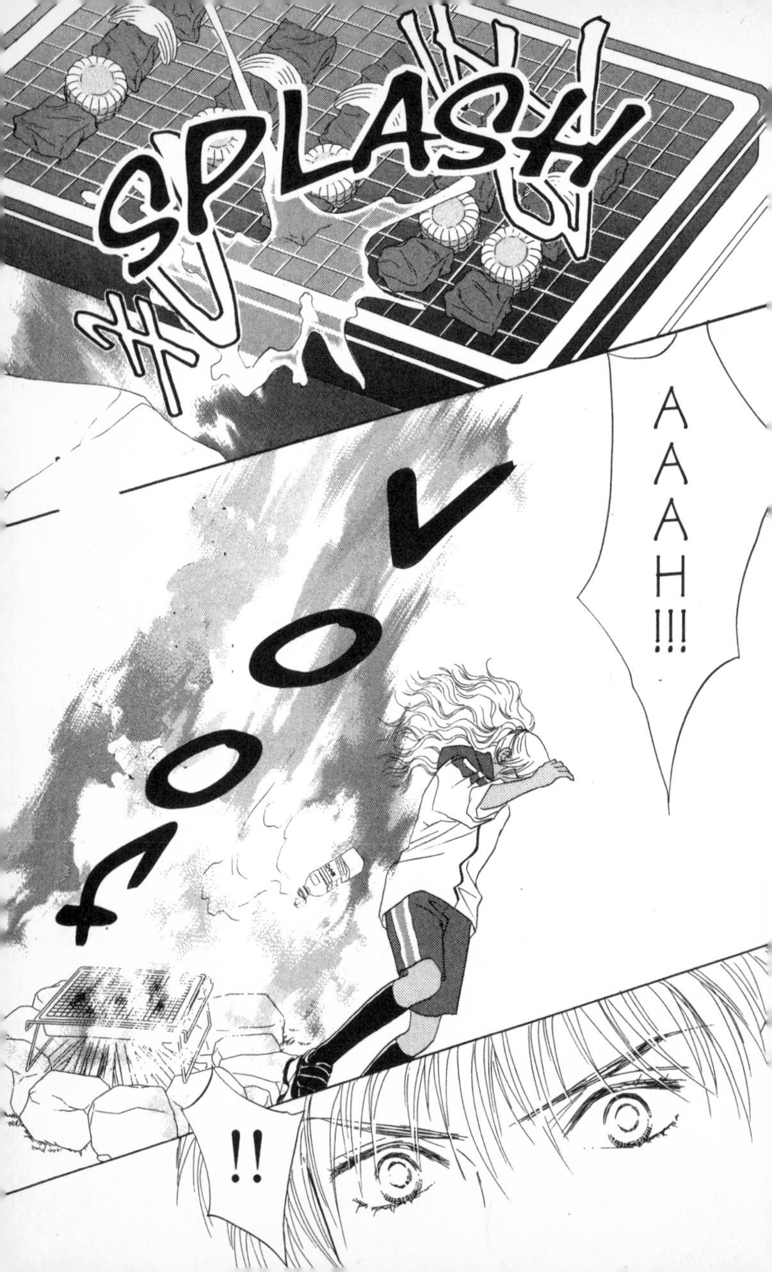
SPLASH
AAAH!!!
VOOOF
!!

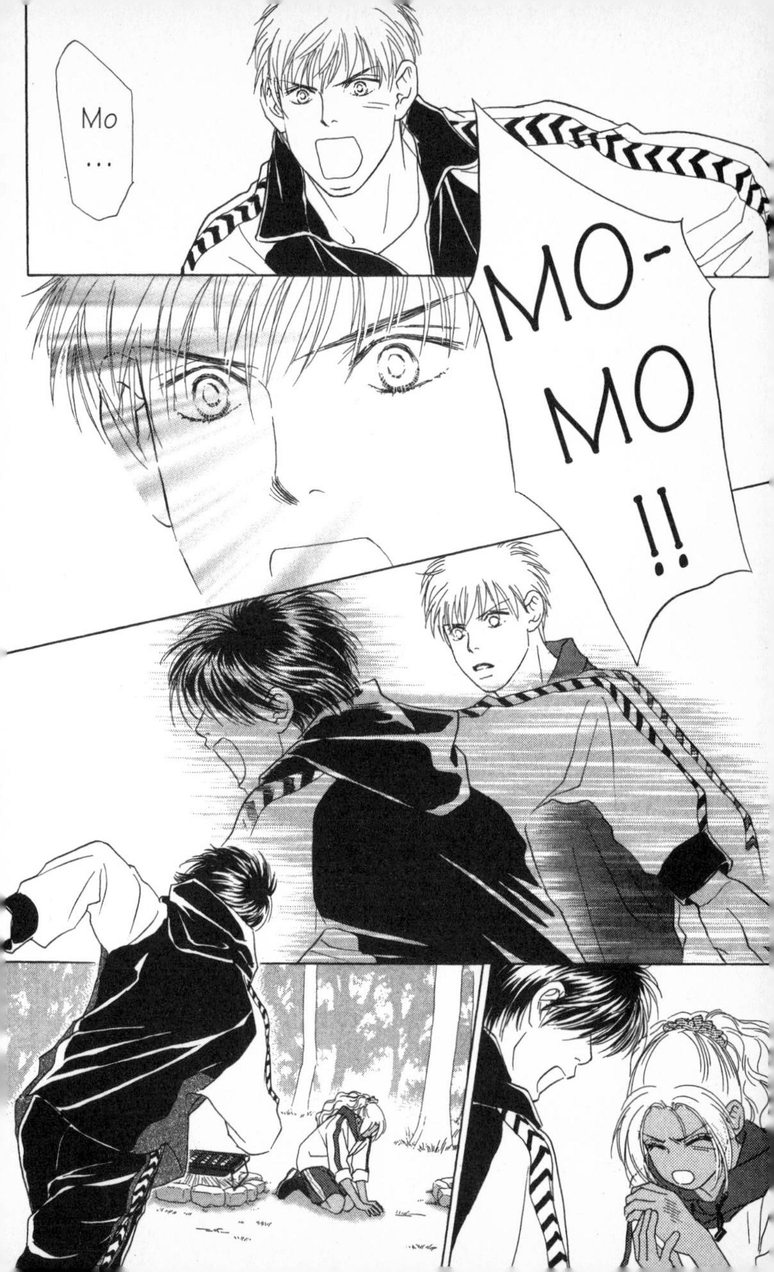
MO-MO !!
Mo ...

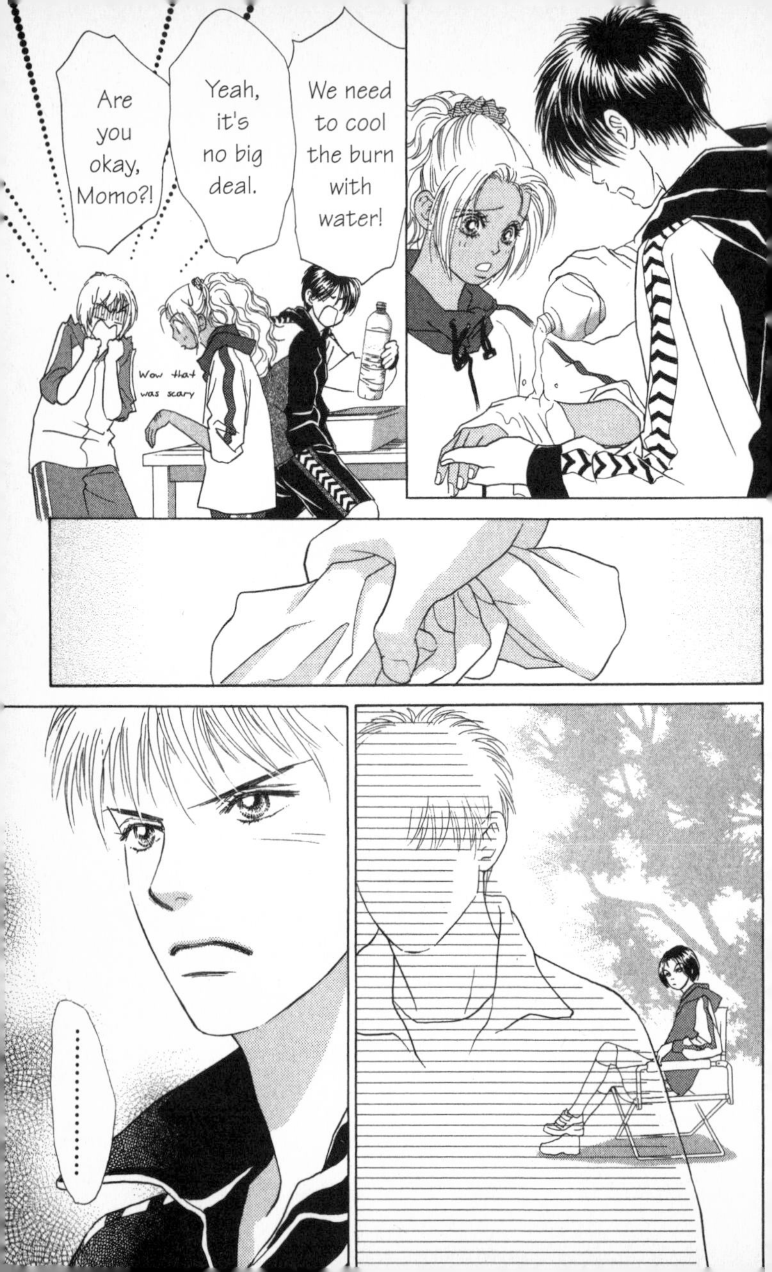
Are you okay, Momo?!
Yeah, it's no big deal.
We need to cool the burn with water!
Wow that was scary
......

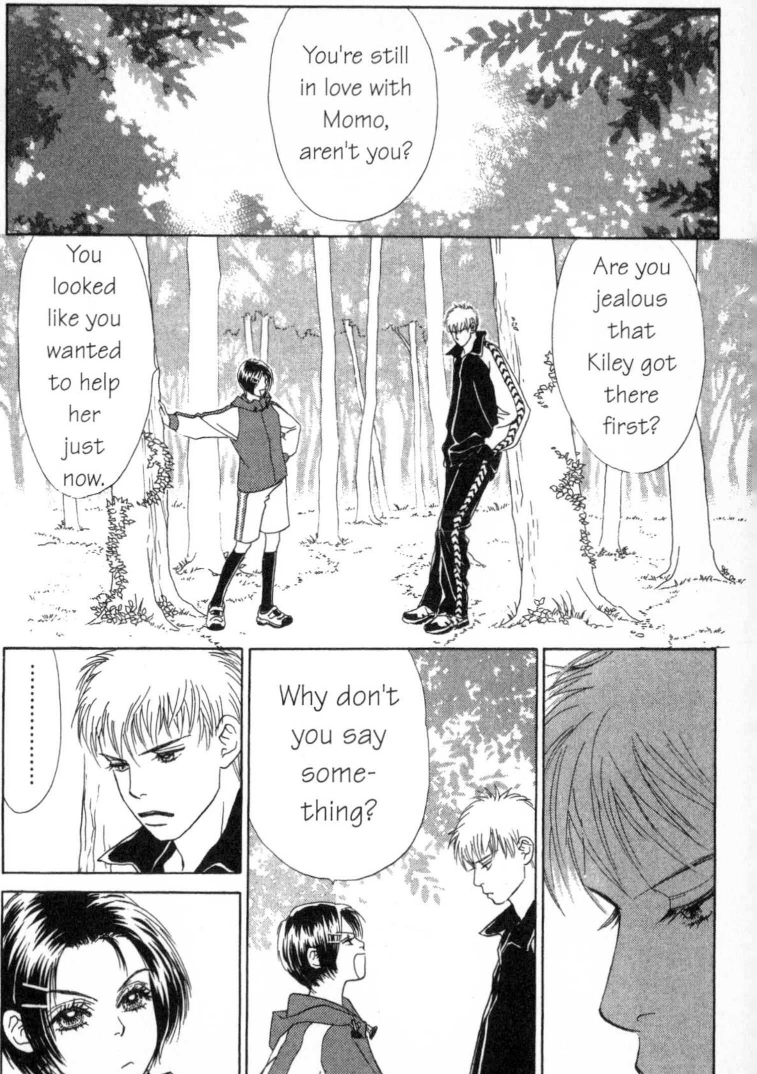
You're still in love with Momo, aren't you?
You looked like you wanted to help her just now.
Are you jealous that Kiley got there first?
......
Why don't you say some-thing?

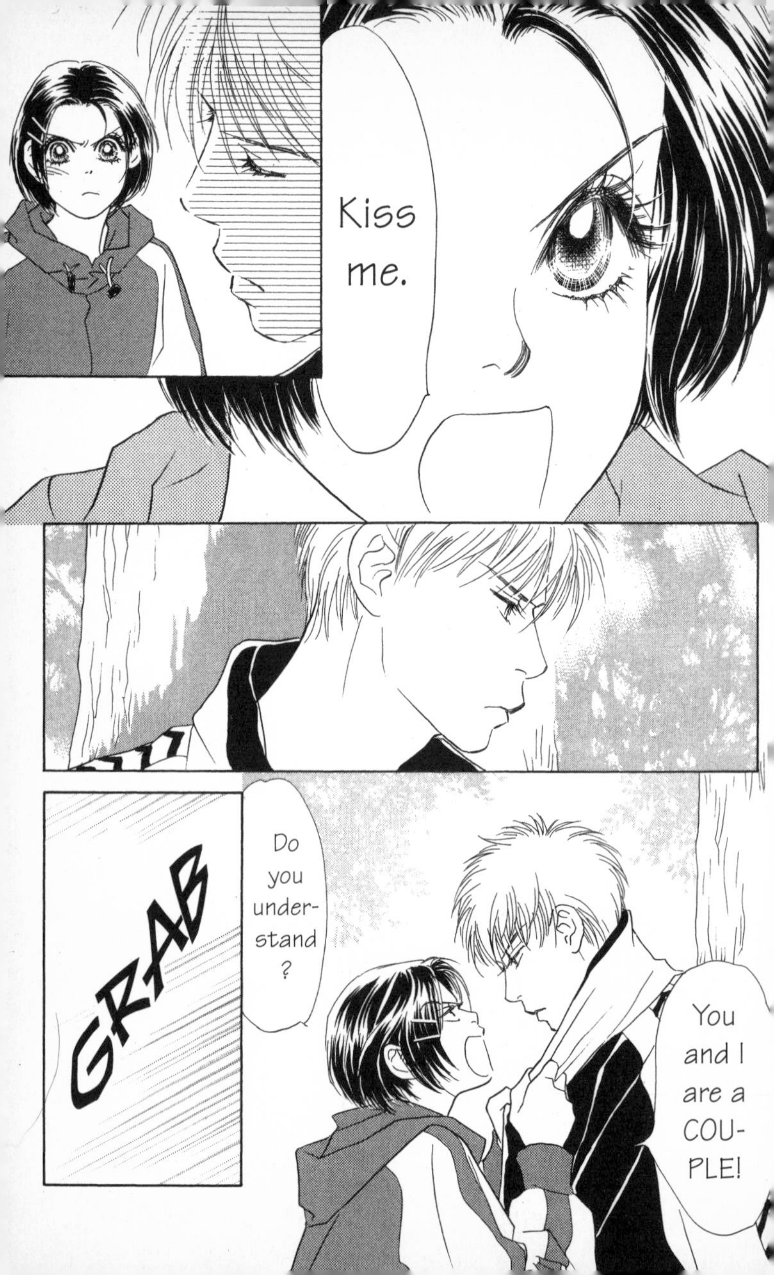
Kiss me.
Do you under-stand?
GRAB
You and I are a COU-PLE!

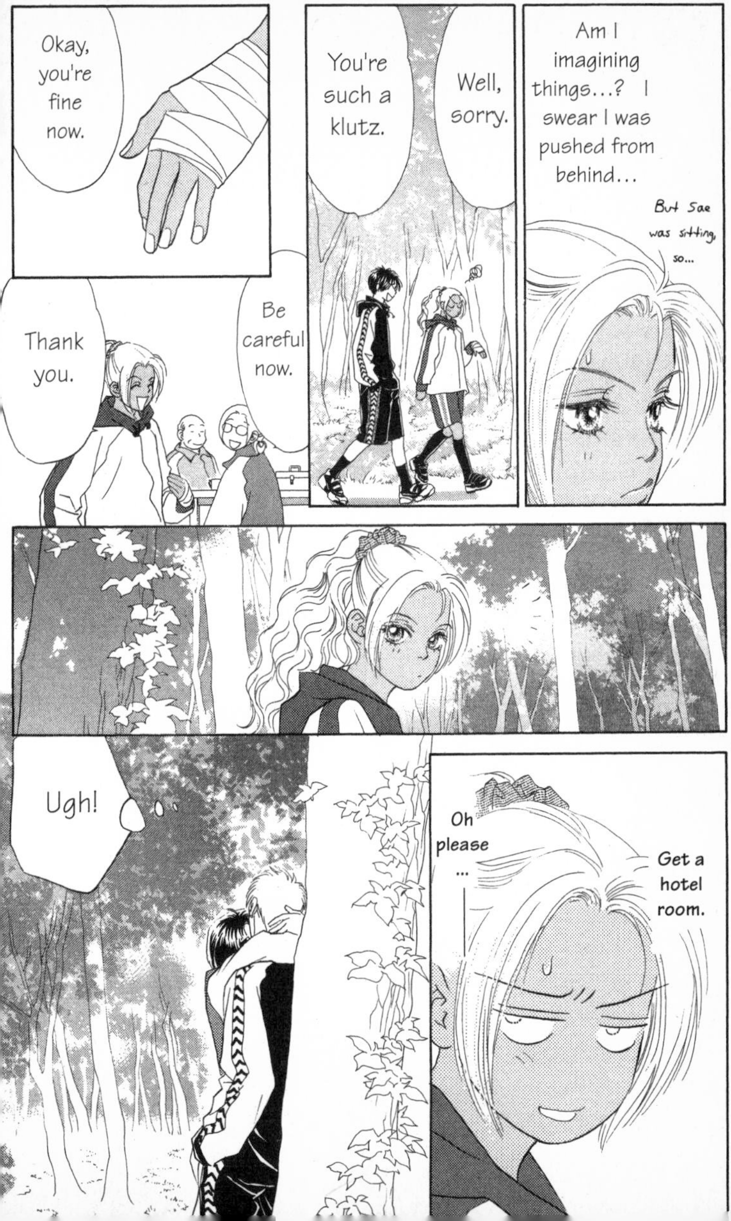
Okay, you're fine now.
Thank you.
Be careful now.
You're such a klutz.
Well, sorry.
Am I imagining things...? I swear I was pushed from behind...
But Sae was sitting, so...
Ugh!
Oh please ...
Get a hotel room.

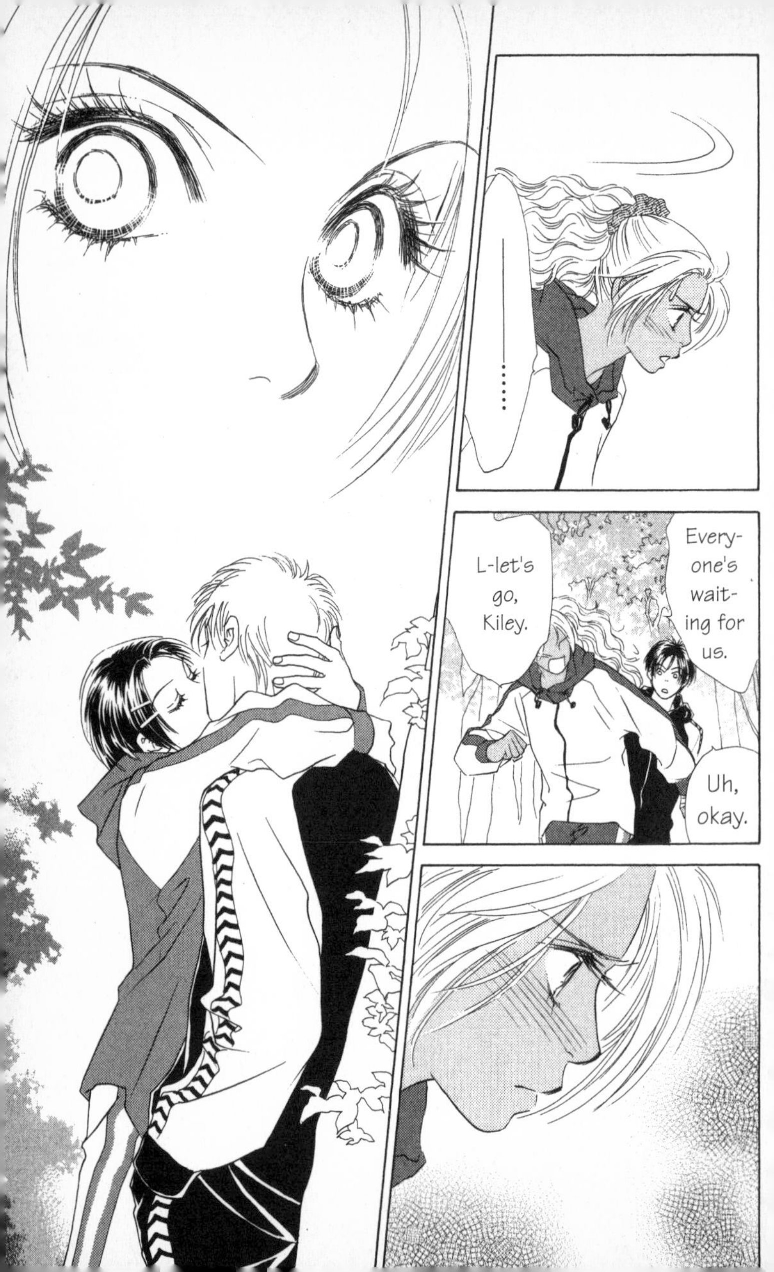
......
Everyone's waiting for us.
L-let's go, Kiley.
Uh, okay.

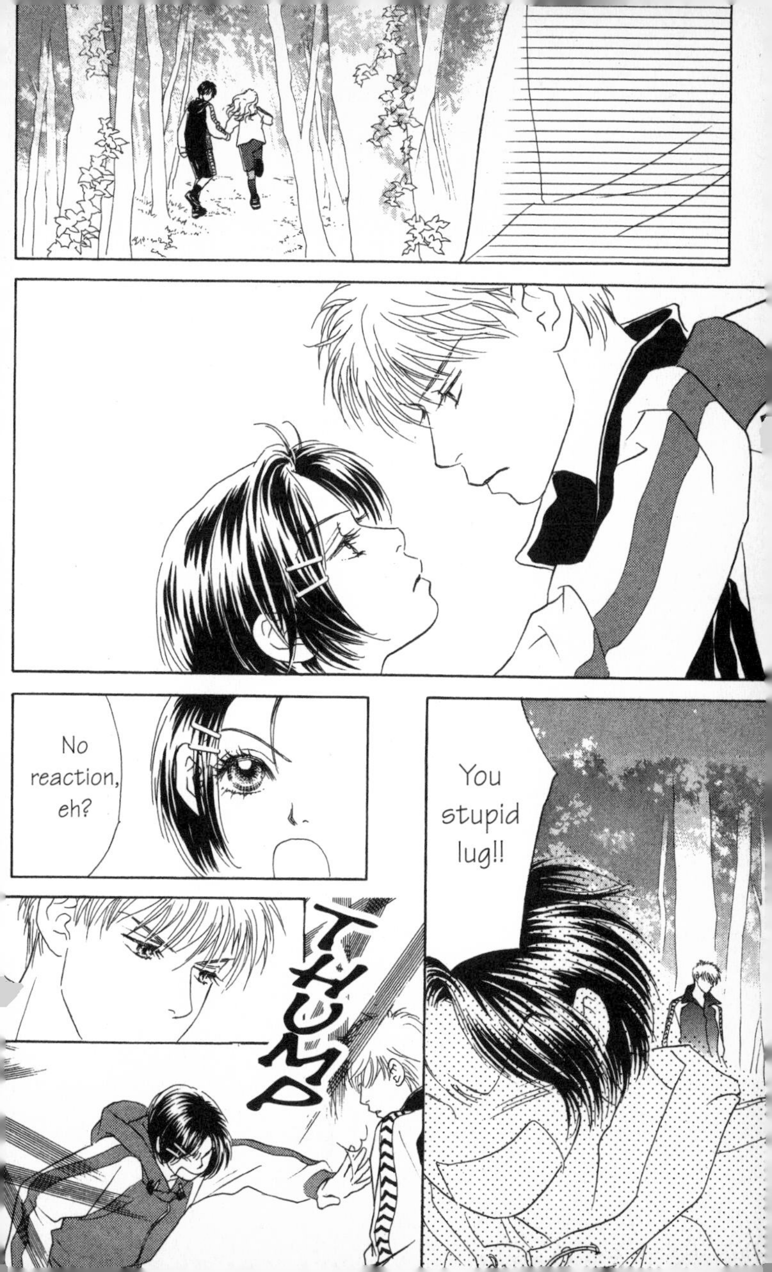
You stupid lug!!
No reaction, eh?
THUMP

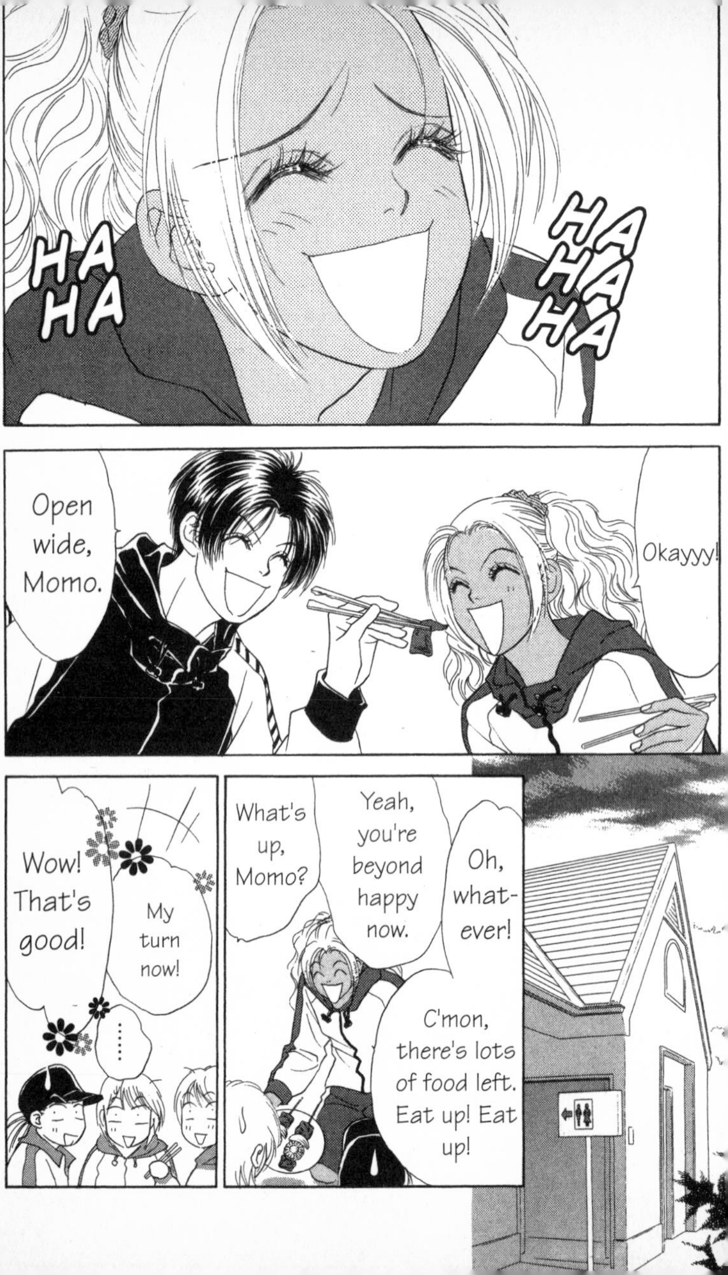
HA HA
HA HA HA
Open wide, Momo.
Okayyy!
Wow! That's good!
My turn now!
......
What's up, Momo?
Yeah, you're beyond happy now.
Oh, whatever!
C'mon, there's lots of food left. Eat up! Eat up!

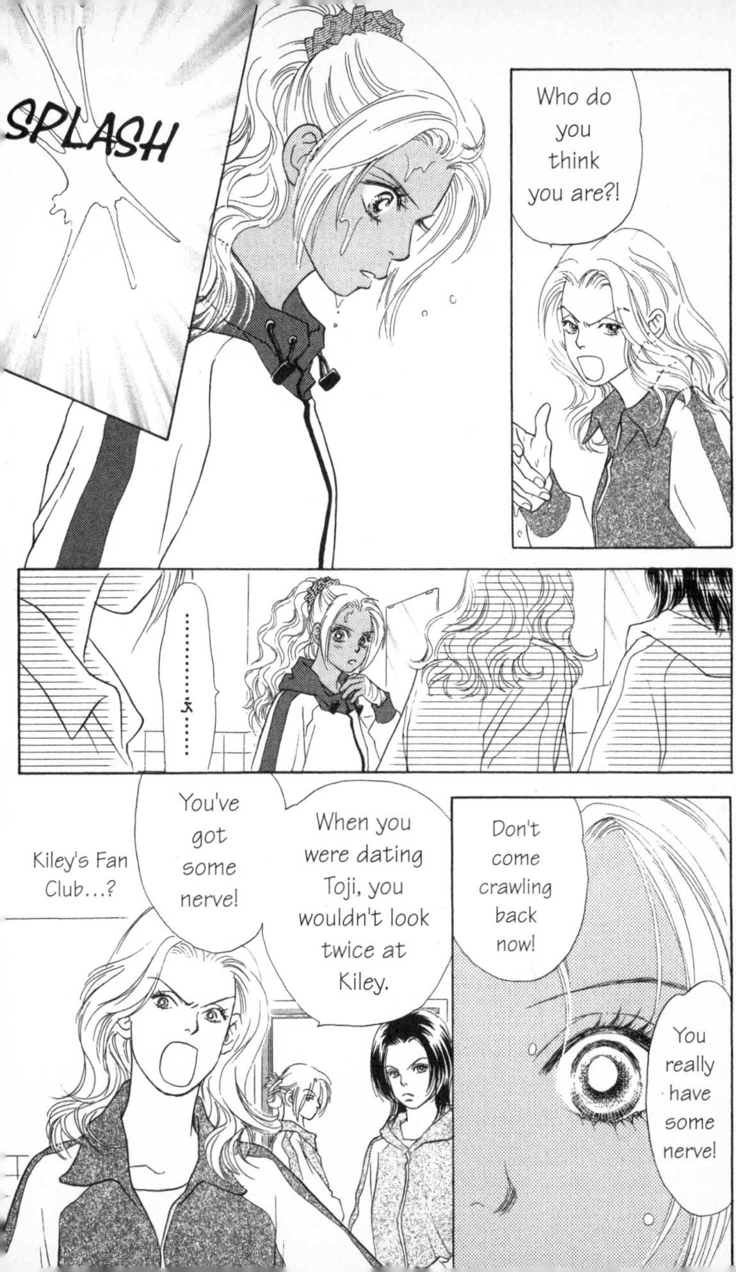
Who do you think you are?!
SPLASH
Don't come crawling back now!
You really have some nerve!
When you were dating Toji, you wouldn't look twice at Kiley.
You've got some nerve!
Kiley's Fan Club…?

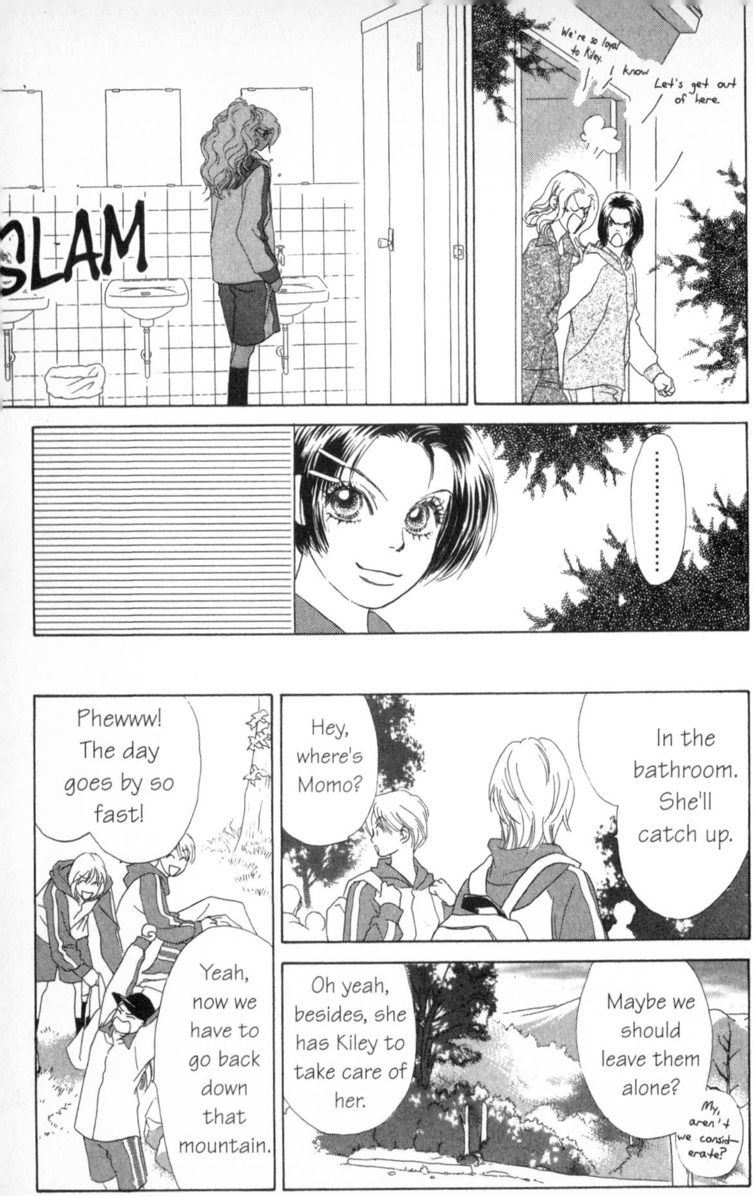
We're so loyal to Kiley.
I know
Let's get out of here.
SLAM
......
Hey, where's Momo?
In the bathroom. She'll catch up.
Oh yeah, besides, she has Kiley to take care of her.
Maybe we should leave them alone?
My, aren't we considerate?
Phewww! The day goes by so fast!
Yeah, now we have to go back down that mountain.

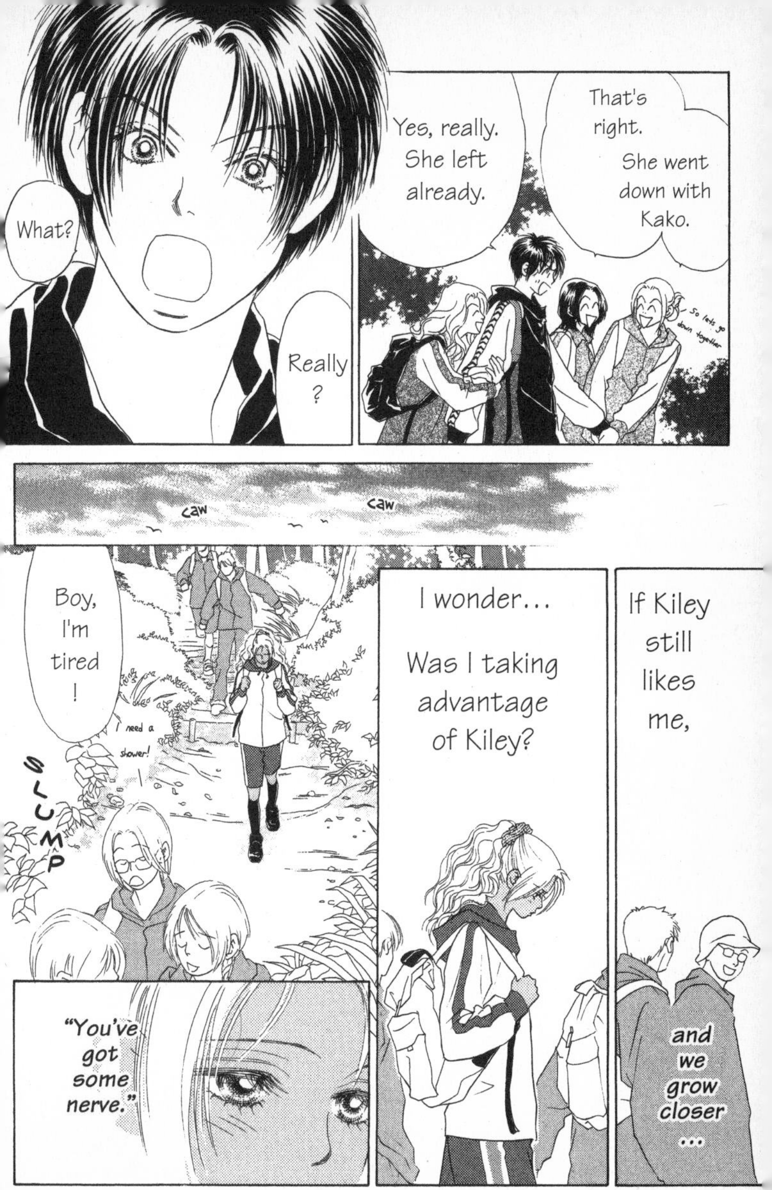
What?
Really?
Yes, really. She left already.
That's right.
She went down with Kako.
So lets go down together
caw
caw
Boy, I'm tired!
I need a shower!
SLUMP
I wonder…
Was I taking advantage of Kiley?
"You've got some nerve."
If Kiley still likes me,
and we grow closer…

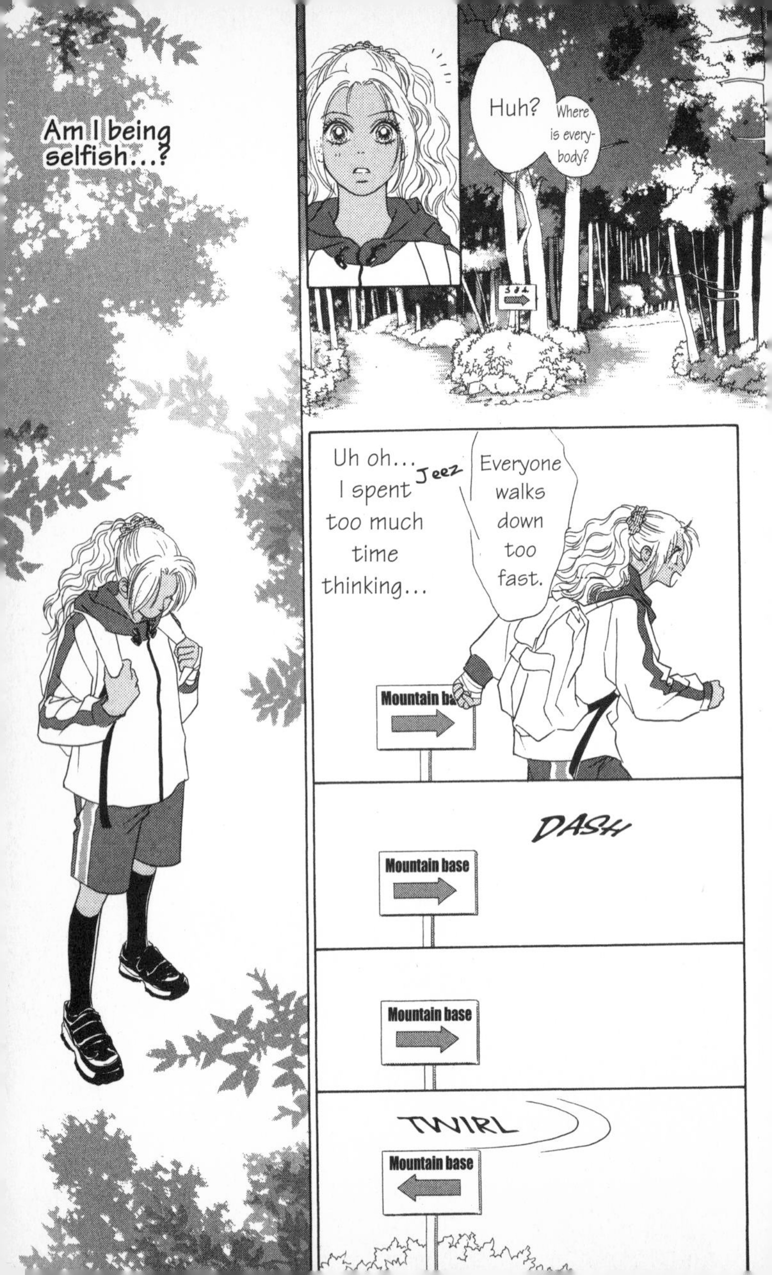
Am I being selfish...?
Huh?
Where is every-body?
Uh oh... I spent too much time thinking...
Jeez
Everyone walks down too fast.
Mountain ba
DASH
Mountain base
Mountain base
TWIRL
Mountain base

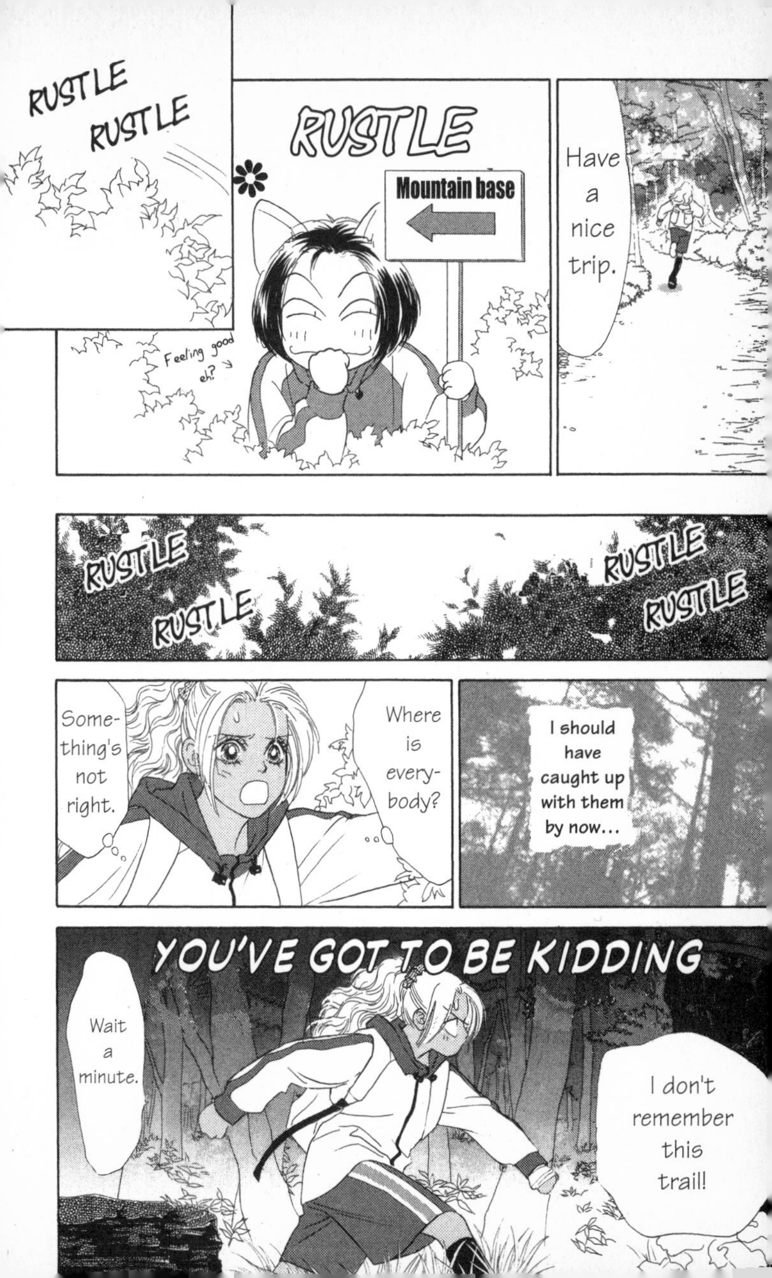
Have a nice trip.
RUSTLE
Mountain base
Feeling good eh?
RUSTLE RUSTLE
RUSTLE RUSTLE
RUSTLE RUSTLE
I should have caught up with them by now...
Where is everybody?
Something's not right.
YOU'VE GOT TO BE KIDDING
Wait a minute.
I don't remember this trail!

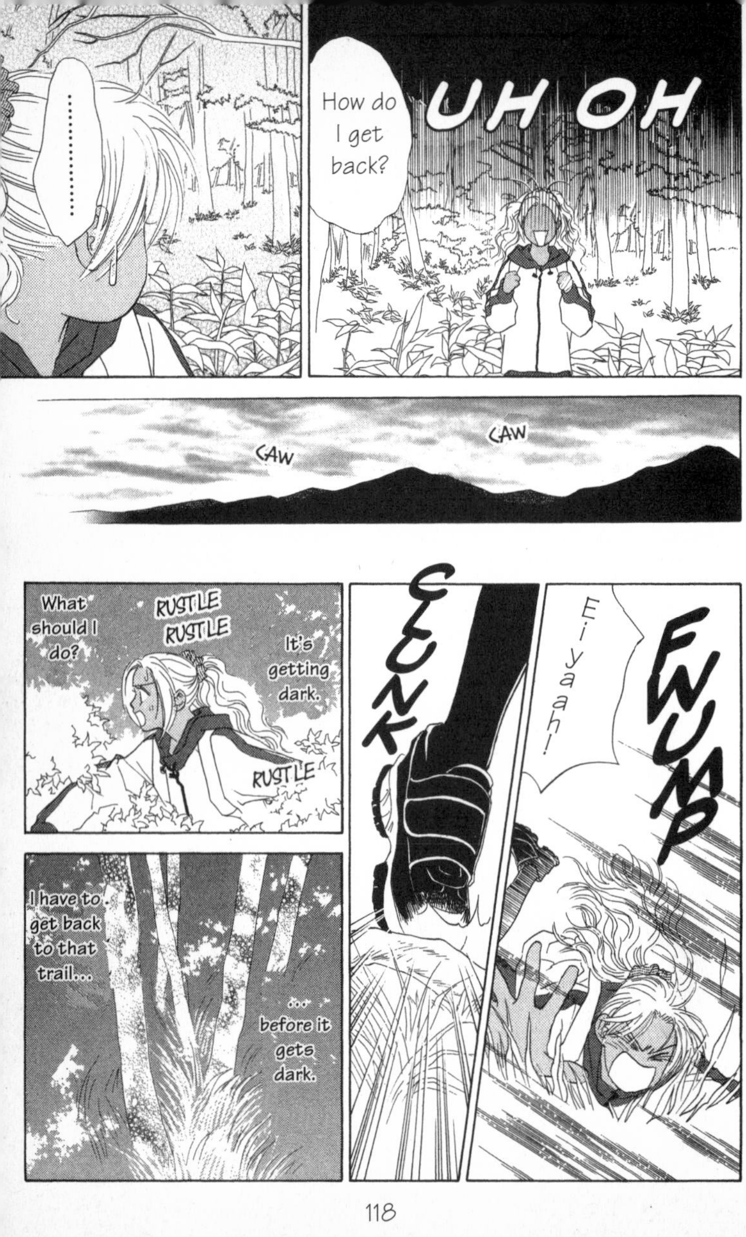

......
How do I get back?
UH OH
CAW
CAW
What should I do?
RUSTLE RUSTLE
It's getting dark.
RUSTLE
I have to get back to that trail...
...before it gets dark.
CLUNK
Eiyaah!
FWUMP

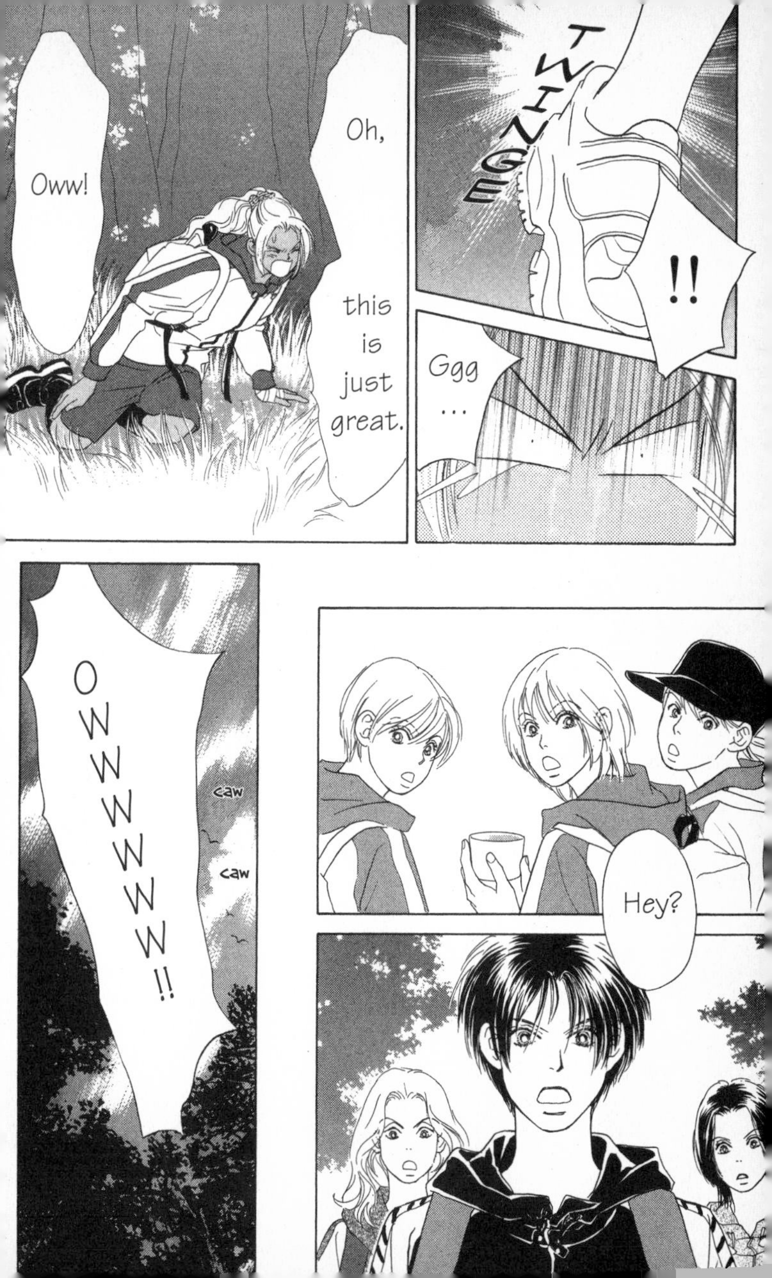
Oww!
Oh, this is just great.
TWINGE
!!
Ggg...
OWWWWWWW!!
caw
caw
Hey?

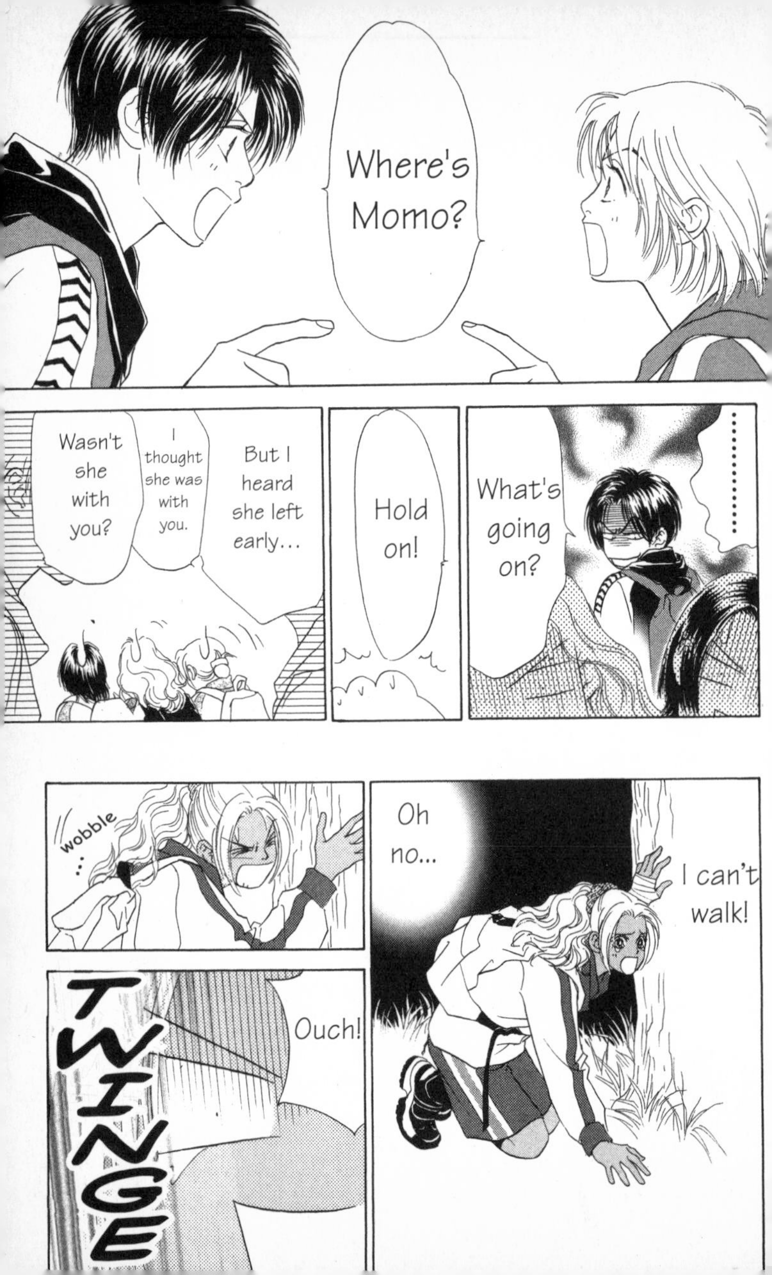
Where's Momo?
Wasn't she with you?
I thought she was with you.
But I heard she left early...
Hold on!
What's going on?
....
wobble
...
TWINGE
Ouch!
Oh no...
I can't walk!

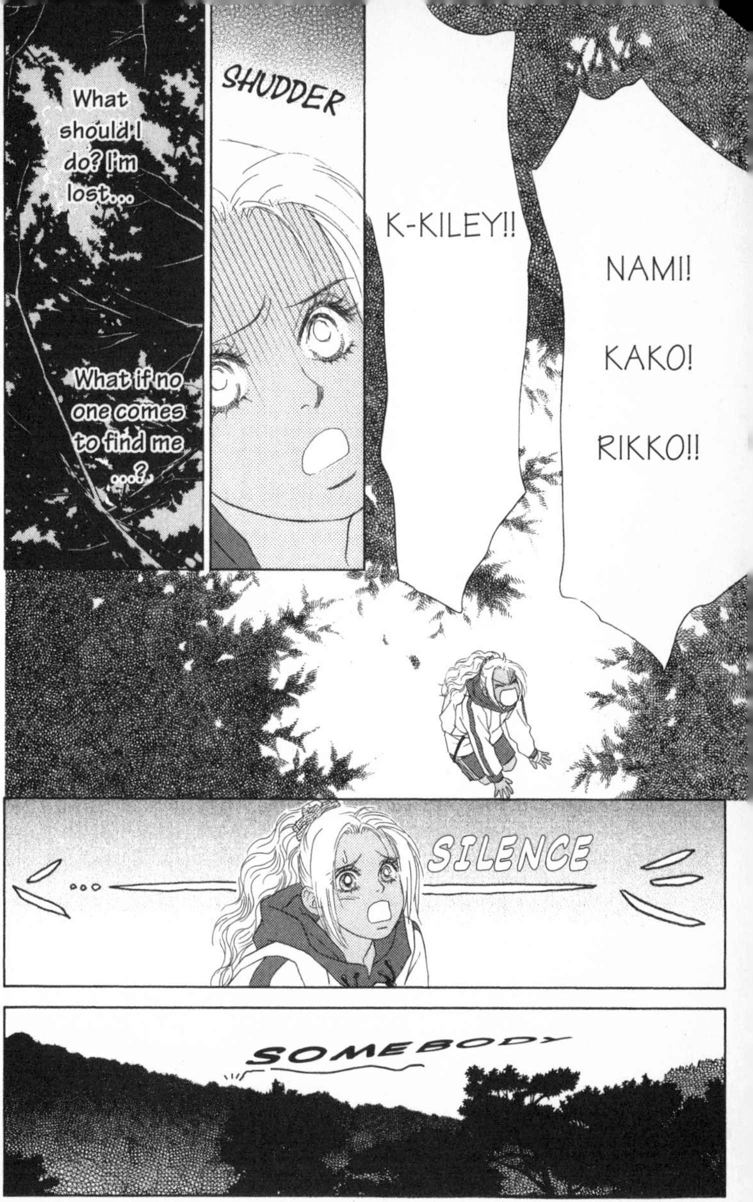
What should I do? I'm lost...
What if no one comes to find me ...?
SHUDDER
K-KILEY!!
NAMI!
KAKO!
RIKKO!!
...
SILENCE
SOMEBODY

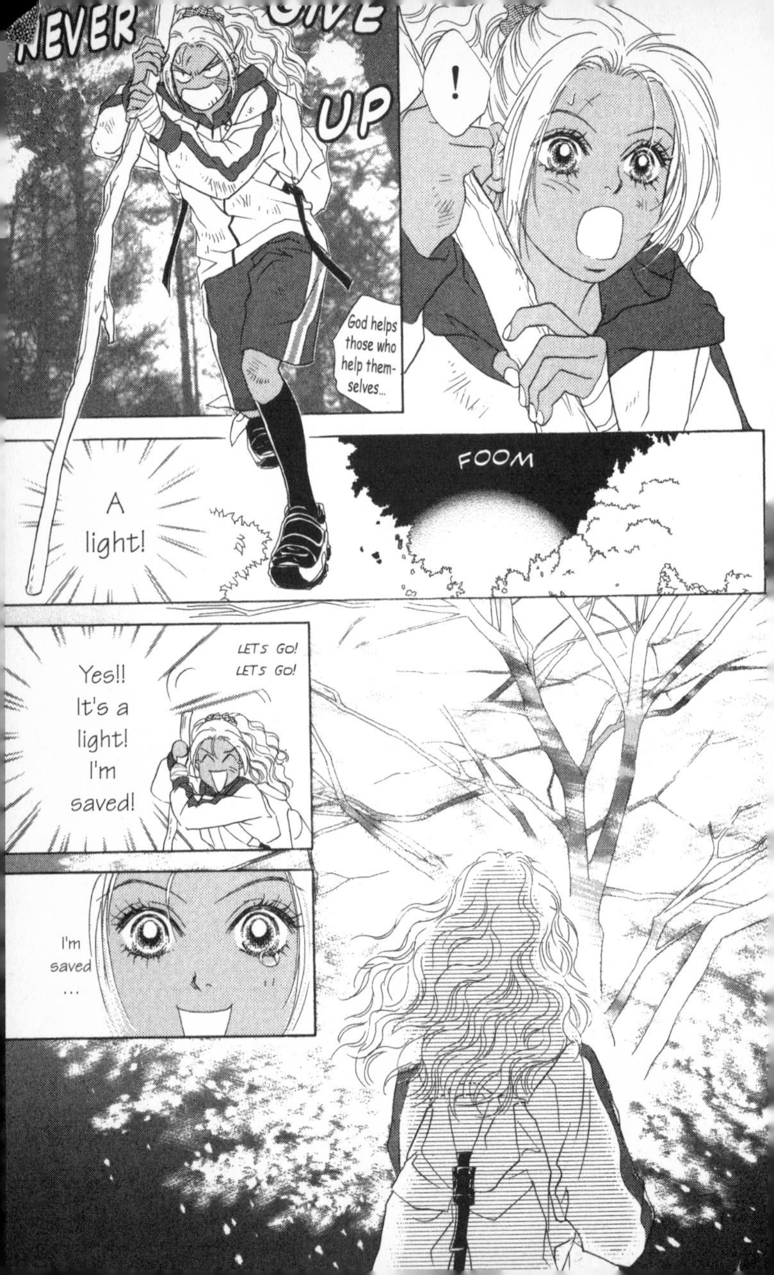
!
NEVER GIVE UP
God helps those who help them-selves...
FOOM
A light!
Yes!! It's a light! I'm saved!
LETS GO! LETS GO!
I'm saved ...

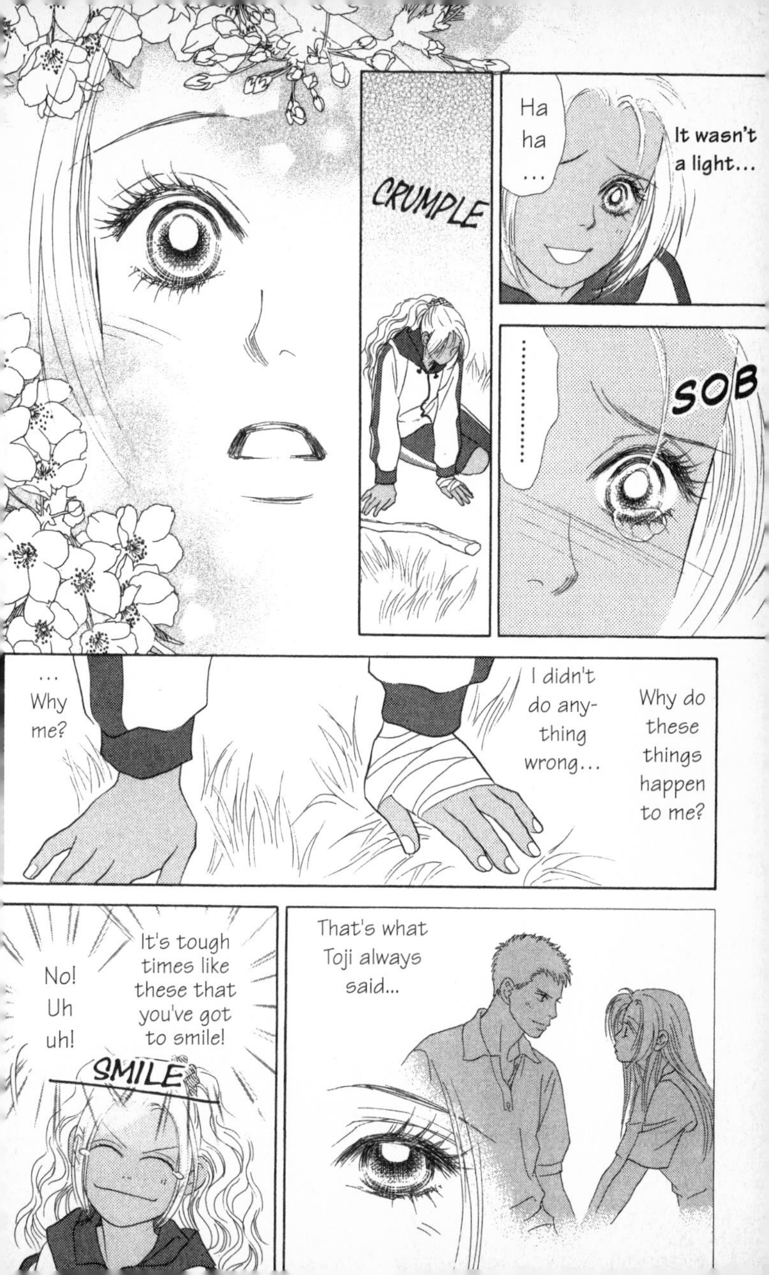
It wasn't a light...
Ha ha ...
SOB
......
CRUMPLE
Why do these things happen to me?
I didn't do any-thing wrong...
... Why me?
That's what Toji always said...
It's tough times like these that you've got to smile!
No! Uh uh!
SMILE

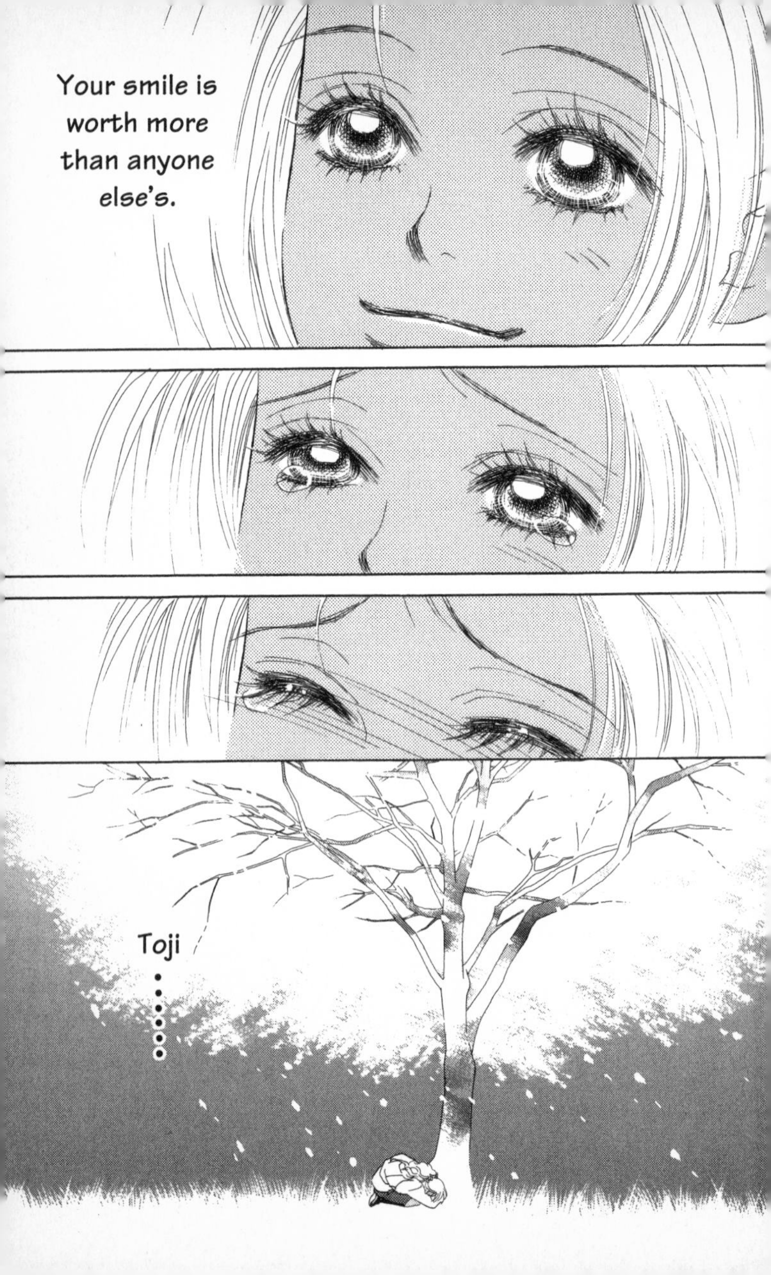
Your smile is worth more than anyone else's.
Toji
......

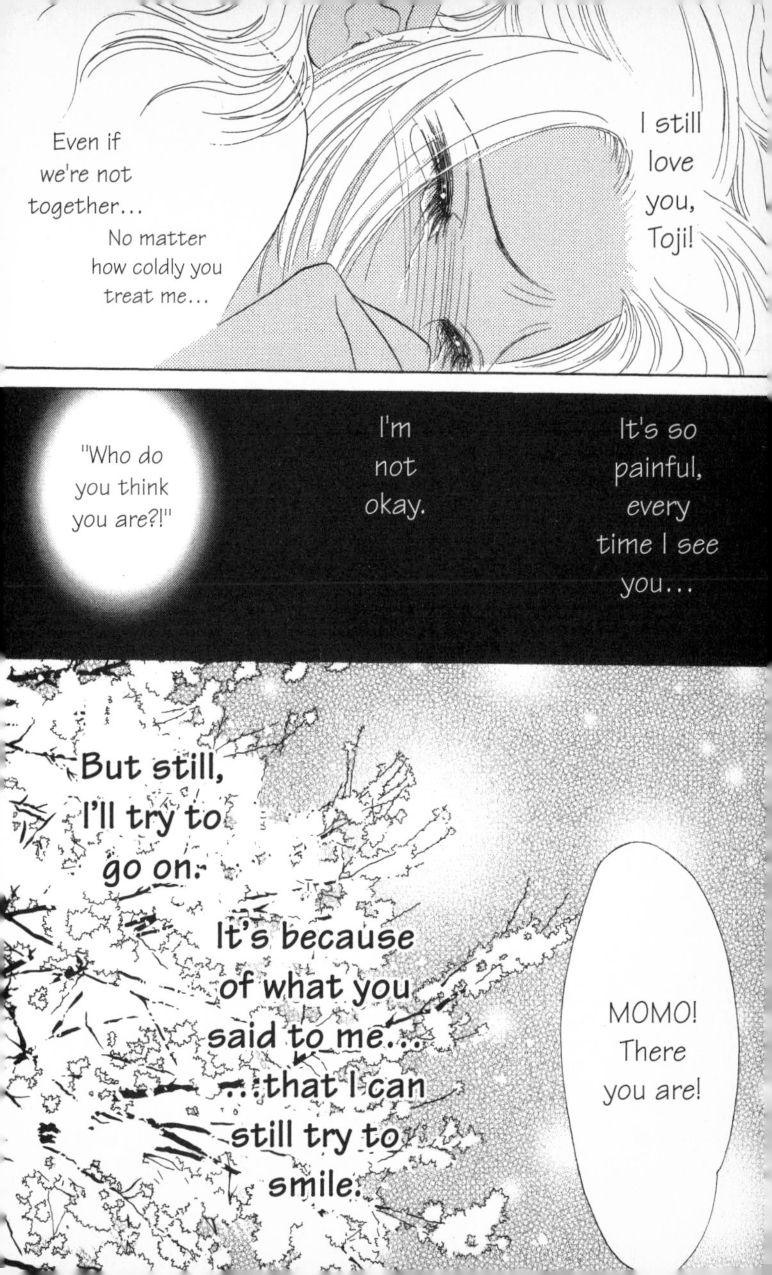
I still love you, Toji!
Even if we're not together…
No matter how coldly you treat me…
It's so painful, every time I see you…
I'm not okay.
"Who do you think you are?!"
But still, I'll try to go on.
It's because of what you said to me…
…that I can still try to smile.
MOMO! There you are!

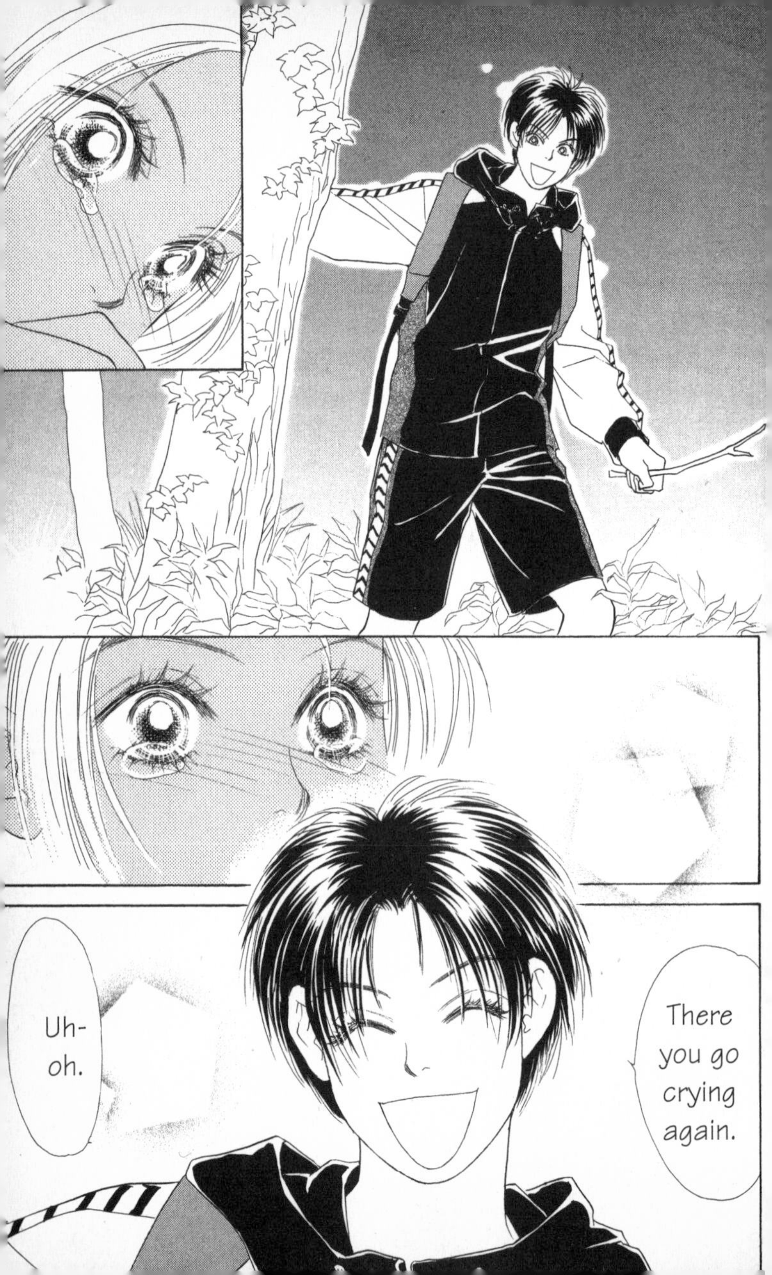
There you go crying again.
Uh-oh.

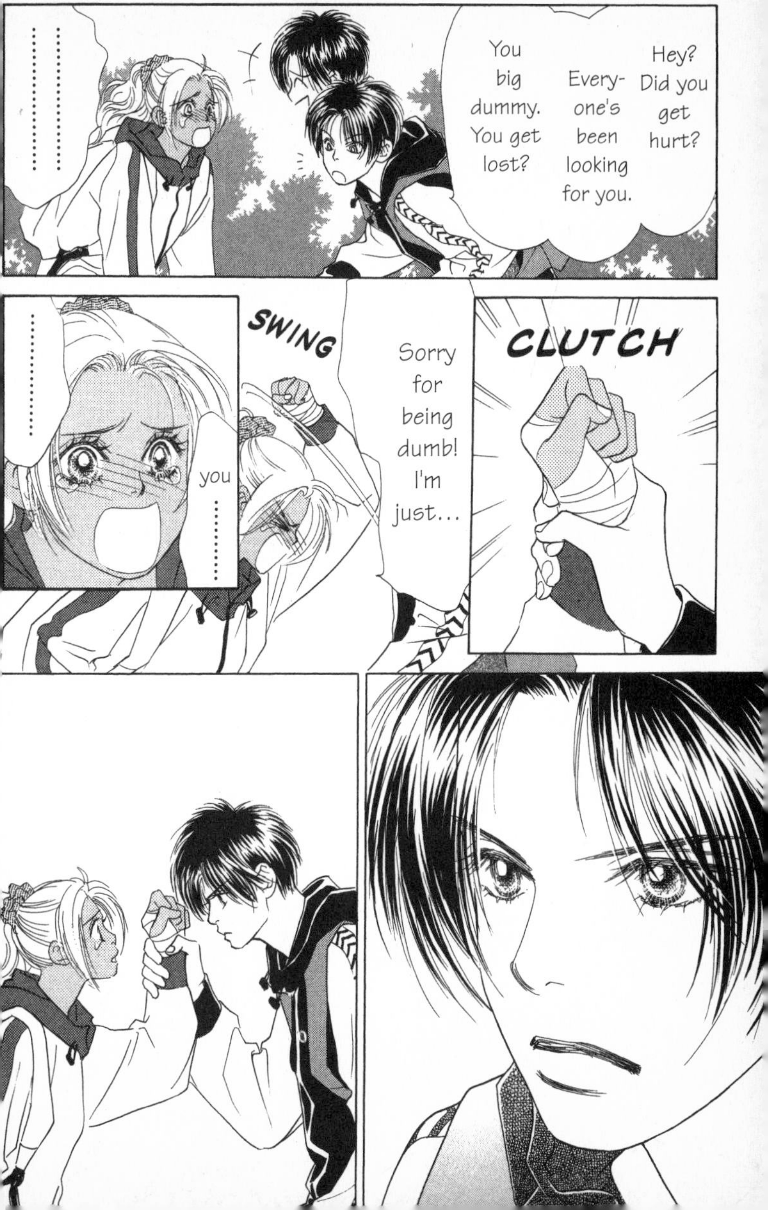

Hey? Did you get hurt?
Every-one's been looking for you.
You big dummy. You get lost?
......
CLUTCH
Sorry for being dumb! I'm just...
SWING
......
you ......

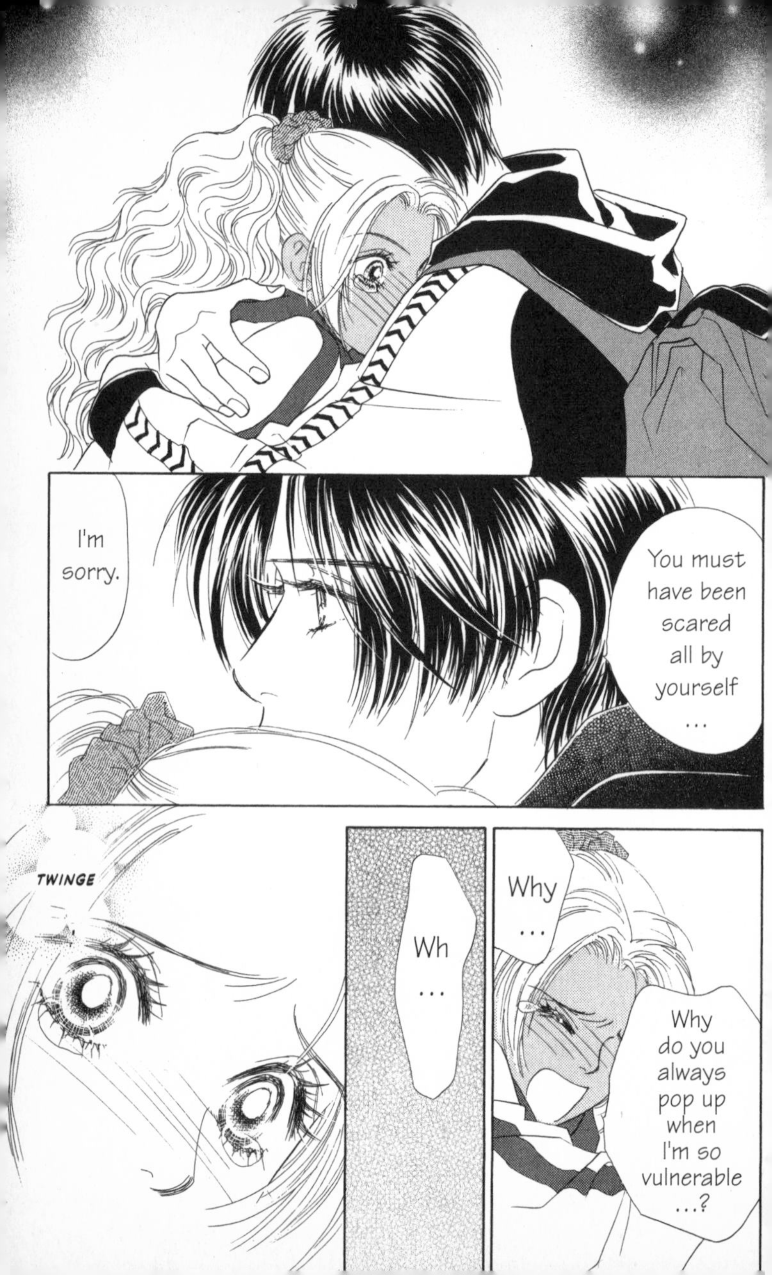
You must have been scared all by yourself ...
I'm sorry.
Why ...
Why do you always pop up when I'm so vulnerable ...?
Wh ...
TWINGE

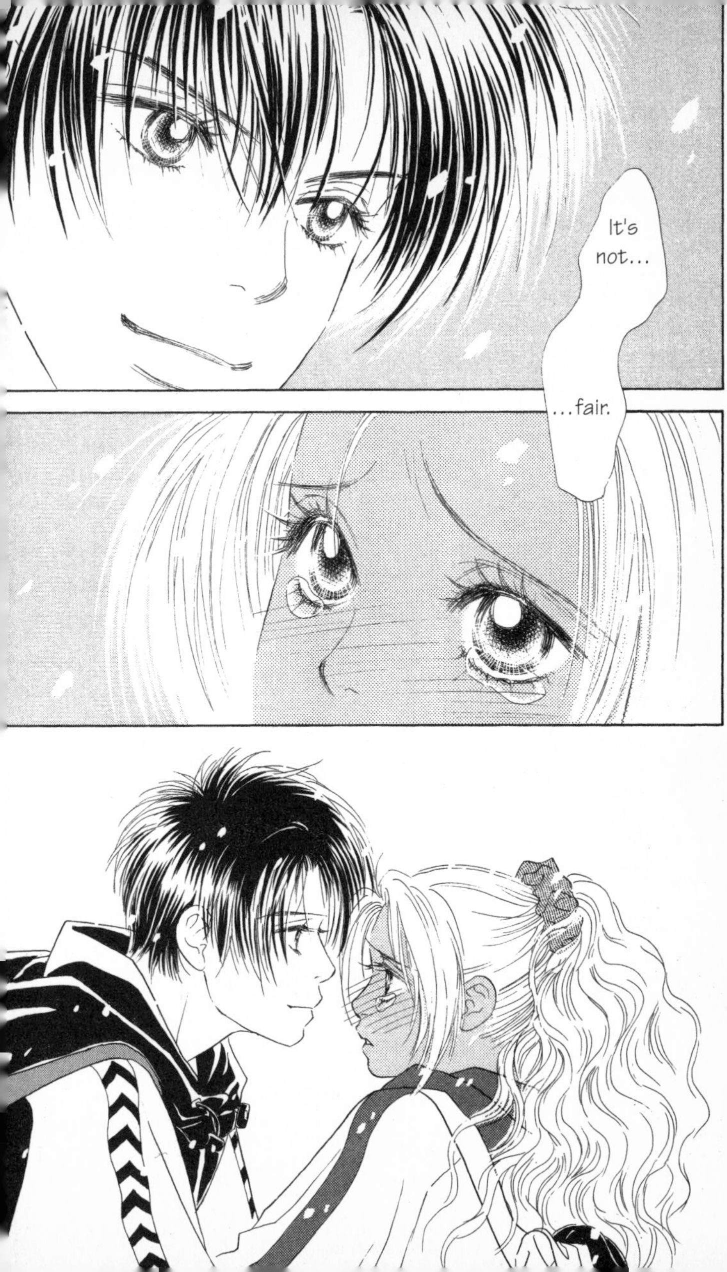
It's not...
...fair.

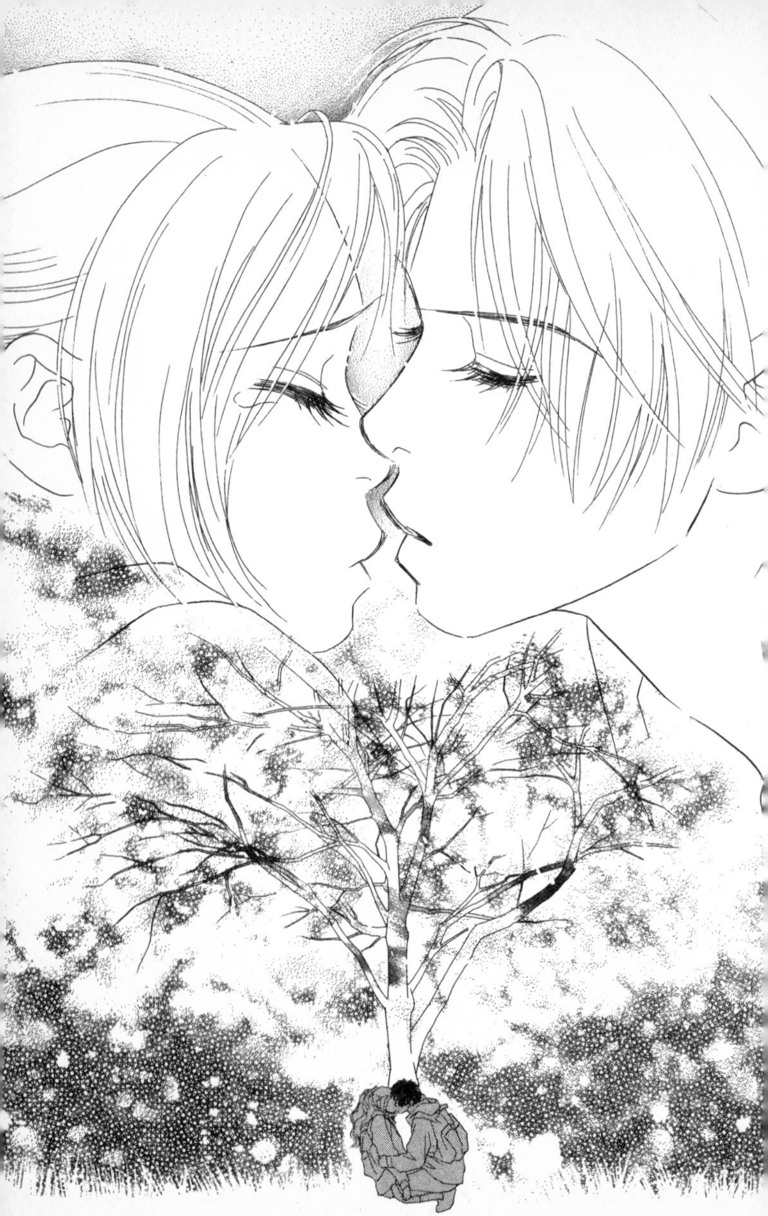

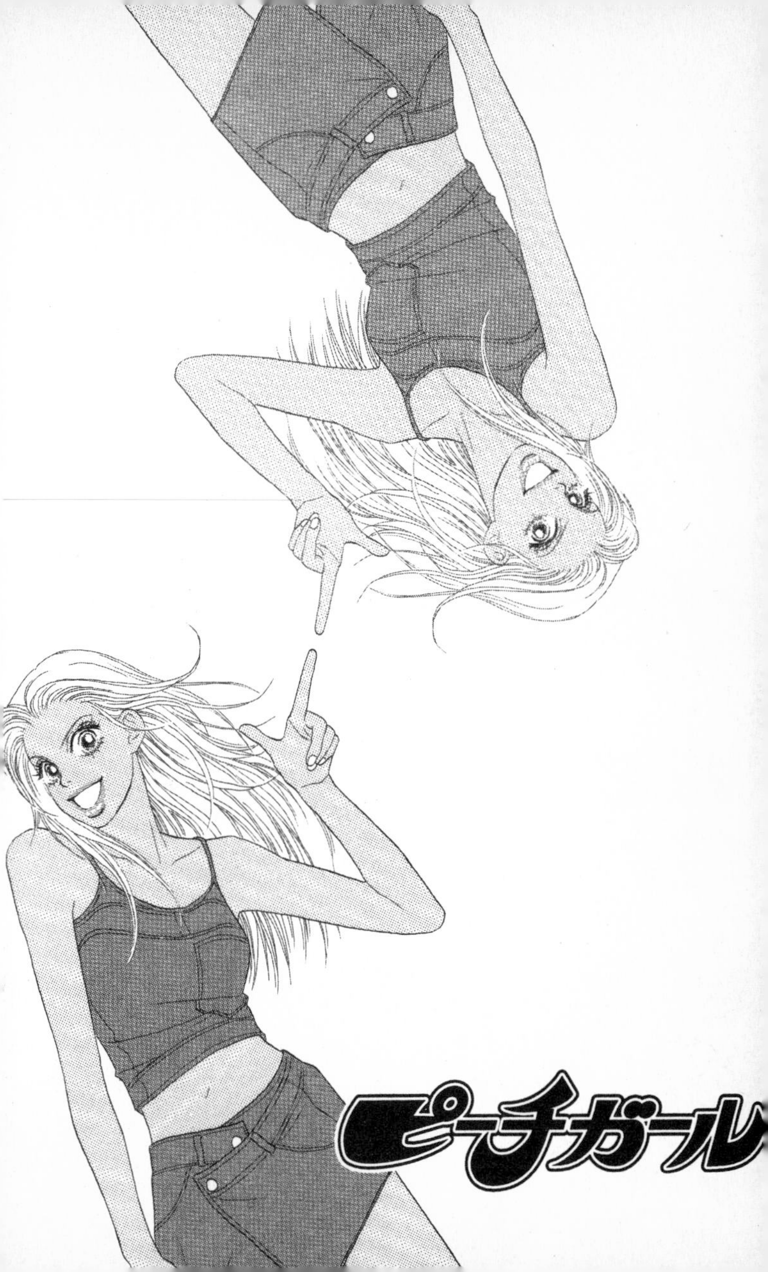
ピーチガール

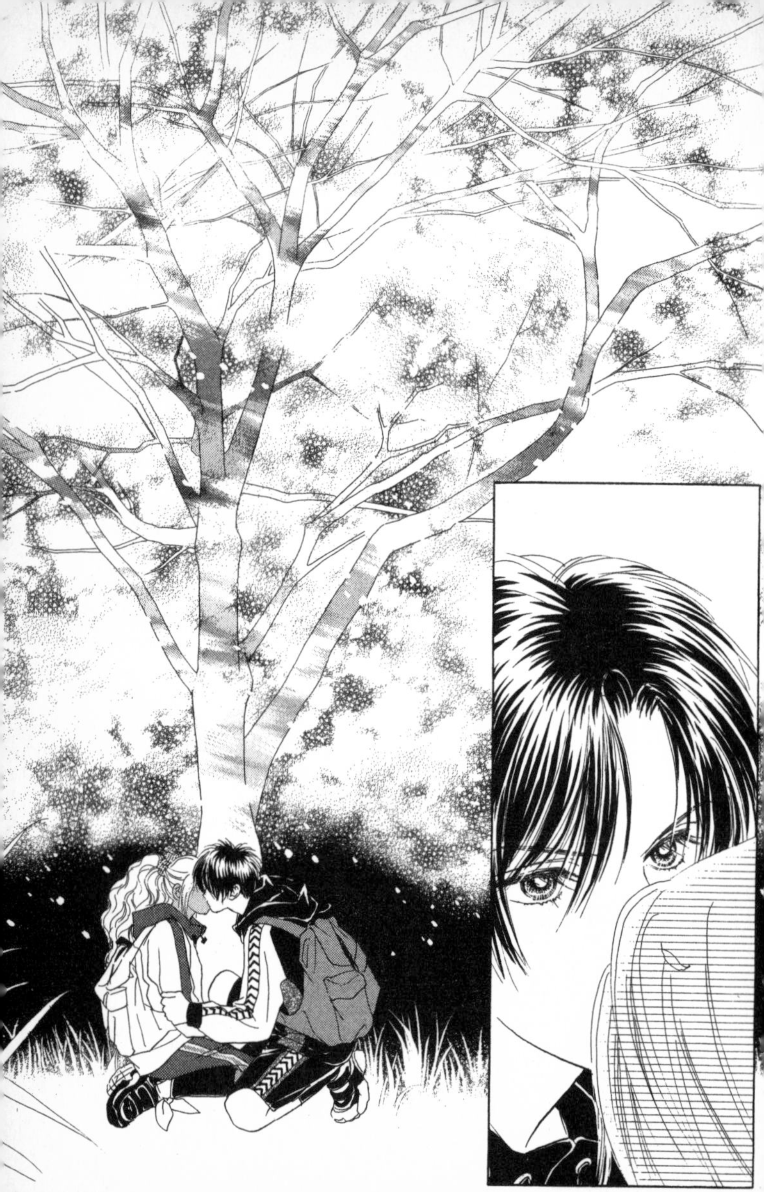

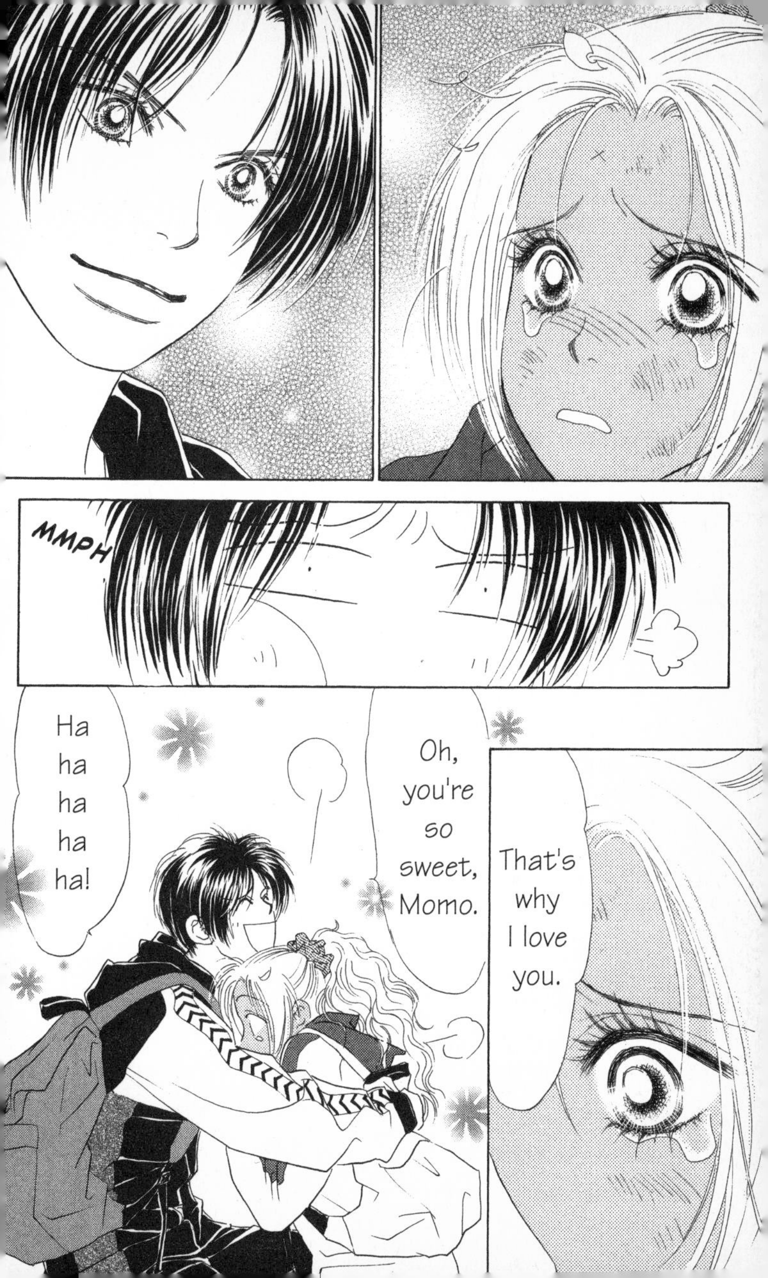
MMPH
That's why I love you.
Oh, you're so sweet, Momo.
Ha ha ha ha ha!

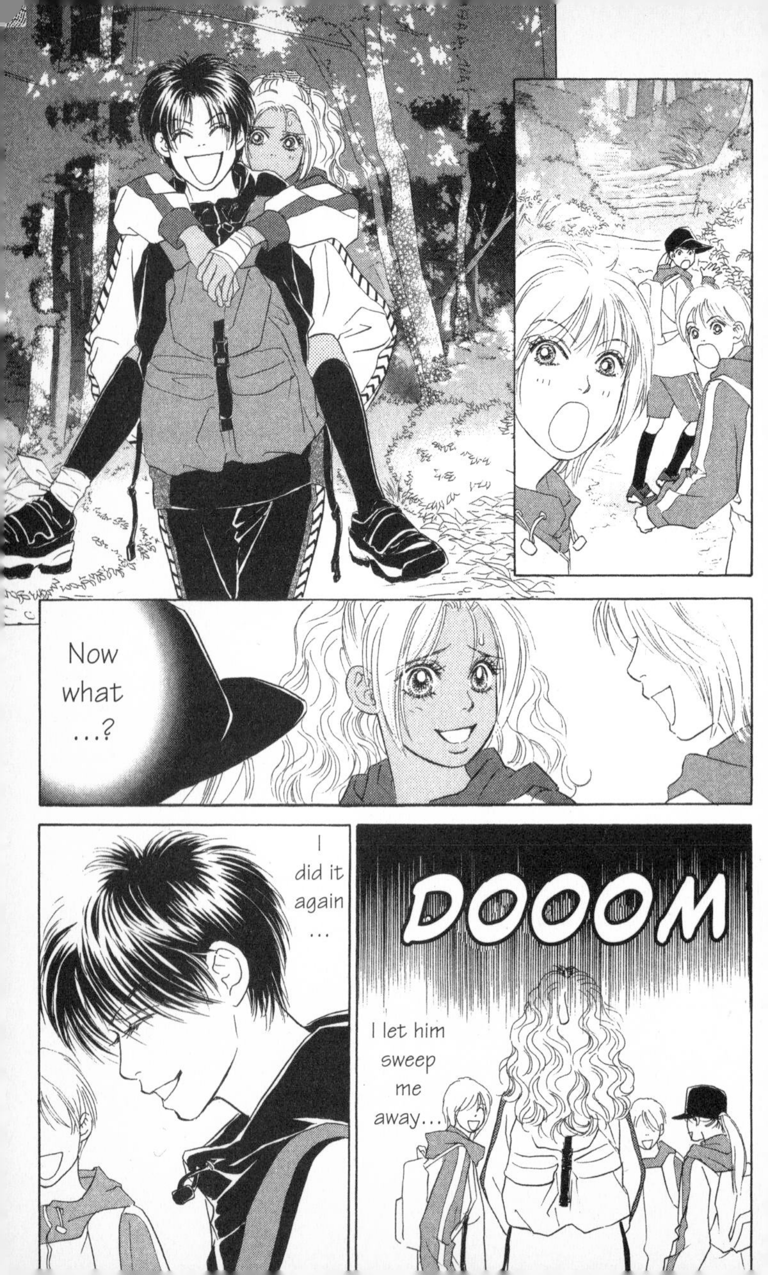
Now what ...?
DOOOM
I let him sweep me away...
I did it again ...

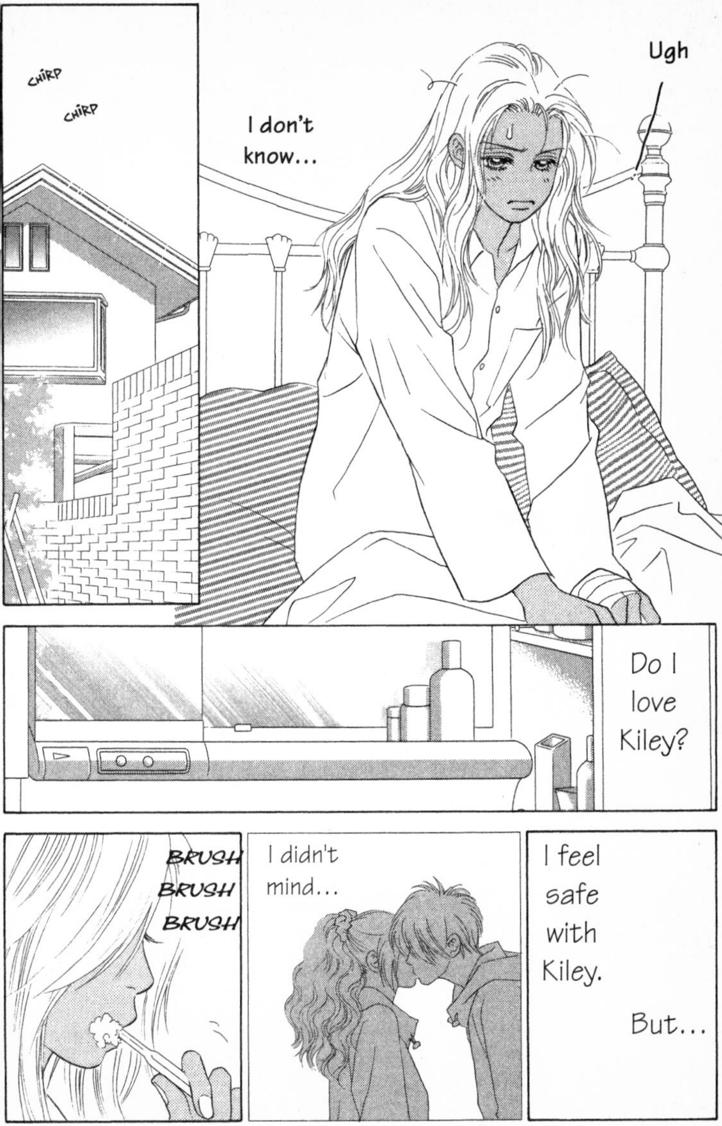
Ugh
I don't know...
CHIRP
CHIRP
Do I love Kiley?
I feel safe with Kiley.
But...
I didn't mind...
BRUSH
BRUSH
BRUSH

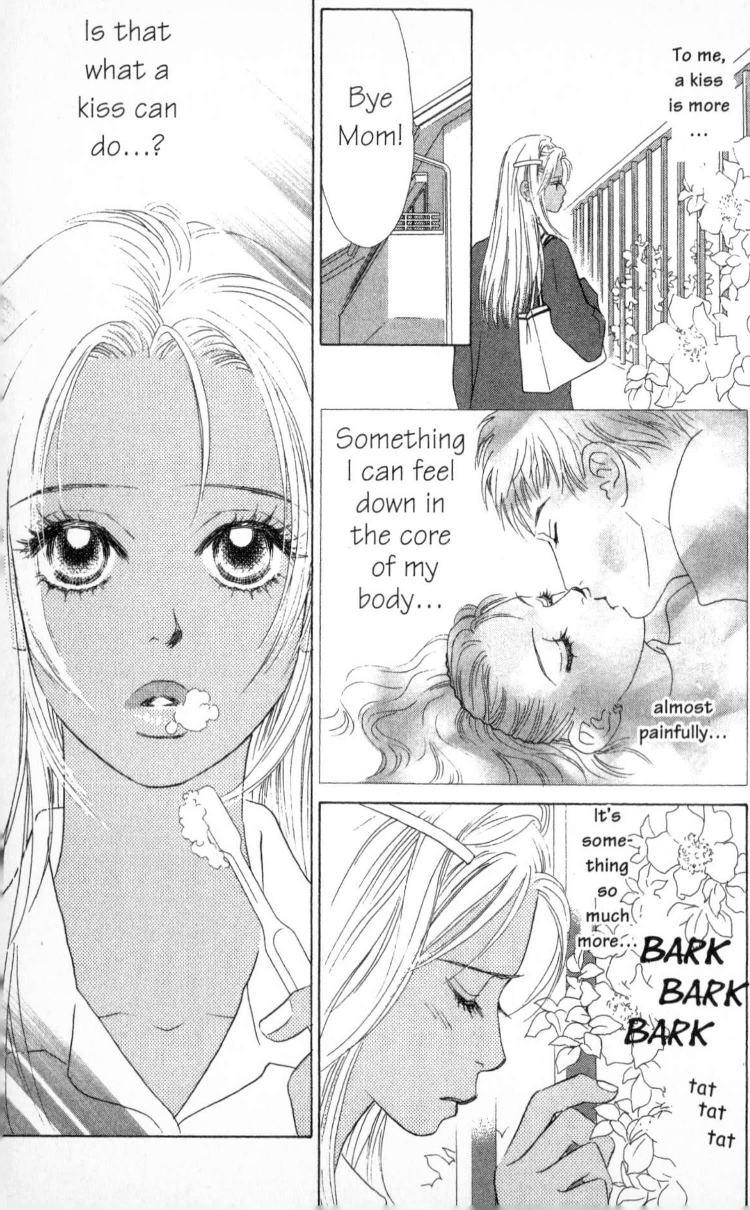

Is that what a kiss can do...?
Bye Mom!
To me, a kiss is more ...
Something I can feel down in the core of my body...
almost painfully...
It's something so much more...
BARK BARK BARK
tat tat tat

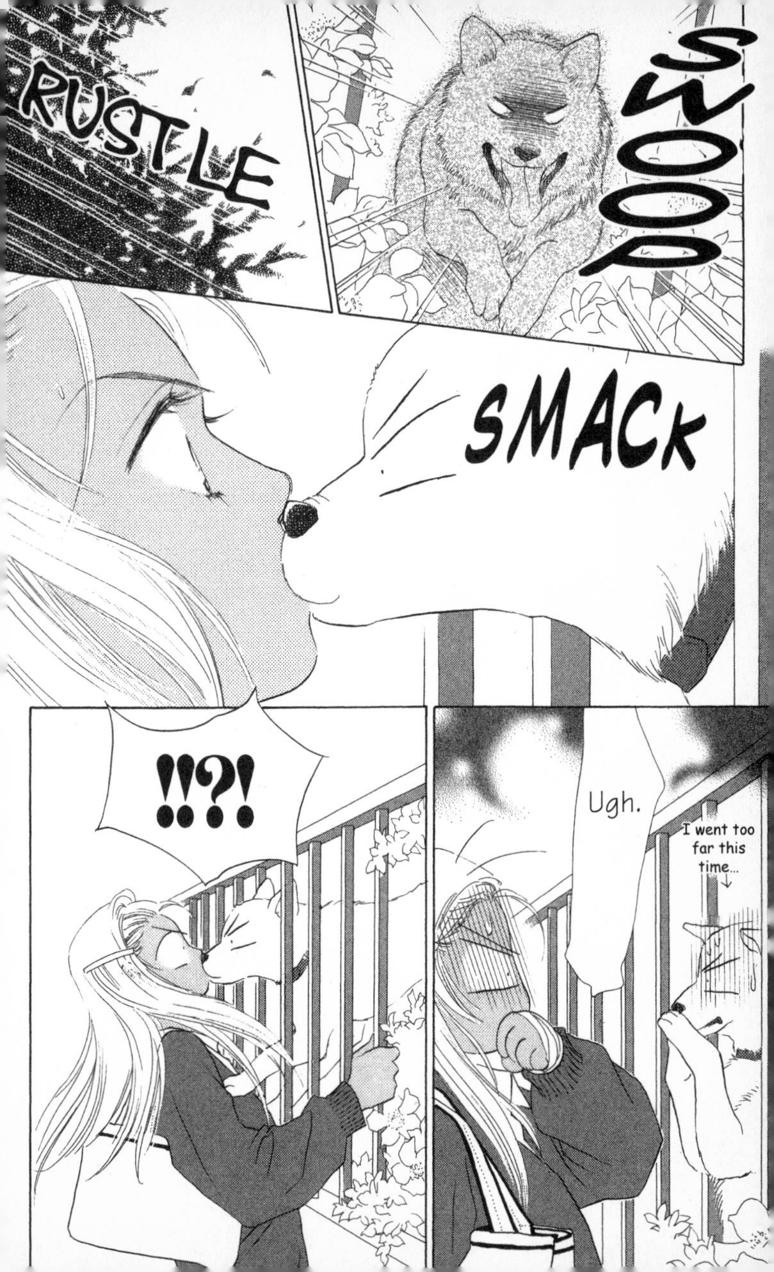
RUSTLE
SWOOP
SMACK
!!?!
Ugh.
I went too far this time...

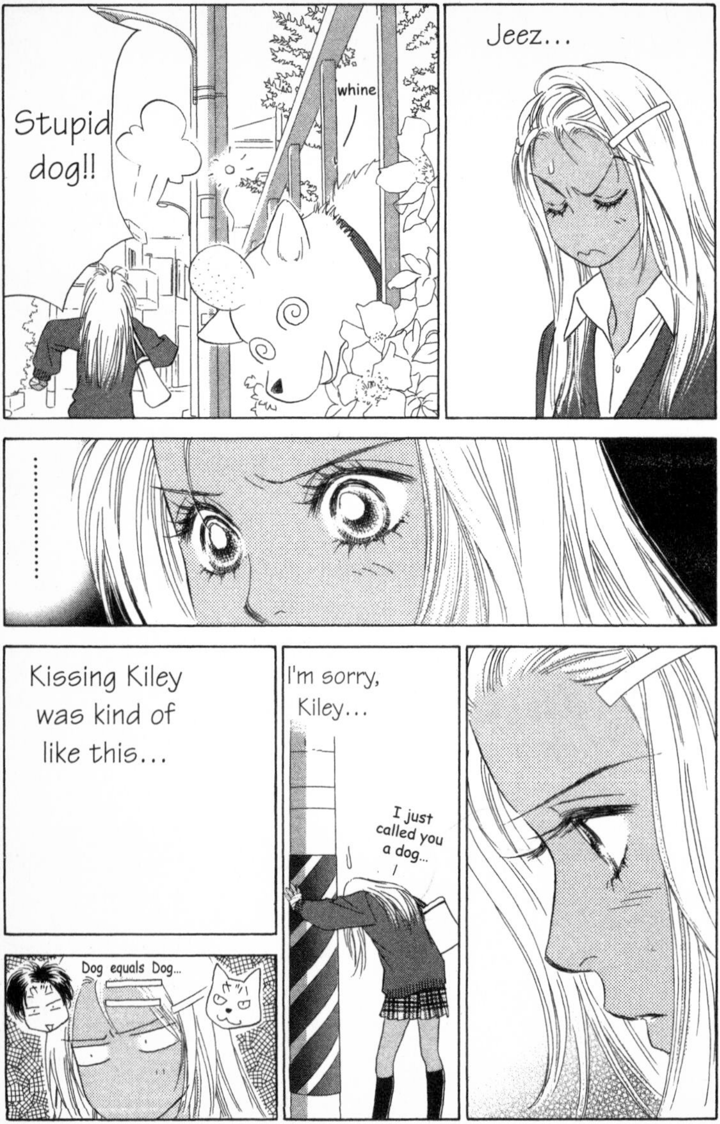
Stupid dog!!
whine
Jeez...
....
Kissing Kiley was kind of like this...
Dog equals Dog...
I'm sorry, Kiley...
I just called you a dog...

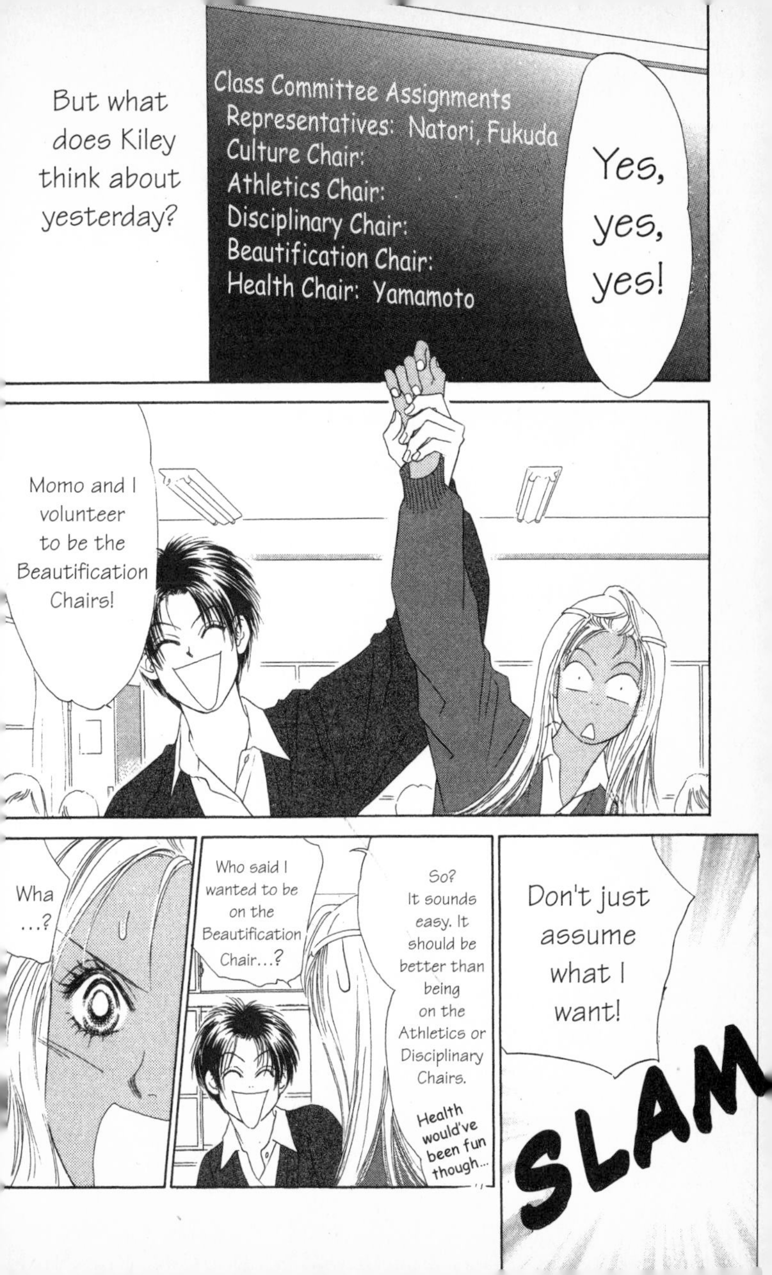
But what does Kiley think about yesterday?
Class Committee Assignments
Representatives: Natori, Fukuda
Culture Chair:
Athletics Chair:
Disciplinary Chair:
Beautification Chair:
Health Chair: Yamamoto
Yes, yes, yes!
Momo and I volunteer to be the Beautification Chairs!
Wha ...?
Who said I wanted to be on the Beautification Chair...?
So? It sounds easy. It should be better than being on the Athletics or Disciplinary Chairs.
Health would've been fun though...
Don't just assume what I want!
SLAM

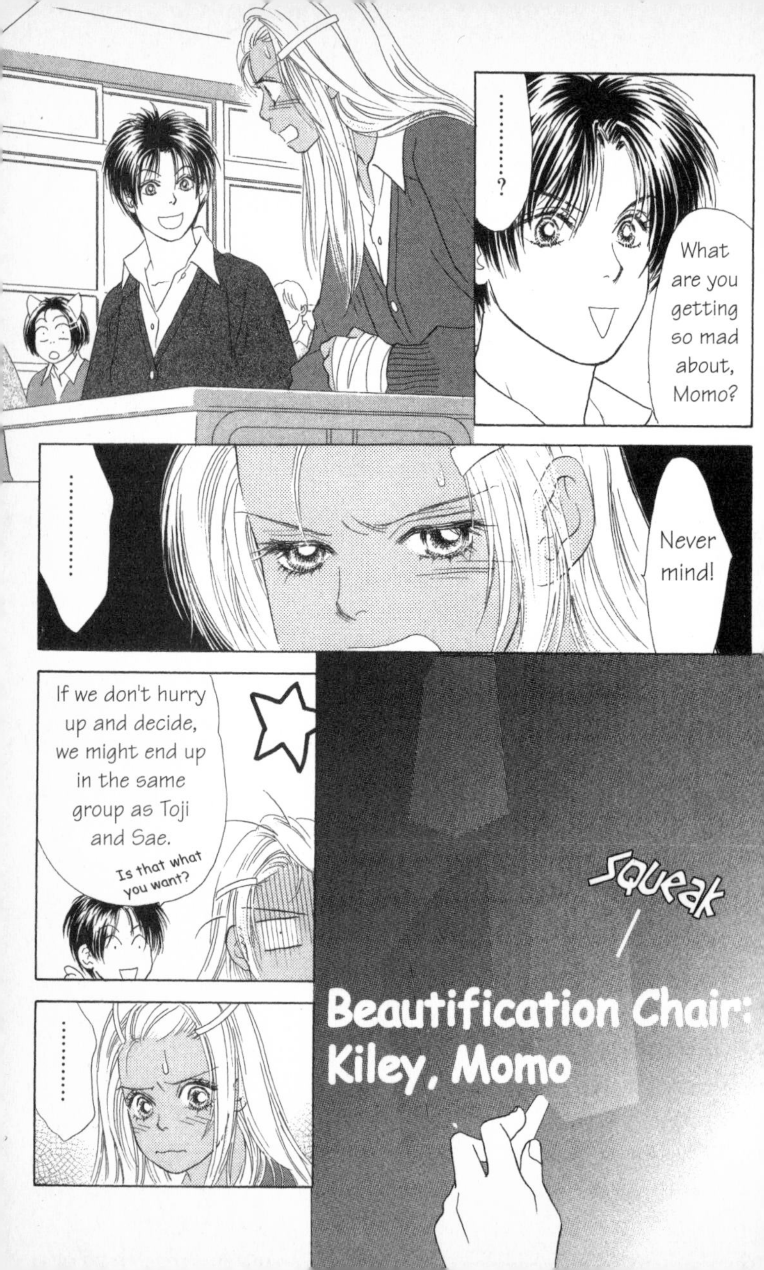
......?
What are you getting so mad about, Momo?
....
Never mind!
If we don't hurry up and decide, we might end up in the same group as Toji and Sae.
Is that what you want?
....
SQUEAK
Beautification Chair: Kiley, Momo

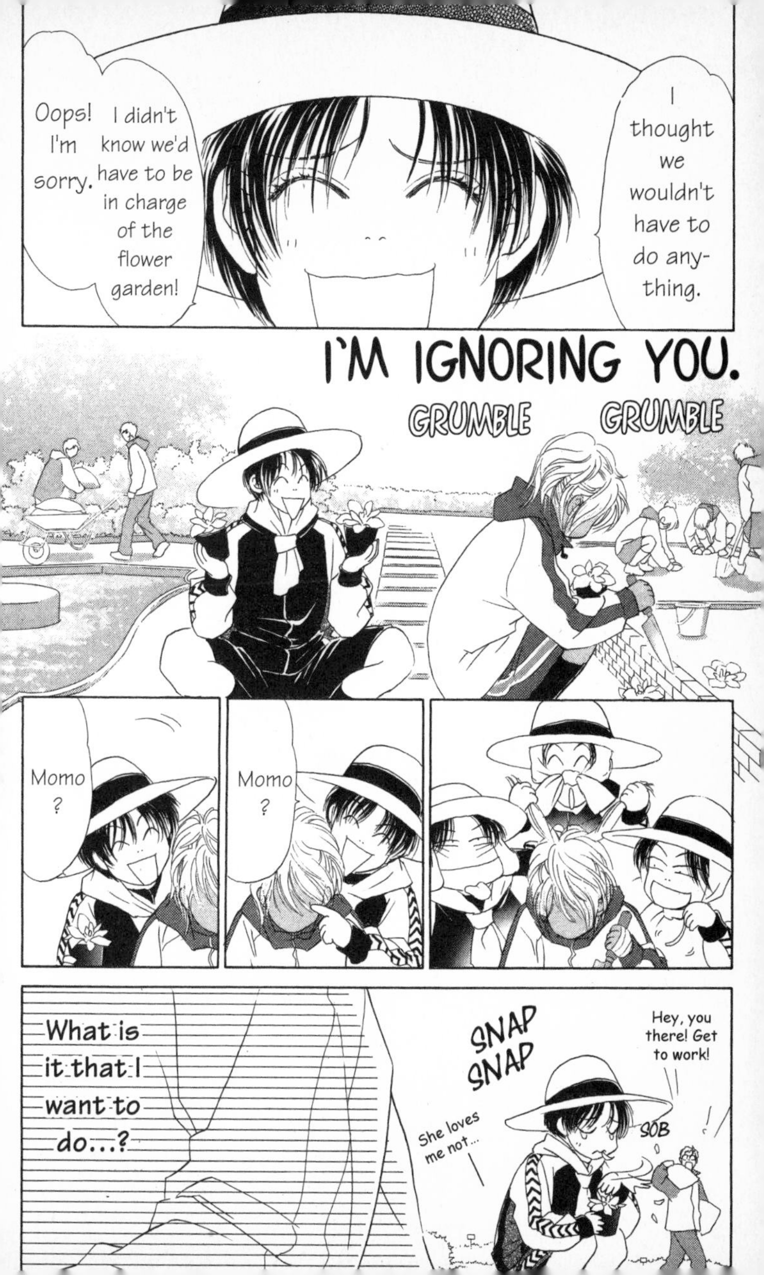
I thought we wouldn't have to do anything.
Oops! I'm sorry.
I didn't know we'd have to be in charge of the flower garden!
I'M IGNORING YOU.
GRUMBLE GRUMBLE
Momo?
Momo?
Hey, you there! Get to work!
SOB
She loves me not...
SNAP SNAP
What is it that I want to do...?

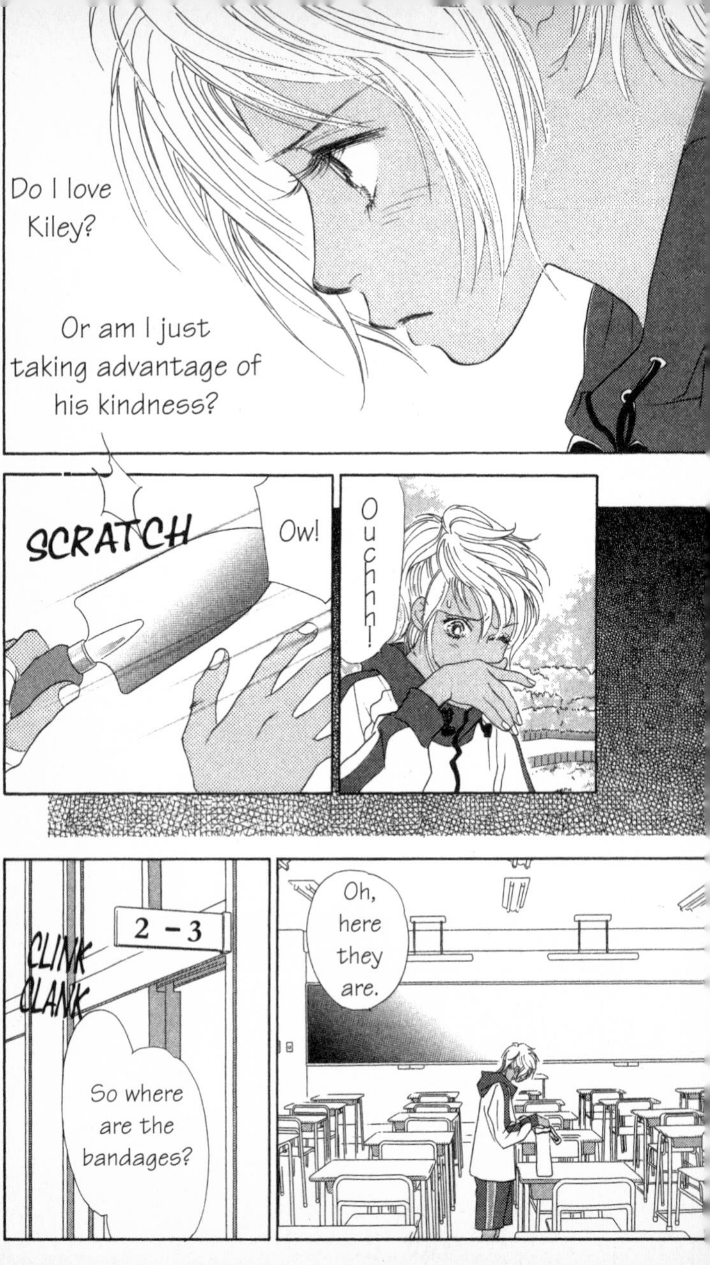
Do I love Kiley?
Or am I just taking advantage of his kindness?
SCRATCH
Ow!
Ouchhh!
CLINK CLANK
2 - 3
So where are the bandages?
Oh, here they are.

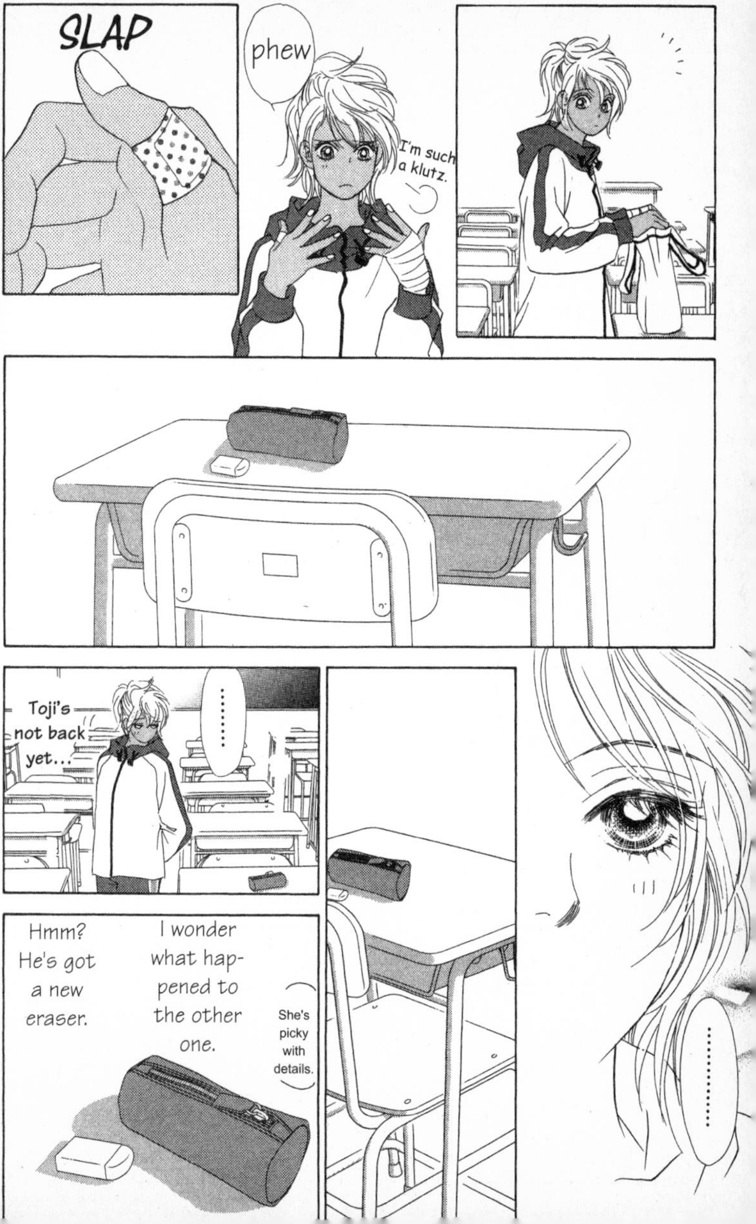
phew
I'm such a klutz.
SLAP
....
....
Toji's not back yet...
Hmm? He's got a new eraser.
I wonder what happened to the other one.
She's picky with details.

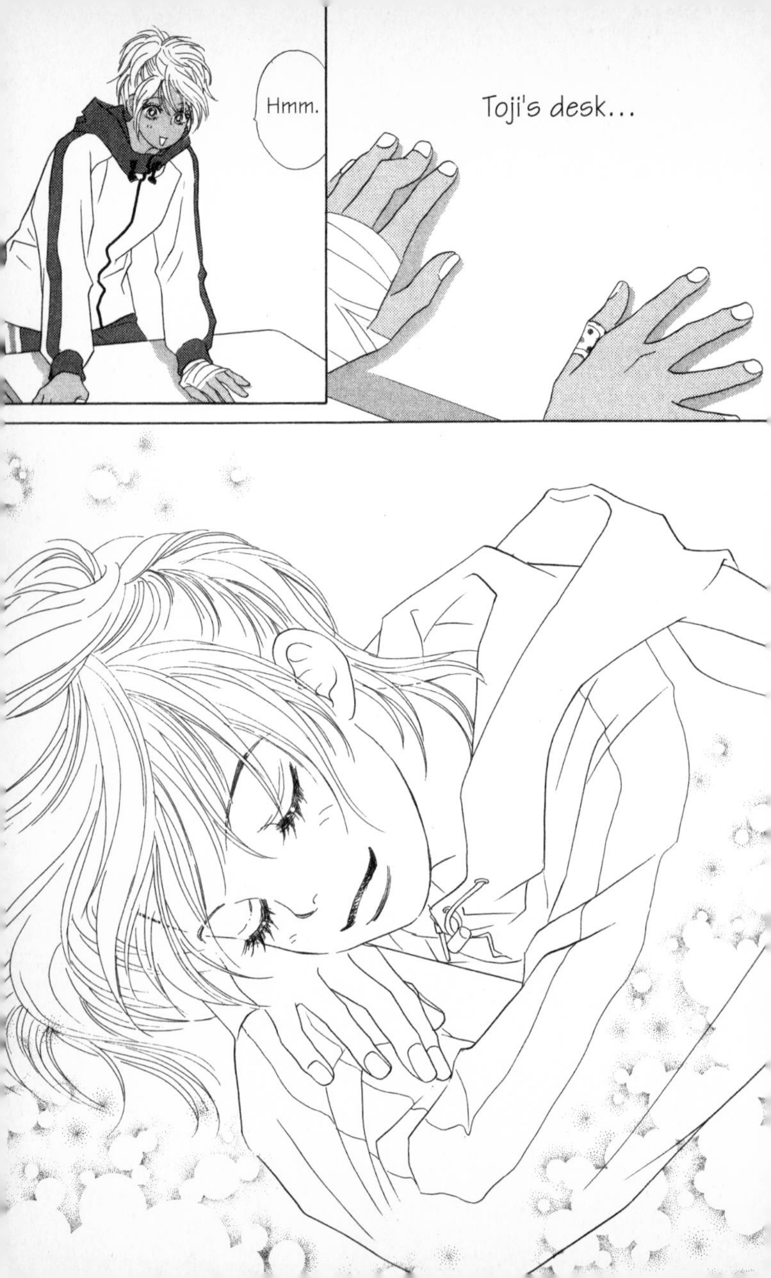
Toji's desk...
Hmm.

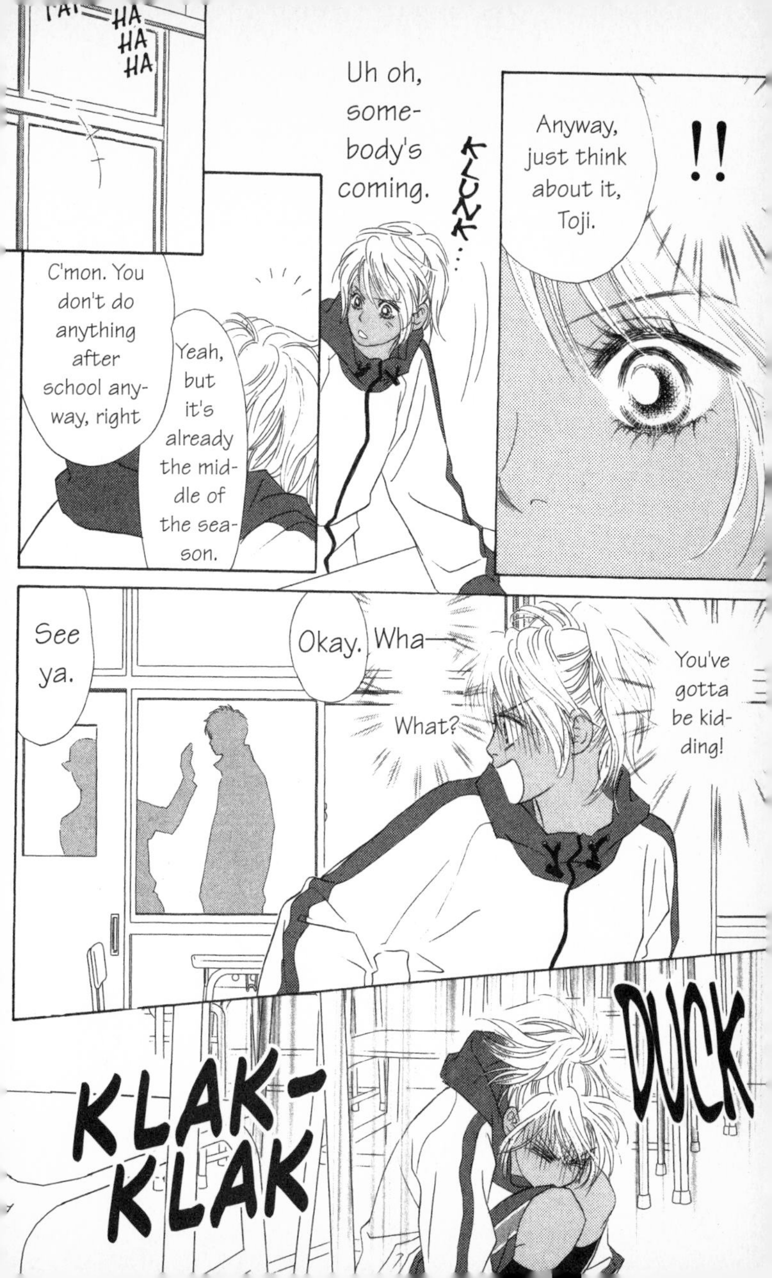
Anyway, just think about it, Toji.
!!
Uh oh, somebody's coming.
KLUNK...
HA HA HA
C'mon. You don't do anything after school anyway, right
Yeah, but it's already the middle of the season.
You've gotta be kidding!
Wha—
What?
Okay.
See ya.
DUCK
KLAK-KLAK

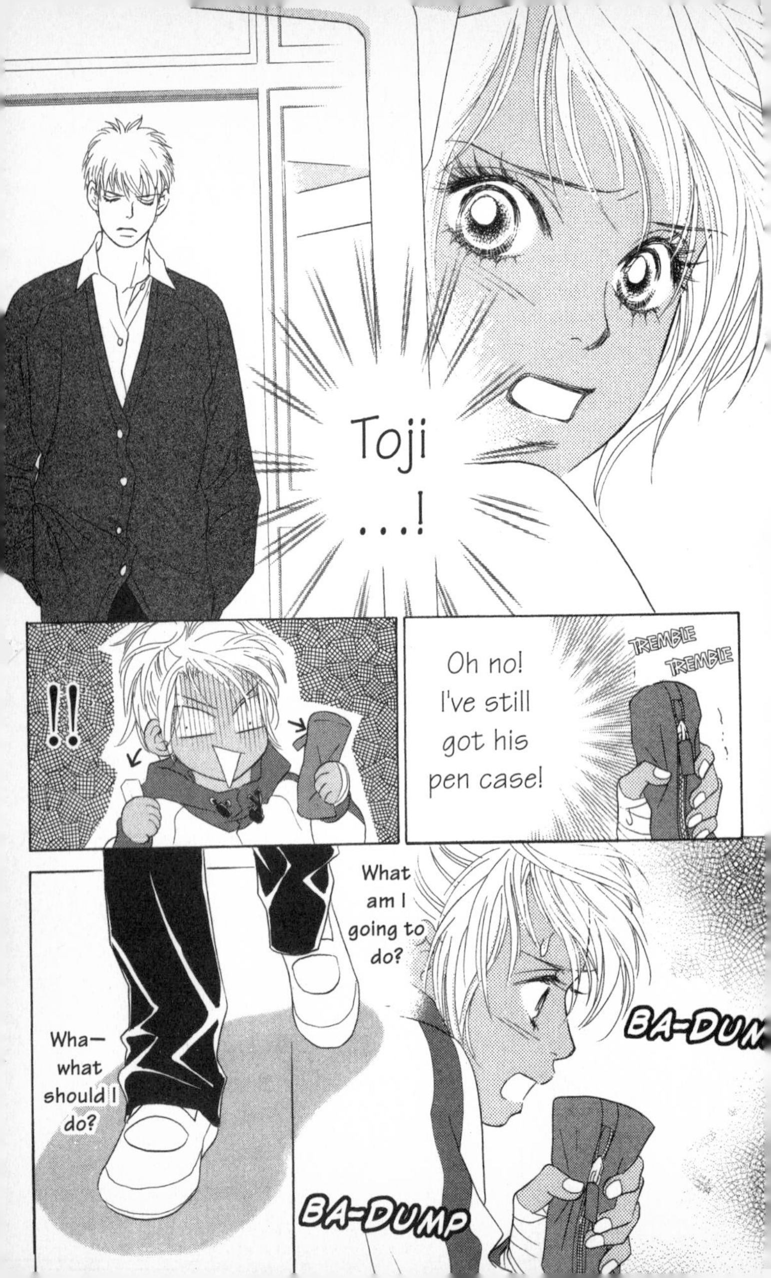
Toji ...!
Oh no! I've still got his pen case!
TREMBLE TREMBLE
!!
What am I going to do?
BA-DUM
BA-DUMP
Wha— what should I do?

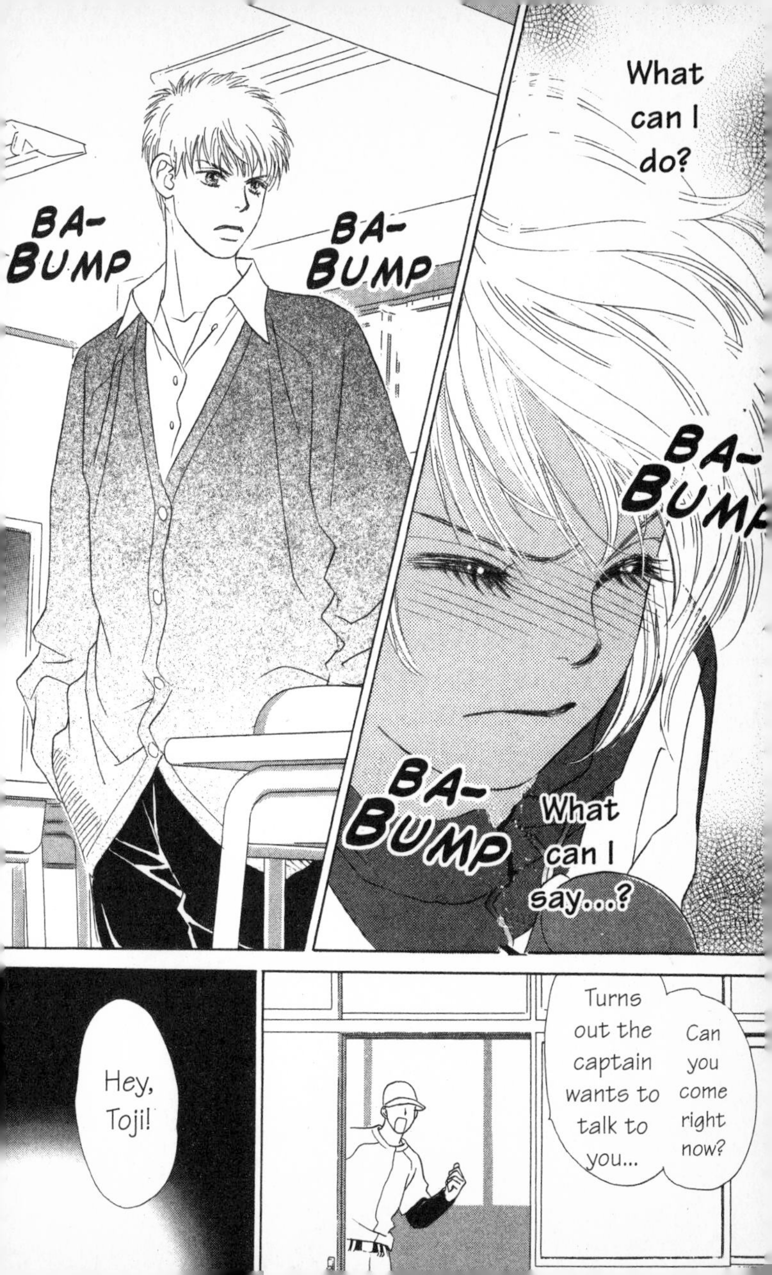
BA-BUMP
BA-BUMP
What can I do?
BA-BUMP
BA-BUMP
What can I say...?
Hey, Toji!
Turns out the captain wants to talk to you...
Can you come right now?

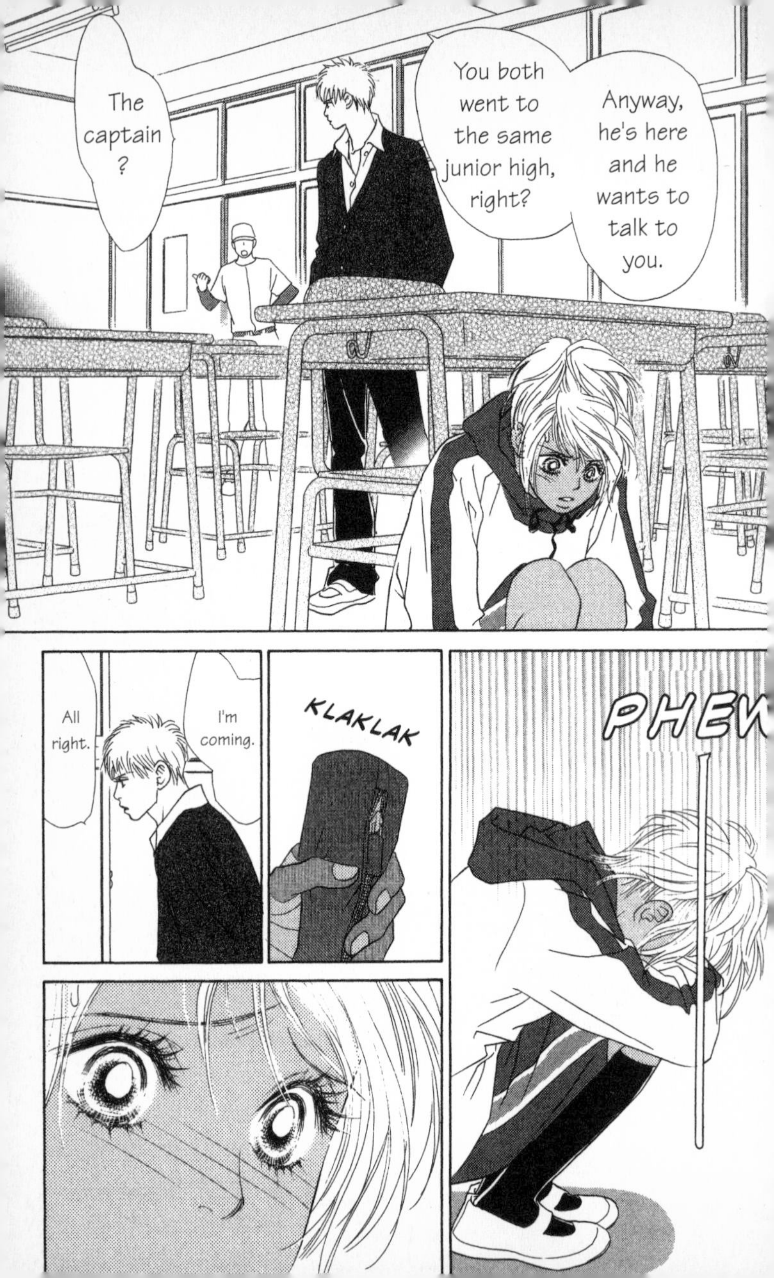
The captain?
You both went to the same junior high, right?
Anyway, he's here and he wants to talk to you.
All right.
I'm coming.
KLAKLAK
PHEW

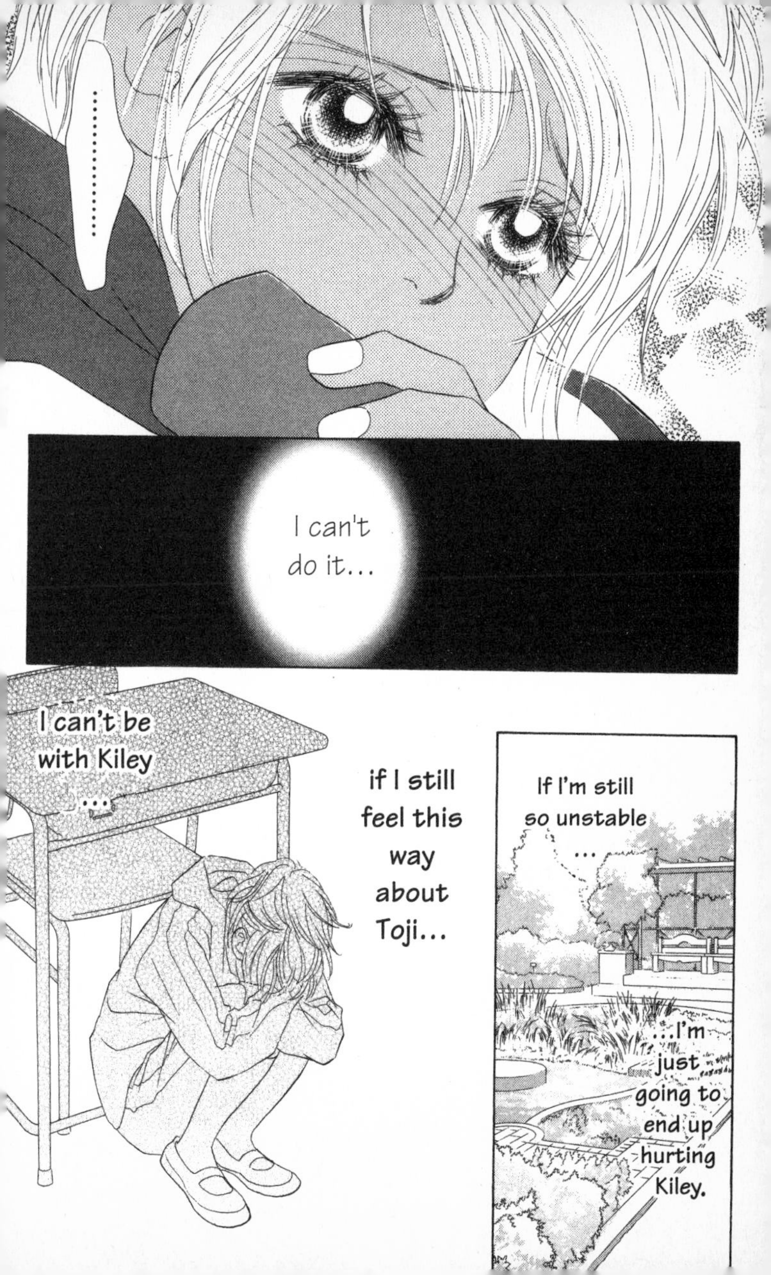
......
I can't do it...
I can't be with Kiley ...
if I still feel this way about Toji...
If I'm still so unstable ...
...I'm just going to end up hurting Kiley.

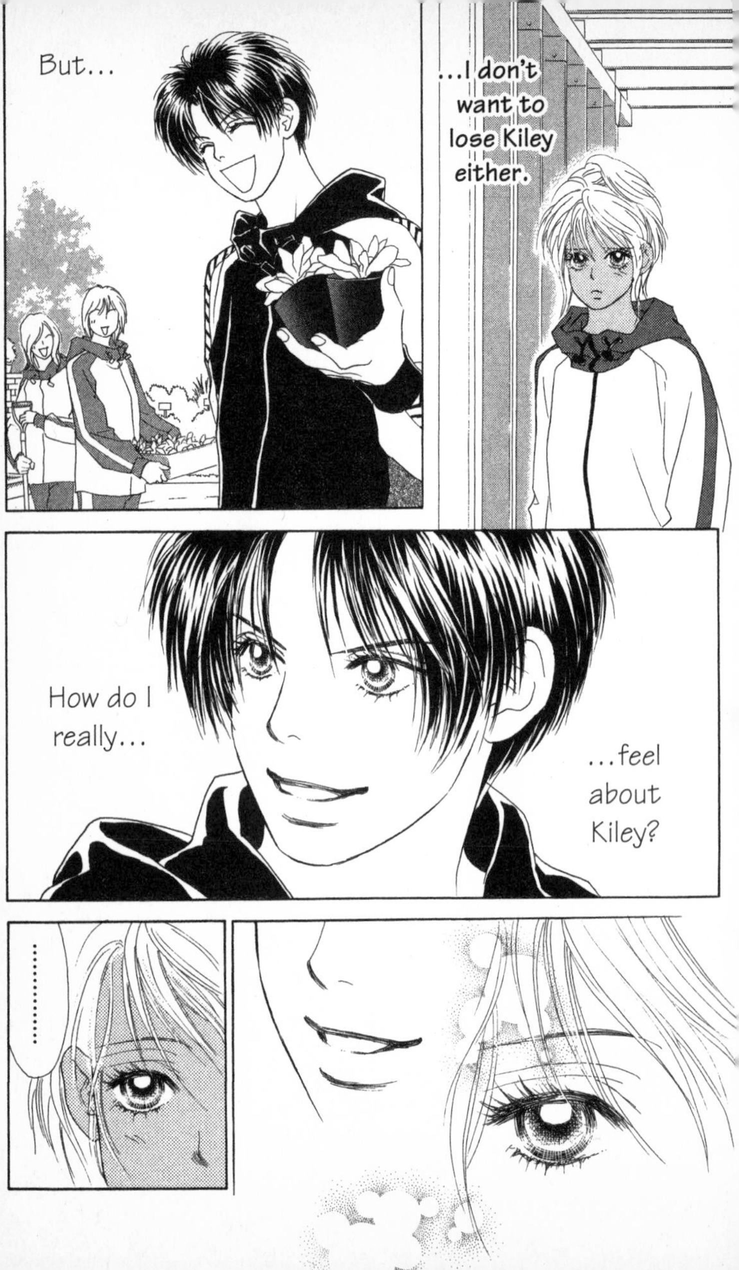
But...
...I don't want to lose Kiley either.
How do I really...
...feel about Kiley?
....

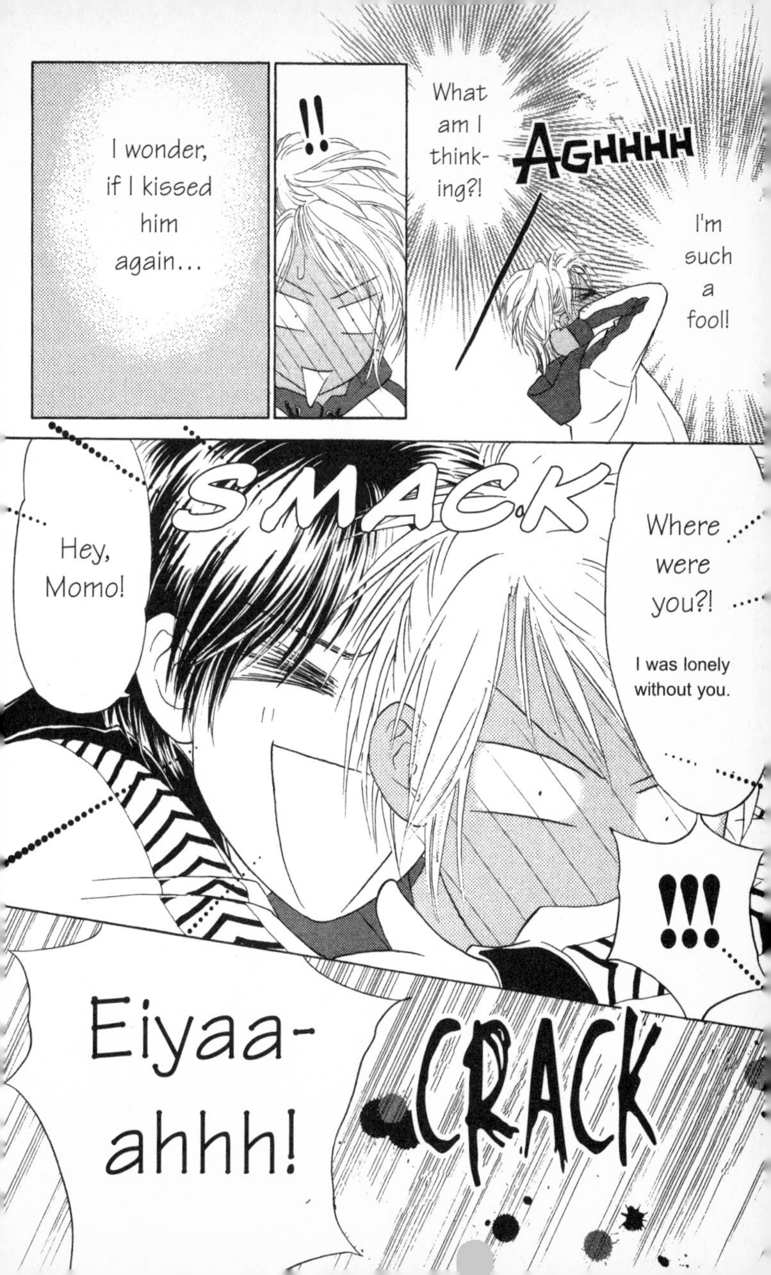
I wonder, if I kissed him again...
!!
What am I thinking?!
AGHHHH
I'm such a fool!
SMACK
Hey, Momo!
Where were you?!
I was lonely without you.
!!!
Eiyaa-ahhh!
CRACK

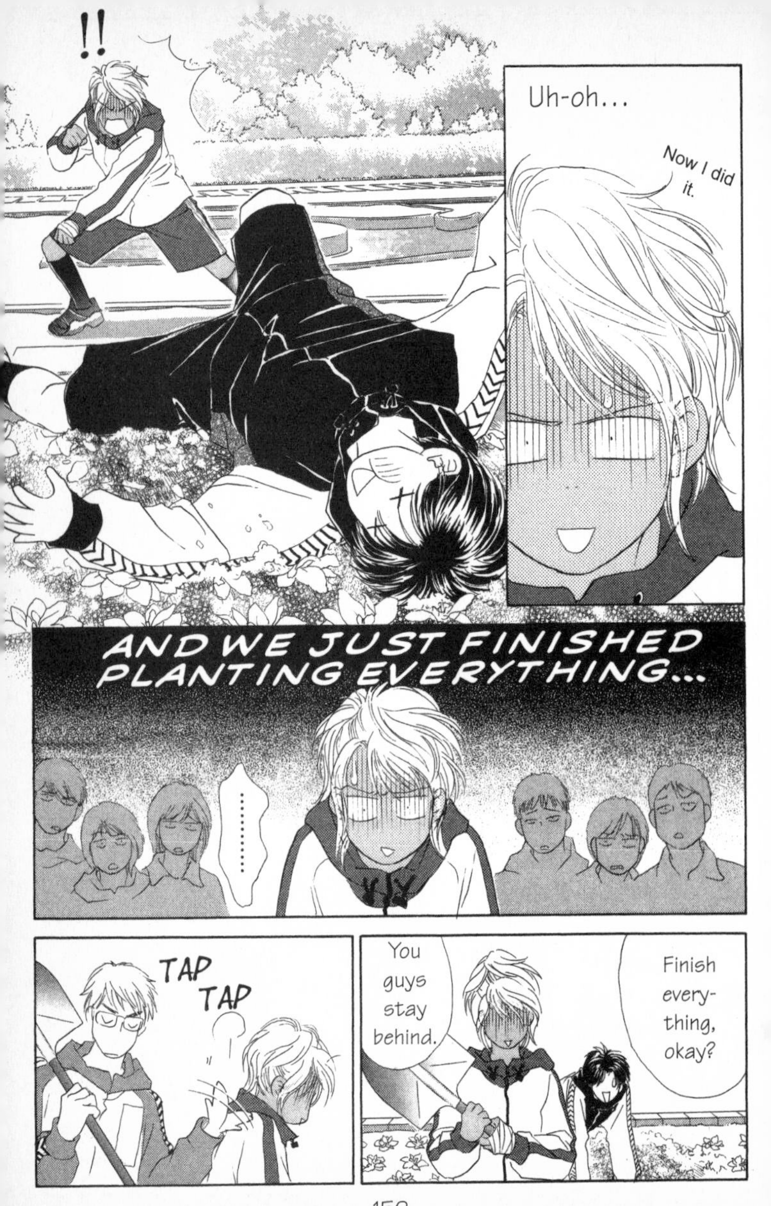
Uh-oh...
Now I did it.
!!
AND WE JUST FINISHED PLANTING EVERYTHING...
....
Finish every-thing, okay?
You guys stay behind.
TAP TAP

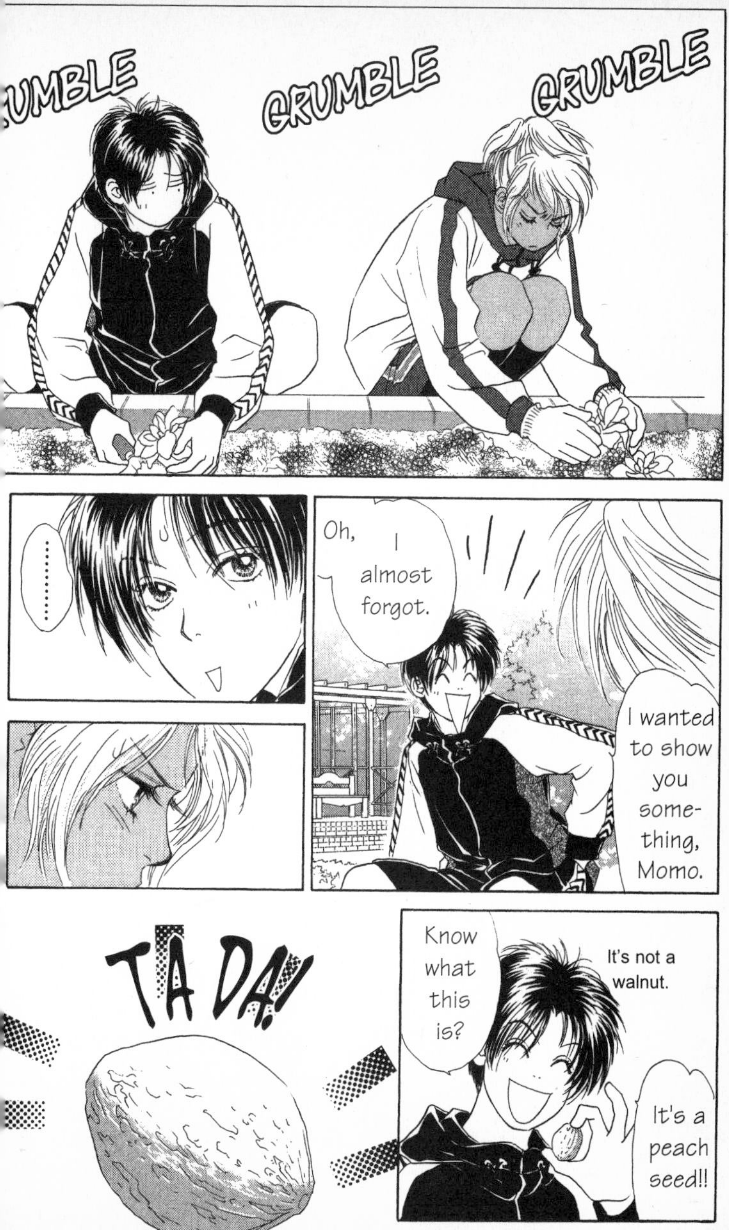
GRUMBLE
GRUMBLE
UMBLE
Oh, I almost forgot.
I wanted to show you something, Momo.
......
Know what this is?
It's not a walnut.
It's a peach seed!!
TA DA!

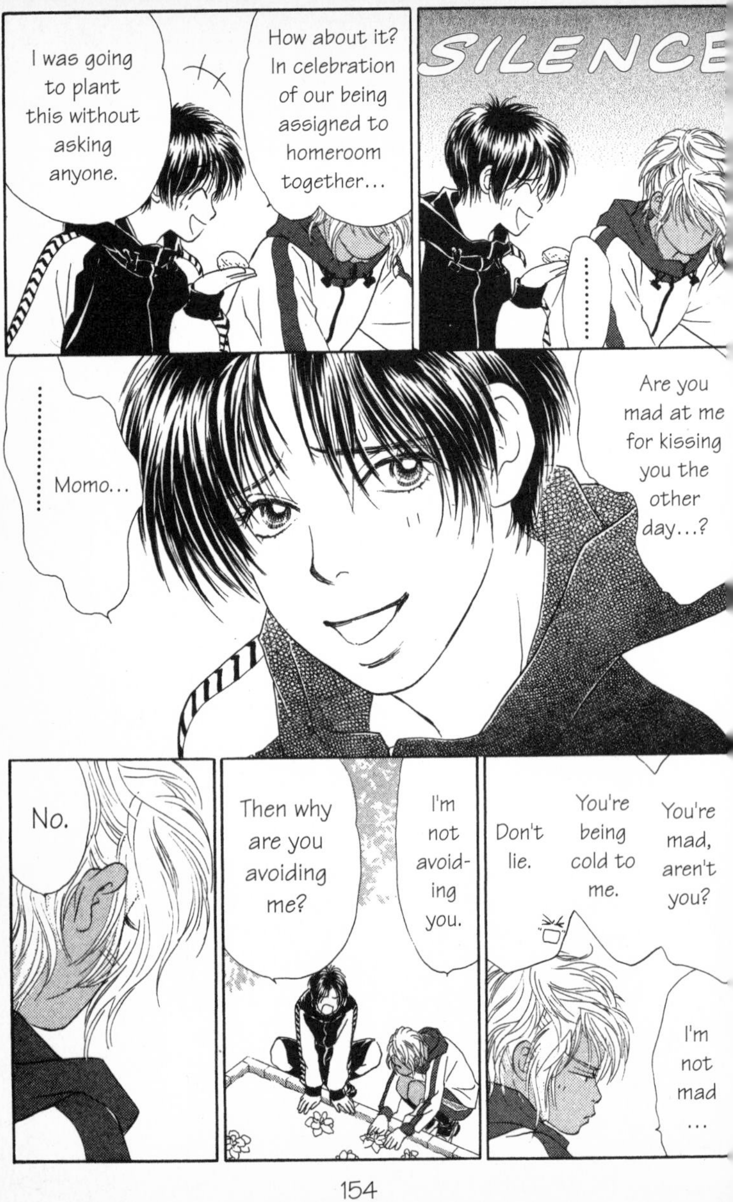
I was going to plant this without asking anyone.
How about it? In celebration of our being assigned to homeroom together...
SILENCE
....
.... Momo...
Are you mad at me for kissing you the other day...?
No.
Then why are you avoiding me?
I'm not avoiding you.
Don't lie.
You're being cold to me.
You're mad, aren't you?
I'm not mad ...

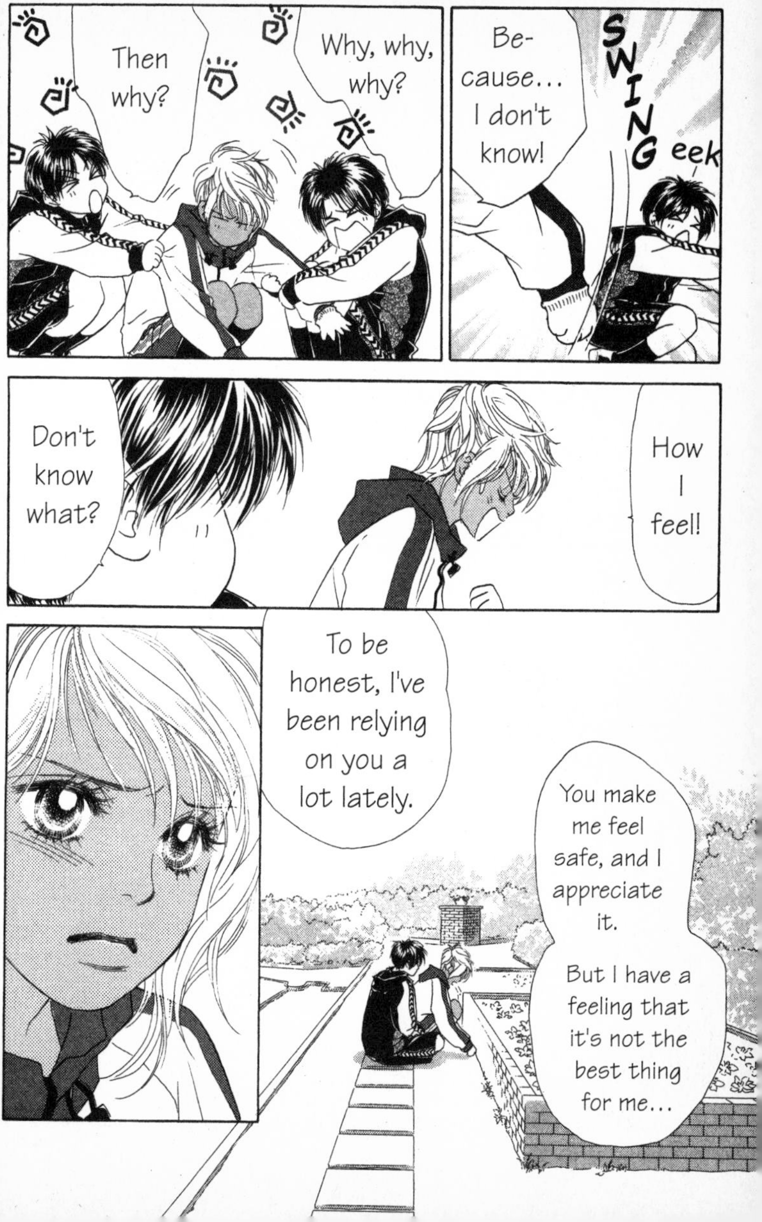
Then why?
Why, why, why?
Be-cause... I don't know!
SWING
eek
Don't know what?
How I feel!
To be honest, I've been relying on you a lot lately.
You make me feel safe, and I appreciate it.
But I have a feeling that it's not the best thing for me...

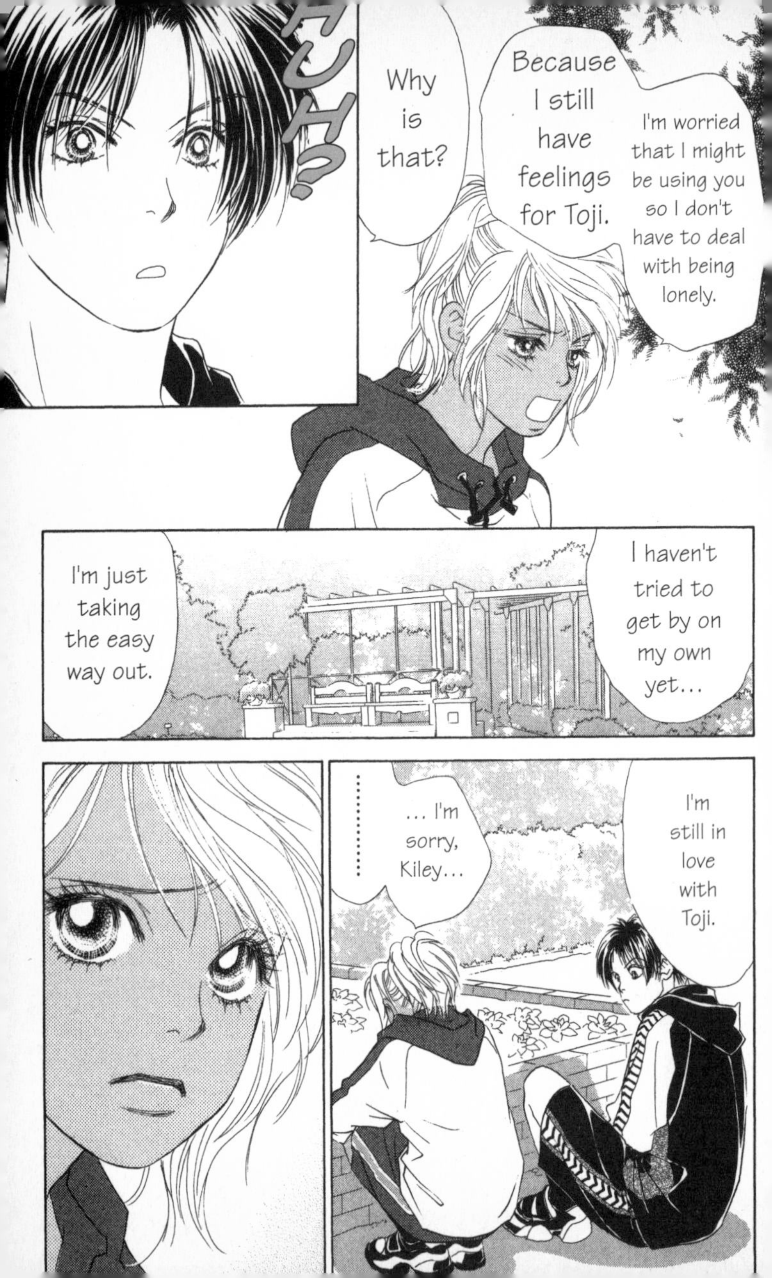
I'm worried that I might be using you so I don't have to deal with being lonely.
Why is that?
Because I still have feelings for Toji.
UH?
I haven't tried to get by on my own yet...
I'm just taking the easy way out.
I'm still in love with Toji.
... I'm sorry, Kiley...
....

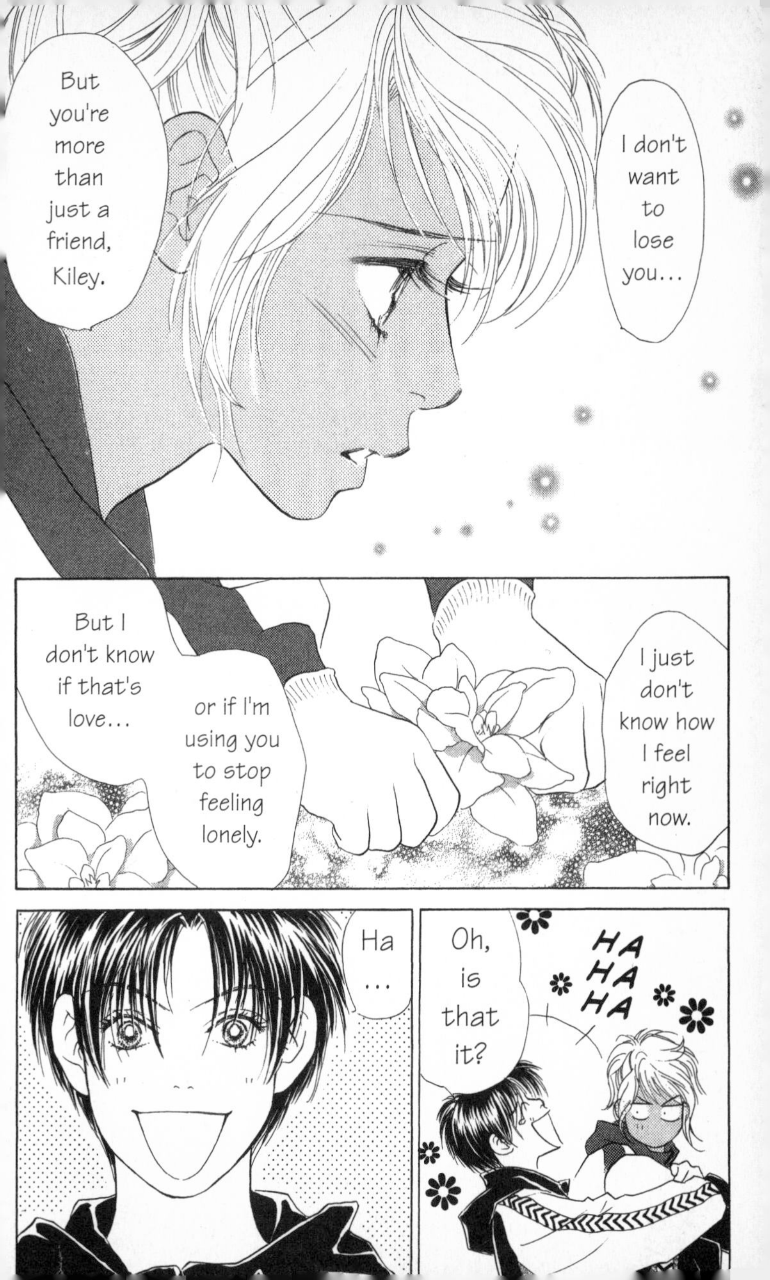
But you're more than just a friend, Kiley.
I don't want to lose you…
But I don't know if that's love…
or if I'm using you to stop feeling lonely.
I just don't know how I feel right now.
Ha …
Oh, is that it?
HA HA HA

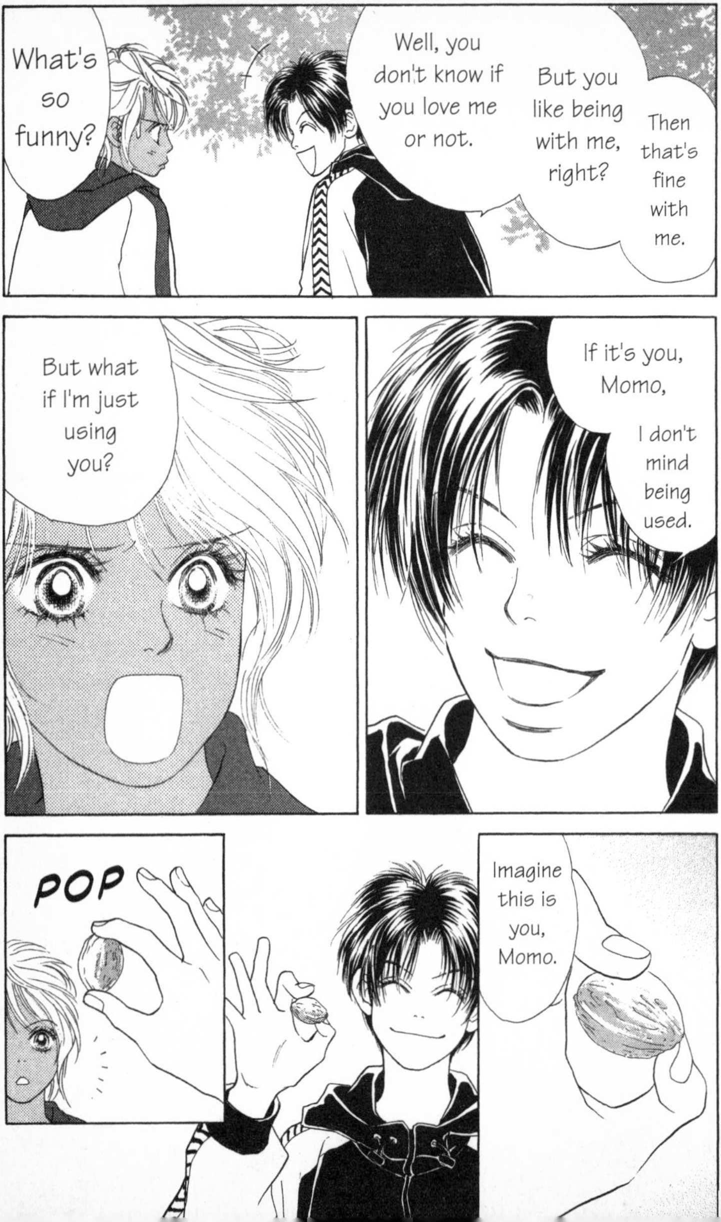
What's so funny?
Well, you don't know if you love me or not.
But you like being with me, right?
Then that's fine with me.
But what if I'm just using you?
If it's you, Momo,
I don't mind being used.
POP
Imagine this is you, Momo.

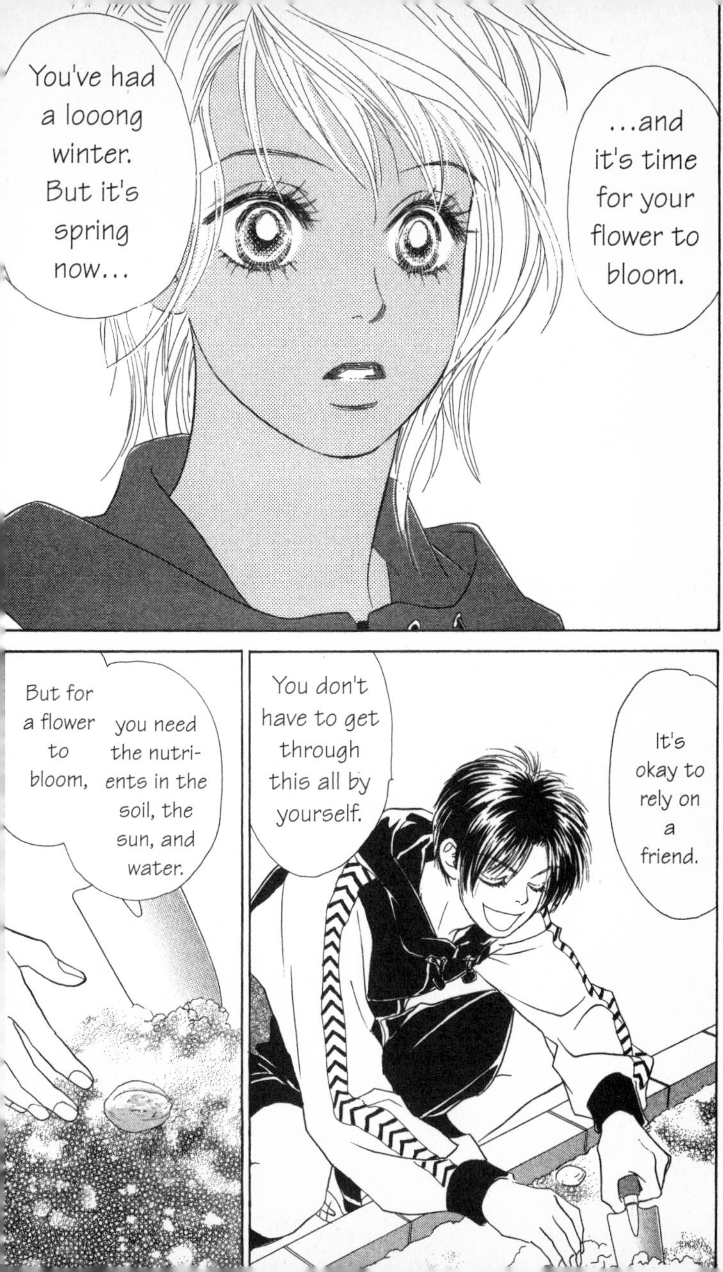
You've had a looong winter. But it's your spring now...
...and it's time for your flower to bloom.
But for a flower to bloom,
you need the nutrients in the soil, the sun, and water.
You don't have to get through this all by yourself.
It's okay to rely on a friend.

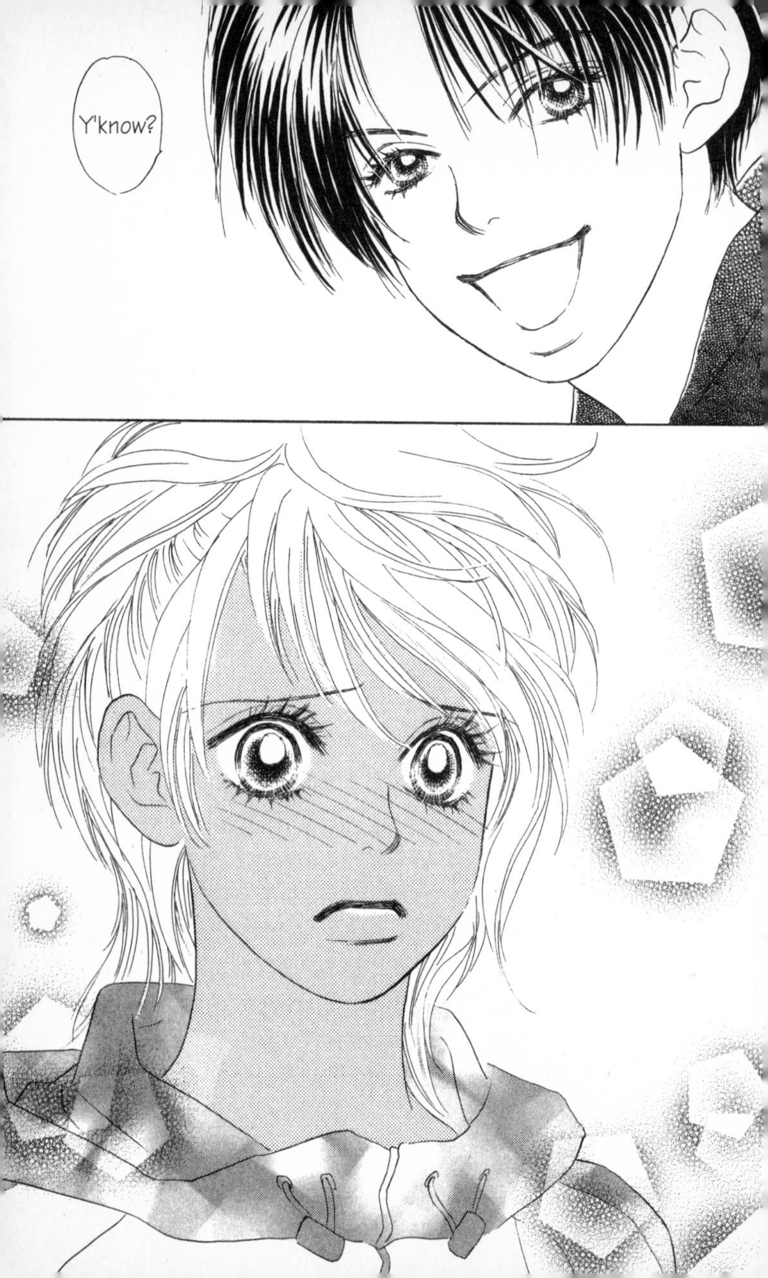
Y'know?

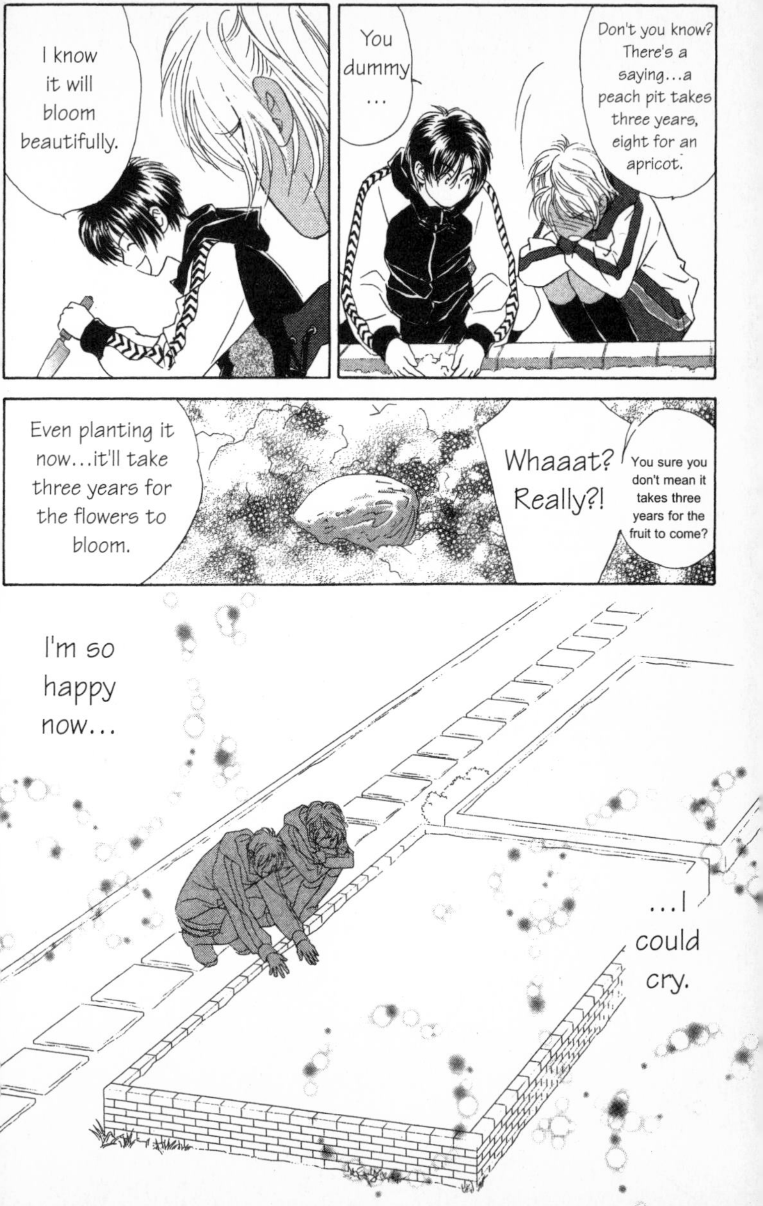
I know it will bloom beautifully.
You dummy...
Don't you know? There's a saying...a peach pit takes three years, eight for an apricot.
Even planting it now...it'll take three years for the flowers to bloom.
Whaaat? Really?!
You sure you don't mean it takes three years for the fruit to come?
I'm so happy now...
...I could cry.

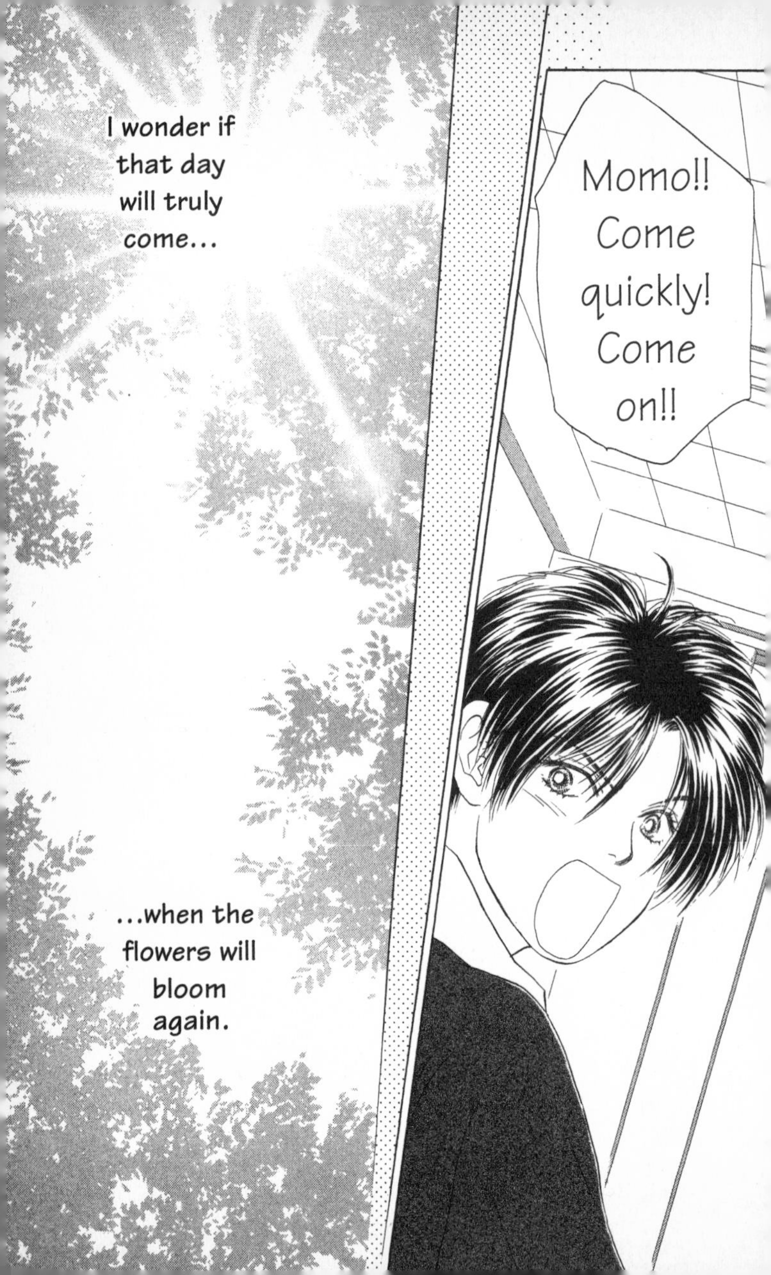
Momo!! Come quickly! Come on!!
I wonder if that day will truly come...
...when the flowers will bloom again.

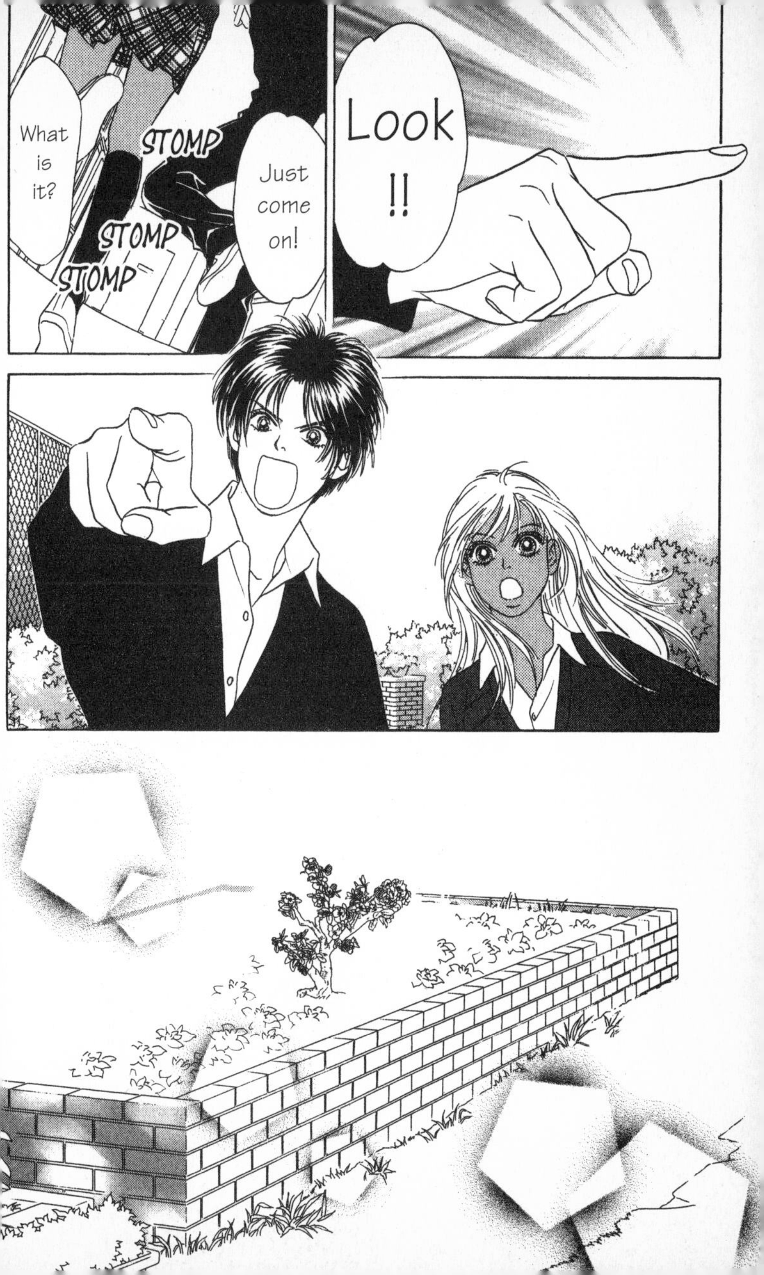
Look !!
Just come on!
STOMP
What is it?
STOMP
STOMP

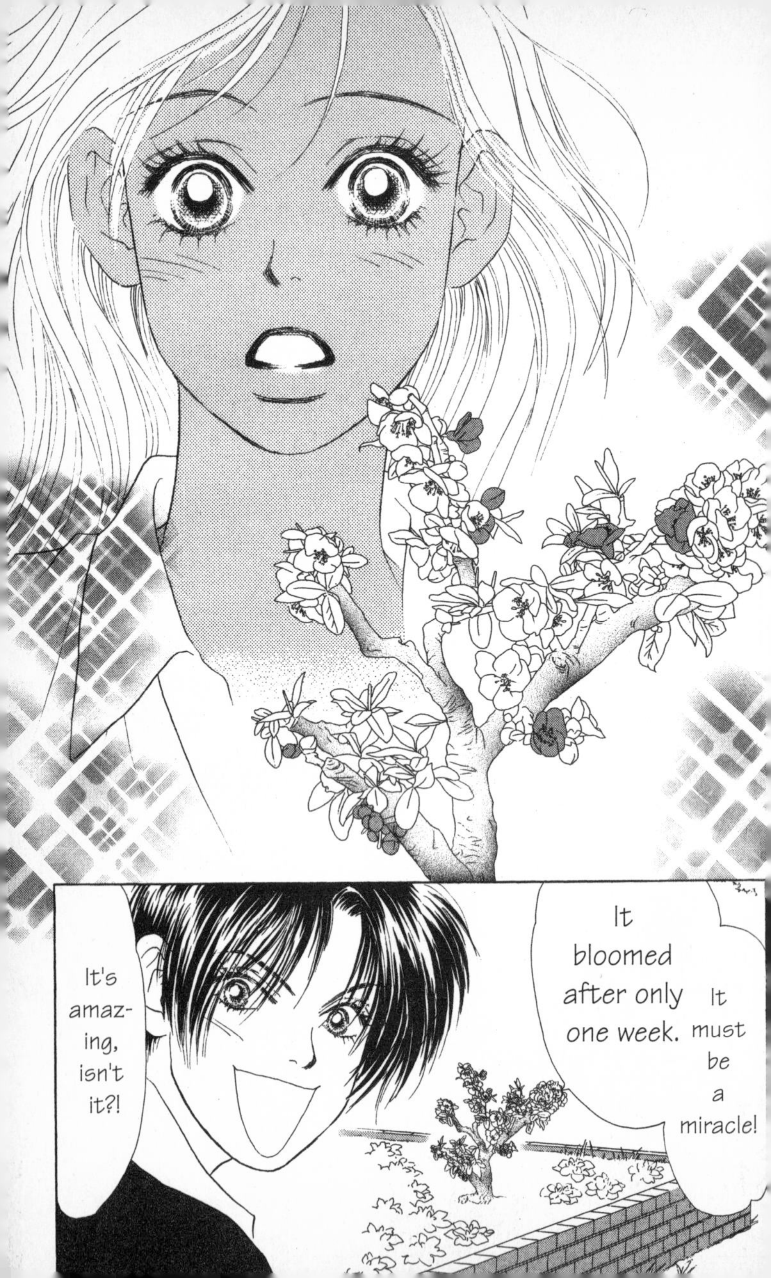
It must be a miracle!
It bloomed after only one week.
It's amazing, isn't it?!

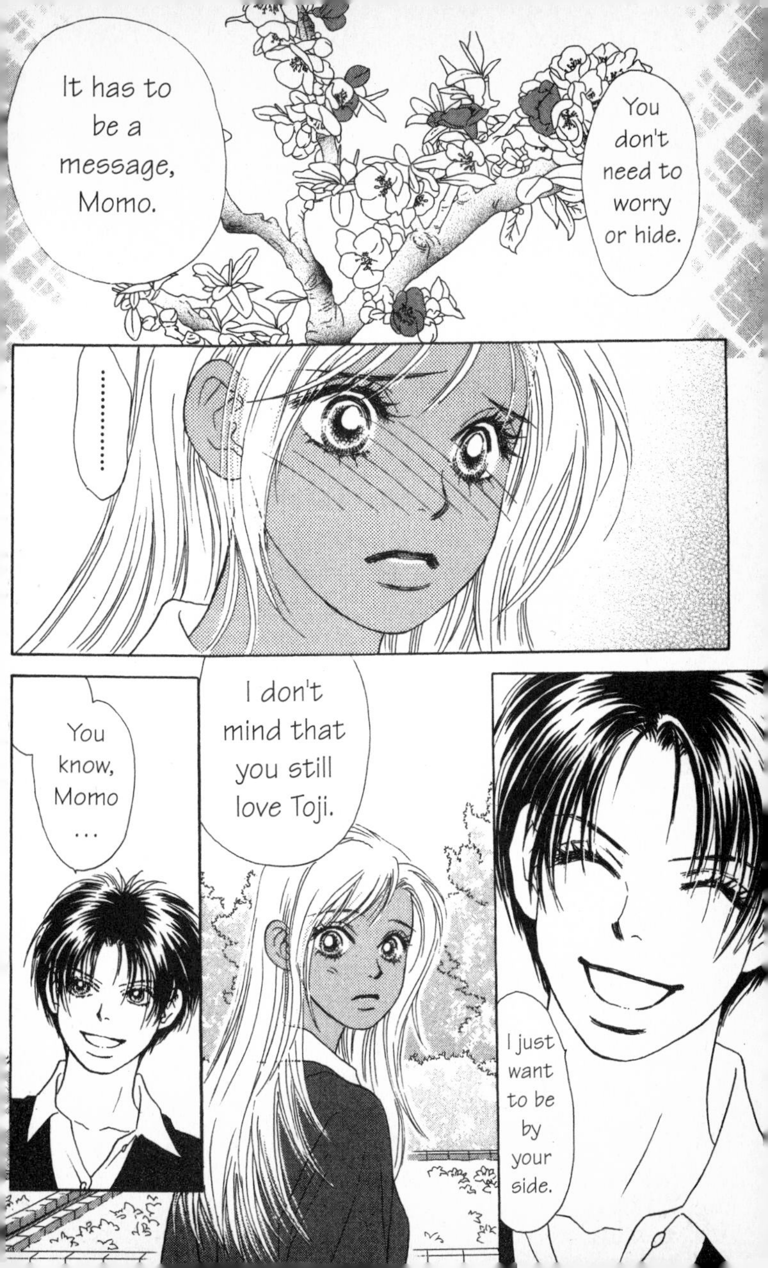
It has to be a message, Momo.
You don't need to worry or hide.
......
You know, Momo ...
I don't mind that you still love Toji.
I just want to be by your side.

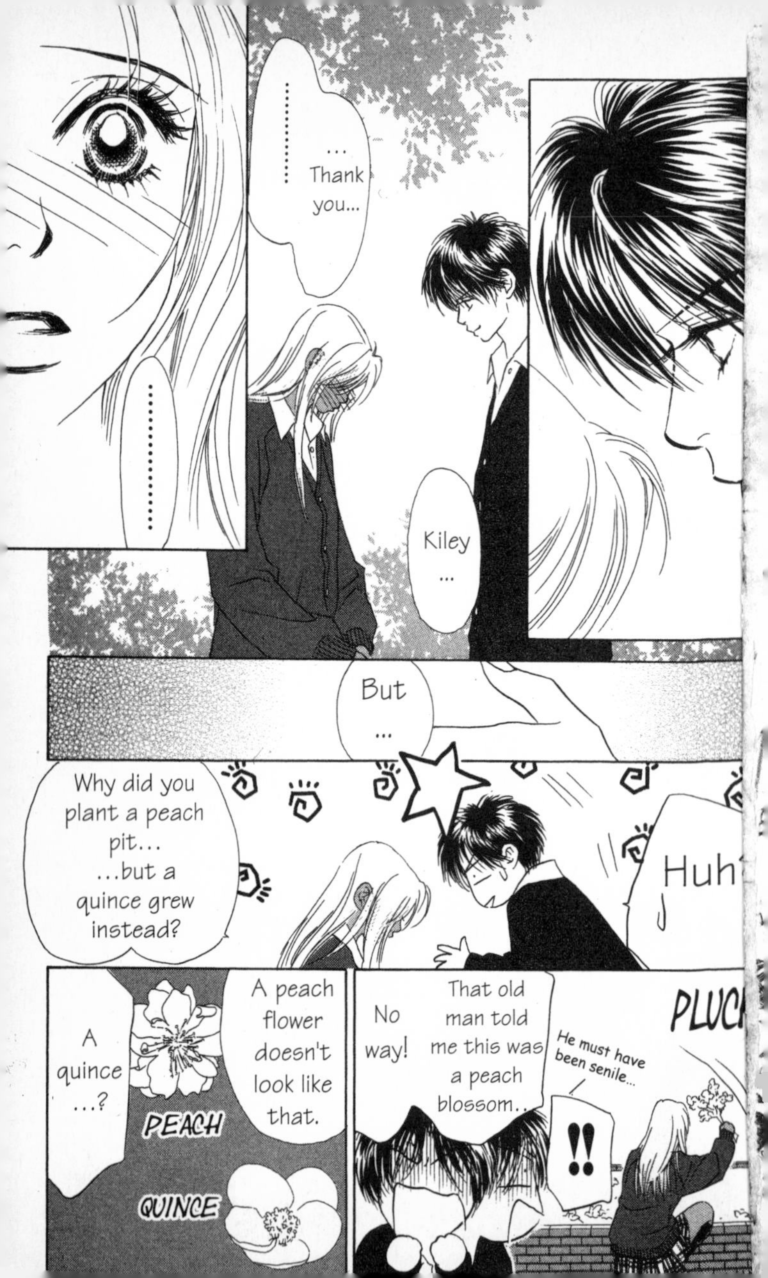

... Thank you...
Kiley ...
......
But ...
Huh?
Why did you plant a peach pit... ...but a quince grew instead?
PLUCK
That old man told me this was a peach blossom..
No way!
He must have been senile...
!!
A peach flower doesn't look like that.
A quince ...?
PEACH
QUINCE

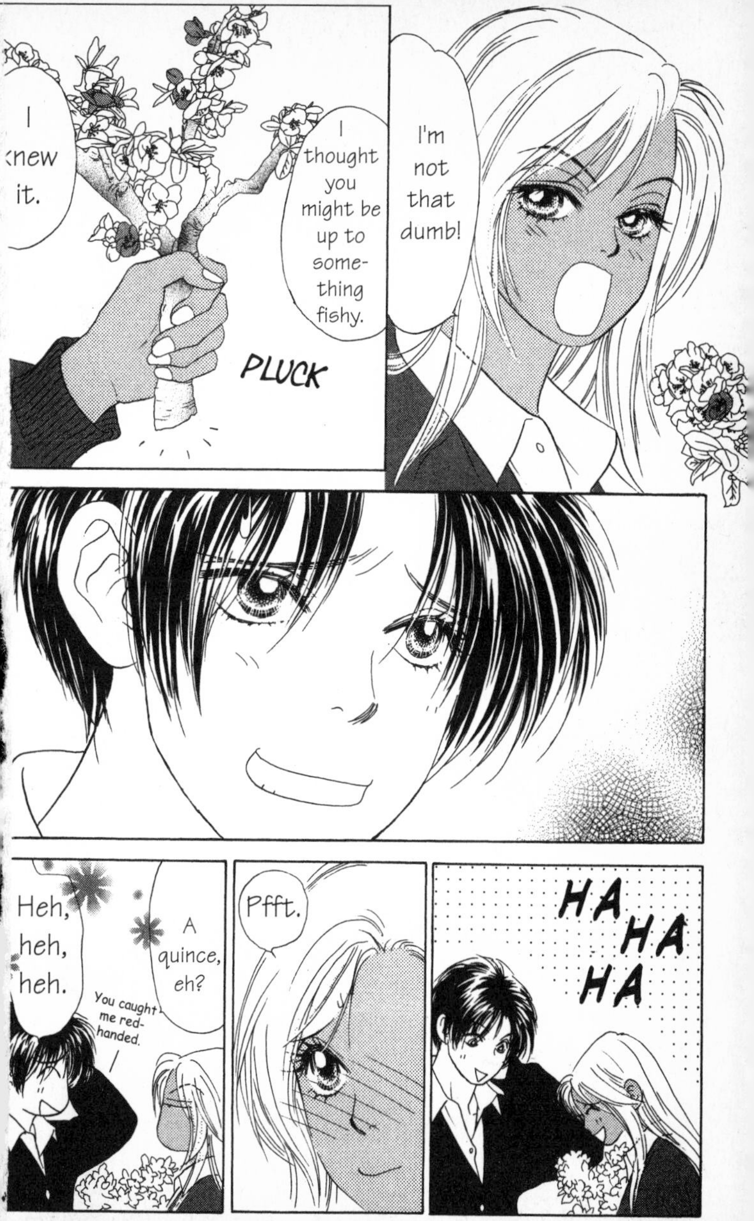
I knew it.
I thought you might be up to something fishy.
PLUCK
I'm not that dumb!
Heh, heh, heh.
A quince, eh?
You caught me red-handed.
Pfft.
HA HA HA

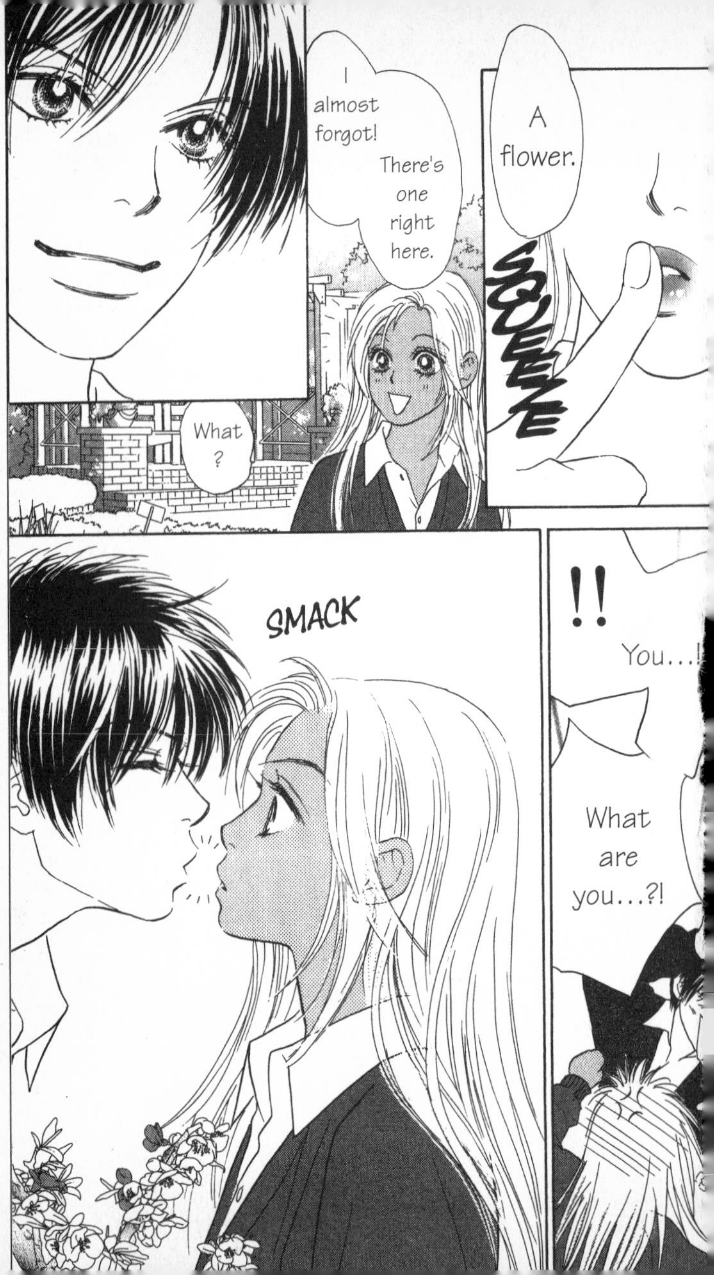
A flower.
SQUEEZE
I almost forgot!
There's one right here.
What?
!!
You...!
What are you...?!
SMACK

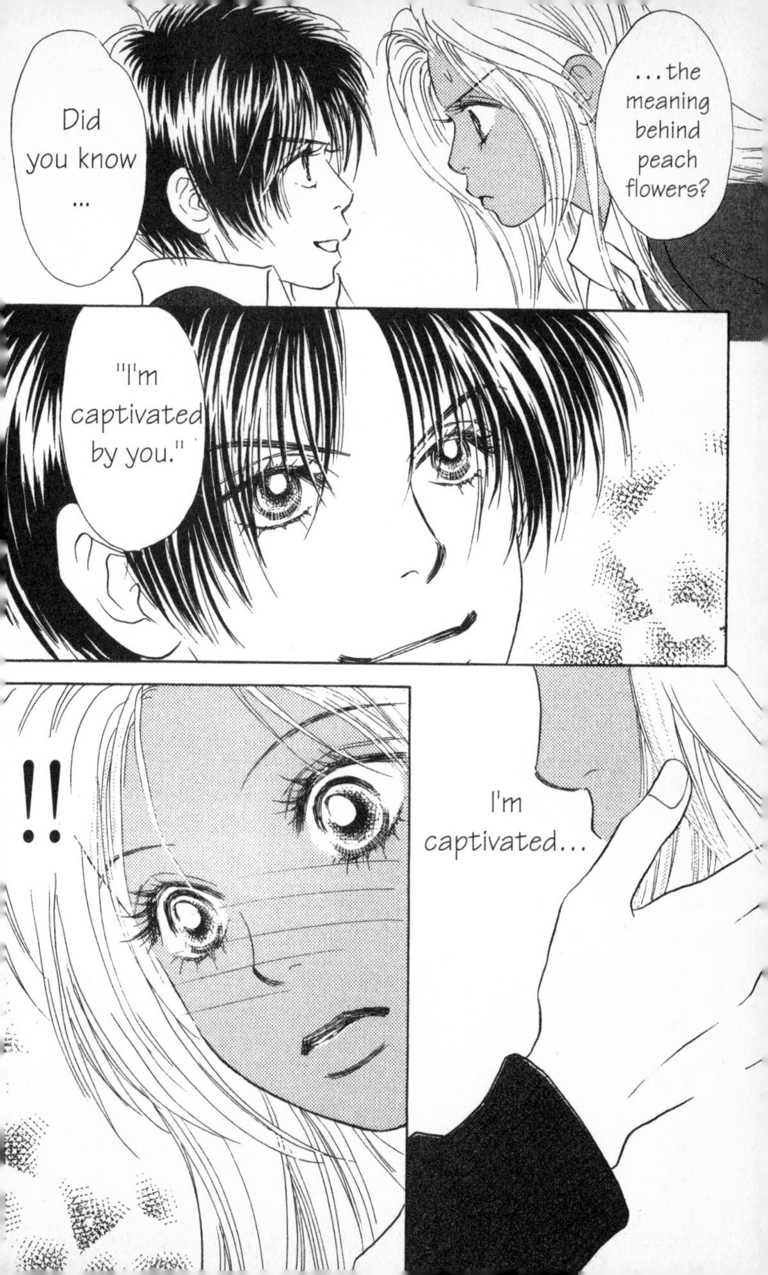
Did you know ...
...the meaning behind peach flowers?
"I'm captivated by you."
I'm captivated...
!!

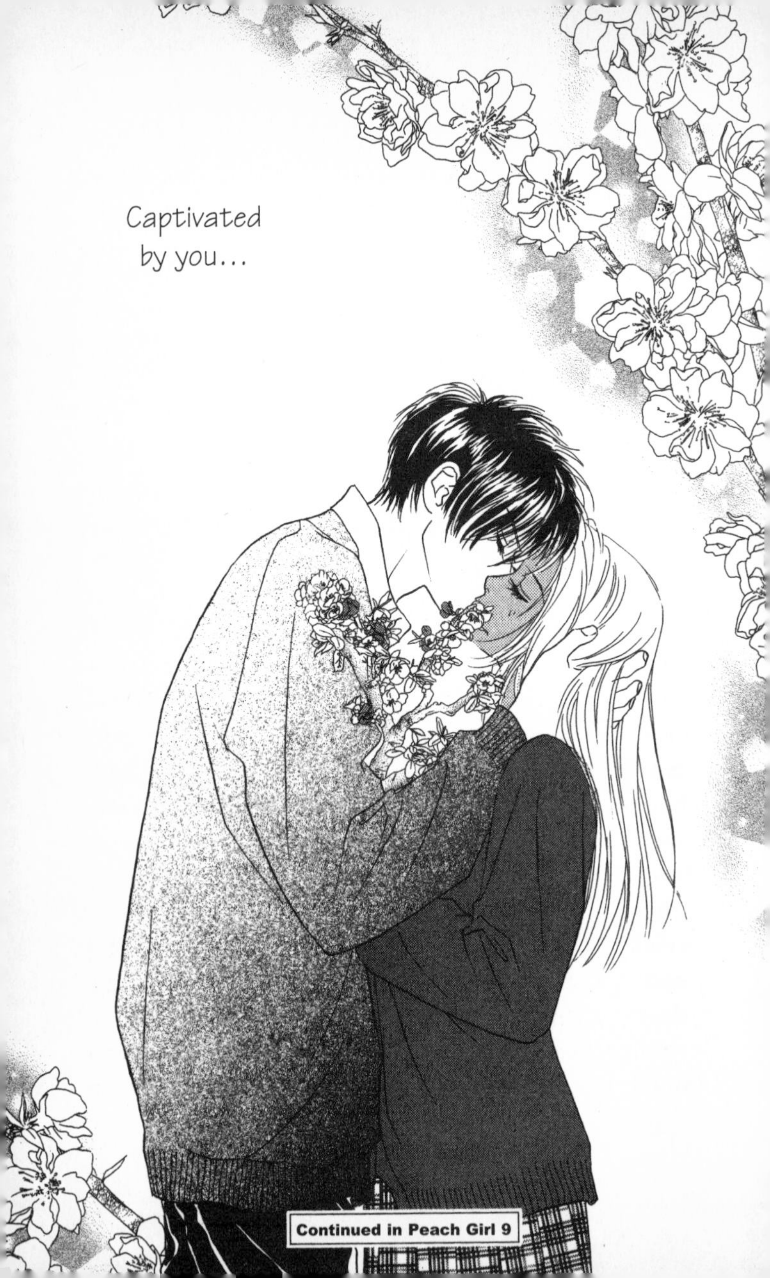
Captivated by you...
Continued in Peach Girl 9

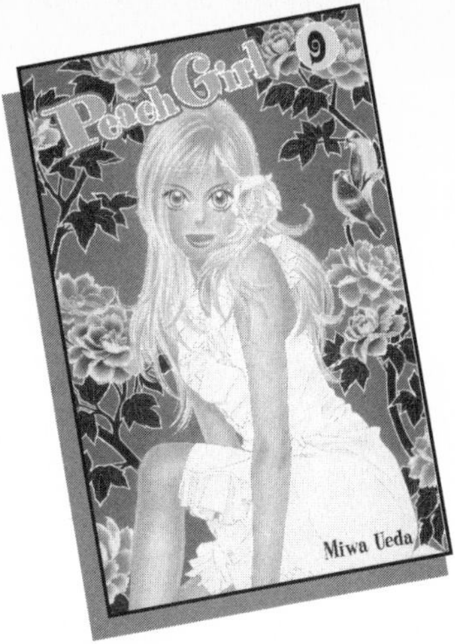
Peach Girl 9
Miwa Ueda

COMING SOON IN PEACH GIRL 9

Momo and Kiley are still hot and heavy...and the Peach Girl's love life seems to be just peachy for once. (Finally!) That is, until Momo's sworn enemy, Sae, plots with Kiley's groupies to break up the happy couple and make Momo's life a living hell. They lure her out to the yard with a fake message from Toji, then threaten to torture her and torch her signature blonde locks. Thankfully, Kiley arrives in time to save his date—and the day. Kiley soon confides in Momo and reveals his deepest, darkest thoughts. This confession makes Momo realize that she still really doesn't know all that much about her new boyfriend. Momo resolves to get to know Kiley better and make this new relationship work...no matter what it takes.

PEACH GIRL LETTERS

OMG! When I read Peach Girl 7 and Toji kissed Sae in the end, I burst out in to tears! I can't believe he went along with Sae! I have never cried over a comic, and I was okay with the tears I shed when Toji said, "Let's break up" but when he kissed her— ohmigod, all hell broke loose and I lost it! I can't believe he did that! He is such a sleeze! He was so nice and I totally liked him. He was my favorite, but now I hate him! I can't believe he would do that to Momo!! She has been through so much—correction: they have been through so much—and I can't believe he would just throw that away. Especially after she said that she didn't know what she would do if he left her!!

—Shannon

Hello,

My name is Rachel Smith. I just wanted to drop a line and say that I LOVE THIS MANGA!!!! ::takes a deep breath and calms down a bit:: I can't wait for number 8 to come out. ::HEE!:: MOMO & KILEY 4 EVER! I hate to say it, I was happy when Toji kissed Sae, the evil one got her way... But now Kiley can finally be happy too, I mean he's got to be hurting watching Momo fantasize over... TOJI. Sure he's a sweetie and all, but along with all my friends who read Peach Girl (10 and counting) WE WANT KILEY AND MOMO TO GET TOGETHER! I was reading the summary for number 8 and starting screaming I was so happy! My dad and dog got kinda freaked out over that, I think... -_-' Heh.

Toodles always,

Rachel

I ABSOLUTELY LOVE PEACH GIRL!!!
It was SO hard for me to read book 7! HOW COULD TOJI DO SOMETHING LIKE THAT??? BAH!

—Rainbowlicious

PEACH GIRL LETTERS

Let me start off with saying I love Peach Girl to death ^-^ I don't know if I'm the only one, but I really think Momo should give up on Toji and go out with Kiley. Toji always seems to fall into Sae's traps. And who always happens to be there? Kiley. Don't get me wrong, I love Toji and all, but I'm rooting for Kiley and Momo ^-^ Can't wait for the rest of the books! (Can you please bring this up somewhere or at least let me know if there are other Kiley/Momo fans out there? Thanks!)

—Brittany

Hey! I have been an avid Peach Girl reader since it started. i just wanted to say that TOKYOPOP has lots of men reading their shoujo graphic novels, especially Peach Girl and Paradise Kiss. Keep up the good work of translating manga. We all appreciate your hard work and the art/writing of the manga creators. I love the style of Miwa Ueda and Ai Yazawa. Thank you very much! You are appreciated more than you think.

— Brad, an avid reader of TOKYOPOP manga

Hey everyone,
Julie here. Thanks for all your cool letters. Keep those e-mails and letters coming! What do you think—should Momo stick with Kiley or get back together with Toji? Drop me a line and let me know what you think. I'd also love to see some fan art so I can publish it in the next volume. Bring it on!
In Peach Girl We Trust,
Julie Taylor, Senior Editor
juliet@tokyopop.com • 5900 Wilshire Blvd., Ste. 2000, Los Angeles, CA 90036

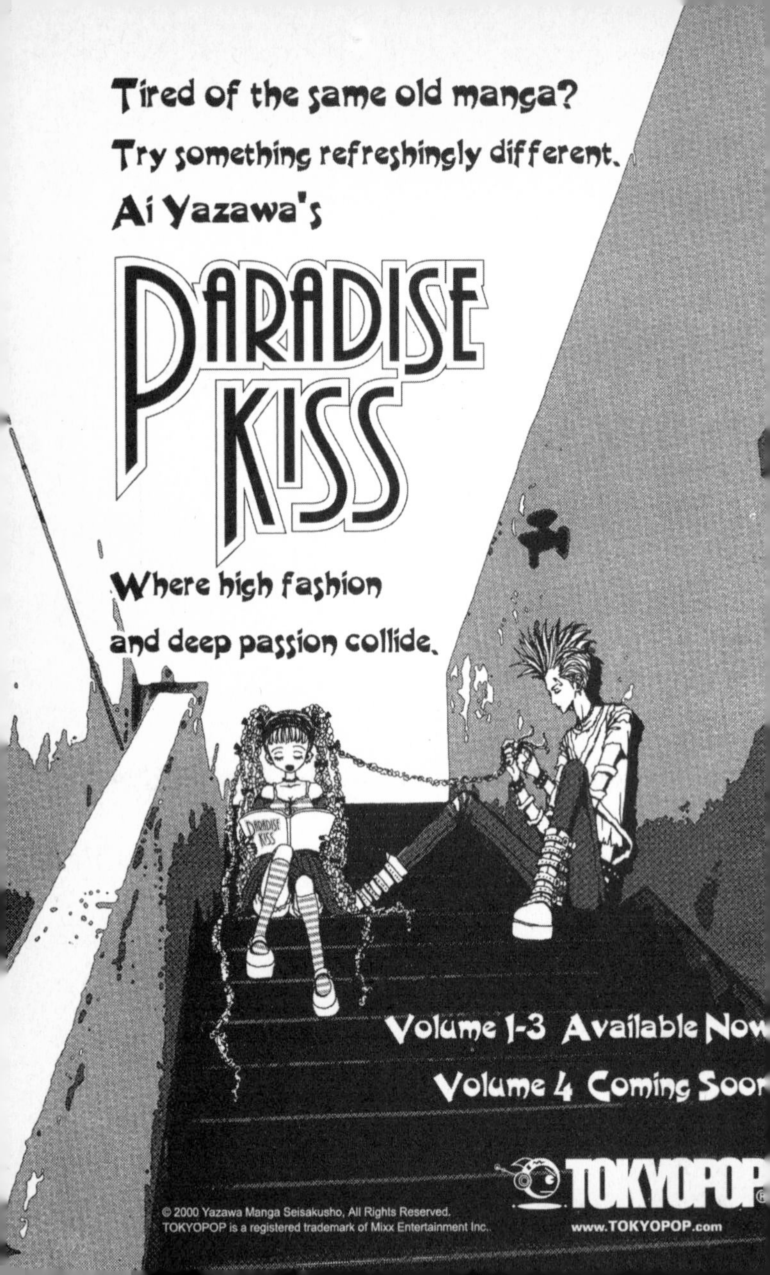
Tired of the same old manga?
Try something refreshingly different.
Ai Yazawa's
PARADISE KISS
Where high fashion
and deep passion collide.
PARADISE KISS
Volume 1-3 Available Now
Volume 4 Coming Soo
TOKYOPOP
© 2000 Yazawa Manga Seisakusho, All Rights Reserved.
TOKYOPOP is a registered trademark of Mixx Entertainment Inc.
www.TOKYOPOP.com

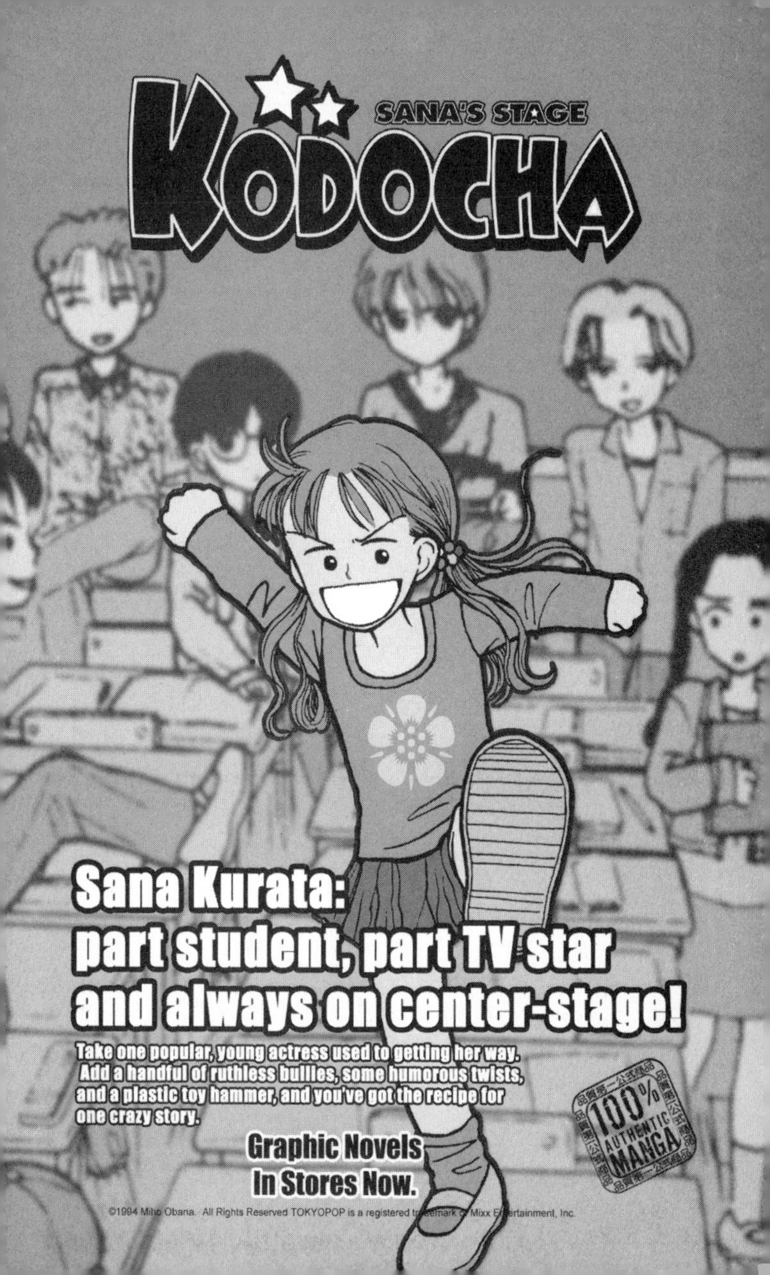
KODOCHA
SANA'S STAGE
Sana Kurata:
part student, part TV star
and always on center-stage!
Take one popular, young actress used to getting her way. Add a handful of ruthless bullies, some humorous twists, and a plastic toy hammer, and you've got the recipe for one crazy story.
100% AUTHENTIC MANGA
Graphic Novels
In Stores Now.
©1994 Miho Obana. All Rights Reserved TOKYOPOP is a registered trademark of Mixx Entertainment, Inc.

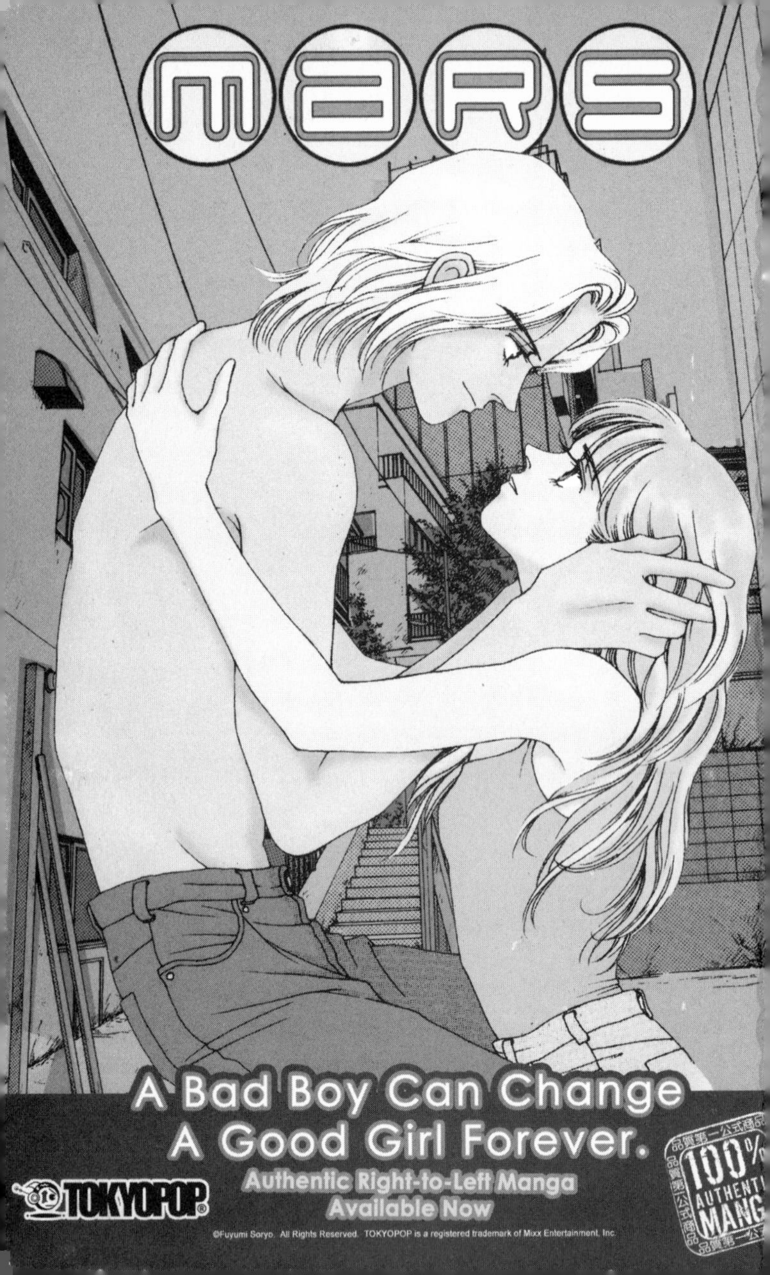
MARS
A Bad Boy Can Change
A Good Girl Forever.
Authentic Right-to-Left Manga
Available Now
TOKYOPOP®
100%
©Fuyumi Soryo. All Rights Reserved. TOKYOPOP is a registered trademark of Mixx Entertainment, Inc.